unasked

Dear Kate
May your
journey be
blessed.
Love Paige

by paige dehart

unmasked

one soul's journey from anonymity to identity

Tate Publishing & *Enterprises*

Tate Publishing
& Enterprises

Unmasked

Cover design by Lynly Taylor
Interior design by Leah LeFlore
Published in the United States of America

ISBN: 1-5988673-6-9
06.12.21

With love and appreciation to Laurel, Hope, Ruthie, Kelly, and Randy . . .
This book is dedicated to you who have ever
felt unworthy of love and forgiveness
and to the One who loves and forgives you.

The unexamined life is not worth living.[1]
Socrates

We must know our inner selves in order to distinguish our own voice from the true voice of God. We must know our secret selfish motives, so that we can set them aside and begin to move in the eternal purposes of God.[2]
John of the Cross

acknowledgements

I would like to thank John Bedunah, my tenth grade English teacher who assigned the journal for class work, and Elizabeth Van Hamersveld, my eleventh grade English teacher who encouraged me to write from a universal perspective.

I would also like to thank Stu Johnson, whose assistance allowed me the opportunity to bring this project to fruition, and Kelly Purselley, whose time was generously donated to encoding the almost-illegible handwritten journals into electronic form.

Finally, I would like to thank any writer, teacher, musician, or thinker who is quoted or mentioned in this book. A piece of me is you.

table of contents

foreword

Our daughter's name is Hope.
This book, *"Unmasked,"* serves to illustrate the reason for her name …
Before recovery,
before God was in our lives,
before Jesus was in our hearts,
there was no hope.

When asked to write the foreword for *Unmasked*, I was not thrilled because I must confess that quite often I am capable of very little faith. The truth is … *I struggle!* I must also admit that in the midst of my bouts with doubt, Paige has *always* been there encouraging me on like the "hopeless optimist." Don't get me wrong, Paige is *not* a "Pollyanna" at all. She simply believes in God and truly knows in her heart that God is going to do what He says He wants to do. So in a sense, this book is for *me* and *you* … for *all* who struggle. This book is for anyone who has ever hoped and prayed for a better life even though all signs pointed to the opposite. It is for those who dare to dream that there *really are* happy endings … as well as for those who dare not dream at all. This book is a testimony to the healing power of the God-ordained Twelve Steps. But most of all, *Unmasked* is a gift to bring *hope* to the hopeless.

Many would fear to bare their soul to the world by publicly exposing their deepest secrets for the good of others … but not my wife, not Paige. She *cares* too much. She *loves* too much! Like Paul of Tarsus, she boasts of her weaknesses, past and present, to comfort and encourage the sick and suffering.

Within the pages of *Unmasked,* Paige has chronicled her hopes and dreams and her despair and failure; as well as the many lessons learned from them. The book is a detailed account of her journey from childhood pain and disappointment through the absolute abyss of bulimia and addiction to the fulfillment of many dreams-come-true. It will take you through her struggle to find the *"God of her understanding"* in the program of Alcoholics Anonymous into the study of Metaphysics and New Age practice to direct experiences with the Lord, Jesus Christ.

Other than our precious ten-year-old daughter, Paige has blessed me with the gift of *hope* many times when I felt hopeless. May the Lord bless you now with her willingness to be used *by Him* and *for Him* that in these pages you may see yourself as He sees you … *His precious child who He loves and adores!*

I invite you to set aside what you think you already know about Religion, the Twelve Steps, and God … that you may have a new experience with Him *now;* and please enjoy *Unmasked: One Soul's Journey from Anonymity to Identity.* You may recognize yourself along the way.

The Rt. Rev. Mark R. (Randy) DeHart
Hope's Daddy!

introduction

The following pages are excerpts from my journal that began as a class requirement in my tenth grade English class. Weeks into the assignment, I became certain that it was an important project that would someday be published. Consequently, I have been obedient to the push from within that has consistently urged me to "write that down." The journal is now twenty-eight years old and twenty-two books long. Beginning with an entry from 1980 when I was eighteen years old and finishing high school, this book has been edited in order to respect your time and patience, but remains raw enough to capture the truth of the person I was at the time of the writing. The names of all but the current people in my life have been changed in order to protect their privacy.

In the first entry, I insinuate that I wish I could go back in time and share with myself the wisdom of experience. With this as one of the objectives of this book, I have used the timeless words of saints, sages, the salvaged, and the Savior to speak wisdom into my circumstances.

However, many of these circumstances have not been pleasant. Although God dramatically entered my life in 1986, I have been an alcoholic, an addict, a compulsively overeating bulimic, a harlot, an adulteress, a child murderer, a manic depressive with psychotic tendencies, a liar, a cheater, and a thief. I am a fallen soul—saved by grace through faith in Jesus Christ and given an entirely new life, from the inside out.

Nonetheless, my journey to redemption has been unconventional. Spiritually, I have been immersed in Alcoholics Anonymous, Unity Church, the

Self-Realization Fellowship, the Pentecostal Church, the Evangelical Bible Church, and the Anglican Church. As a self-educated college drop-out, my intellectual pursuits have been Psychology, Quantum Physics, Sociology, and World Religion. I have found pieces of truth, as well as error, in all of these places, but have been able to reconcile my learning into a comprehensive worldview. Consequently, another objective of this book is to share this reconciliation with you; to educate you on the nature of addiction and the vital ingredients necessary for permanent and effective Twelve Step sobriety, to clarify the distorted truths of New Age Thought, and to illuminate the universal truths of life as well as the unique Truth of Christianity.

However, the most important objective of this book is to bring hope to those of you who feel as though you are lost beyond retrieval. I pray that my experience will encourage you to believe that there is nothing that you can do or have done that is capable of separating you from the love of God—if only you will turn to Him and *follow Him*. I have exposed my deepest and most shameful secrets that you may know that you are not alone.

It is my prayer that all of us may learn that the one true God desires and is able to meet us *where we are* with the ultimate purpose of *unifying us* for the perfection and peace of His world. I encourage you to move through these pages with honesty, open-mindedness, and willingness to stretch beyond your previous boundaries of knowledge and understanding in order to have a fresh perspective of yourself, your companions in life, and the world in which you live.

Ralph Waldo Emerson said, "*What lies behind us and what lies before us are tiny matters compared to what lies within us.*"[3] May God Himself lead you personally and profoundly into the deep reality of this statement; into an *experience with Him* as the endless well of Life, Love, and Truth. *This* is the hope of glory.

Paige DeHart
Bedford, Texas
August, 2006

We differ from others only in what we do or don't do, not in what we are.[4]
Anthony DeMello

.1. childish whims

May 12, 1980 – November 30, 1982

When I was a child, I spoke as a child,
I understood as a child, I thought as a child.
1 Corinthians 13:11

My husband and I are the founders of a Christian Twelve Step ministry. One of the locations for our ministry is Fort Worth's county jail; where inmates are counseled through worksheets that are completed for the ministry's review. One of the questions on the first worksheet is, *Describe the most painful event from your childhood.* Amazingly, a strong majority of the inmates answer that question with, *The divorce of my parents.*

My parents divorced when I was seven; after which my mother suffered a nervous breakdown and was hospitalized for an extended period. My two younger sisters and I then lived with Dad in a big, beautiful house that was not a home. Dad was a successful oil man so we enjoyed material wealth, but he was also a busy workaholic. The majority of my adolescence was spent yearning for his attention while mourning the loss of my mother's presence.

Shortly after the separation from my mother, I began to battle a serious weight problem. By the sixth grade, I weighed 202 pounds. By the seventh grade, after the summer at a weight loss camp in San Diego where I lost a substantial amount of weight, I ventured into sex, drugs, alcohol, and rock and roll. The effect produced by this powerful combination was so seductive that pursuing it became a way of life for me.

Even though I eventually gained the weight back, my new lifestyle gave me a sense of power and confidence that I had never known before. Alcohol and drugs eased the pain of loneliness, sex provided the male attention that I craved, and the songs of Led Zeppelin, Pink Floyd, and The Who gave me something new to think about.

Although extremely foolish, I was also creative, ambitious, and intelligent so I was able to succeed in a prestigious private school in spite of my unconventional lifestyle. My template for behavior did not concern what was "right" or "wrong," but whether or not I could "get away with it." In what would prove to be a grave disadvantage, I "got away" with many things.

At seventeen, I had a serious car accident that kept me hospitalized for a week and in a cast for over a month. During that time, I had my first "born again" experience and became involved with Young Life. I went to a priest at the Episcopal Church where I had been baptized at twelve and asked to be re-baptized, but I was disregarded. As soon as I was out of the cast and back behind the wheel of my car, the party resumed and my salvation experience became a faint memory.

My relationship with Dad was tumultuous so I moved out of the house shortly after my eighteenth birthday and became a waitress. By the end of my senior year, I believed that I was destined for greatness and that the way to obtain it was to get what I wanted in as painless, easy, and fun a way as possible.

I've heard that many spiritual awakenings are preceded by rude awakenings. This was the truth for me.

May 12, 1980

I feel as though I am becoming an apathetic person. School is almost out and I'm not even dazed. I thought I would be hysterical. I feel like I'm sitting here waiting for my last bit of naiveté to float off into the sunset; but it's no big deal. I'm very sad about that.

I feel as though I have drastically changed. I look back on who I was even as recently as three months ago and feel that I was a ridiculous fool at times. I want to go back to myself and say, *You don't even know what's ahead of you.*

If only I had known.

May 30, 1980

It's hard to grasp the fact that I've outgrown everything that was once important to me. When I look at my life, my feelings, and myself, I don't even recognize who and what I see.

What the caterpillar calls the end of the world, the master calls a butterfly.[5]
Richard Bach

June 8, 1980

From now on, I'm living for today and not the tomorrows that never really come. I've been reflecting on past problems. I spent hours-on-end being miserable because things didn't work out the "way I wanted them to." I've spent too much time planning and manipulating. I now realize that I cannot dictate the course of my life because too many things change. Life is so strange. I really can't explain my feelings because, even though I'm content, there is always that recognition in me that nothing is perfect.

The mass of men lead lives of quiet desperation.[6]
Henry David Thoreau

June 28, 1980

I'm starting to like a guy at work named Chris. I really enjoy hanging out with him, but as always, the fear of our friendship not working out has set in. Besides, he likes another girl.

Chris is a lot like me in many ways. I think we're both suffering from disillusionment. We can both hear the little voice within us that wants to keep on caring, but we are also both starting to doubt if things that really matter even exist.

Many young people are convinced that there is something terribly wrong with the world in which they live and that cooperation with existing models of living would constitute betrayal of themselves.[7]
Henri J. M. Nouwen

July 6, 1980

I wish I could be happy, but for some reason, I've convinced myself that there's no such thing as happiness. It seems that I don't understand *anything* anymore—not even myself. I hate myself for chalking defeat off to growing up. I used to think that the world was mine, but now I've lost my hope. I wonder why.

This fearful generation which rejects its fathers and quite often rejects the legitimacy of every person or institution that claims authority is facing a new danger: becoming captive to itself.[8]
Henri J. M. Nouwen

July 17, 1980

Lately I've been making myself miserable. Chris holds me when I'm upset and it makes me feel safe. I wish he'd hold me when I'm not upset. I like Chris, but I fear that he is going to fade out of my life. I don't know why I spend so much time worrying about things that *could* happen.

I just don't understand the simplest things anymore and I'm becoming more and more of a pessimist. I wish that I could stop feeling sorry for myself. I don't understand where all of my hope went—probably hanging out somewhere with my belief in God. I don't believe in anything anymore—not even reality. I have no idea what I want to do.

Life is not *anything* like I thought it would be. I guess that's what I get for thinking—or at least for having preconceived notions. I just want to scream my head off until things start making sense again. I want to dream again and understand what is going on inside of me. I try to count my blessings, but I feel as though I am coming up short.

Sometimes, I want to give up and cash it all in due to plain old lack of interest. Most of the time, I just want to cry. I've got so much boiling inside of me, but I'm not even sure of what it is.

I think I'm going crazy—literally. I have this horrible feeling of dread inside of me, but I don't even know what I'm dreading. Even worse, I don't know what I'm looking forward to. I guess I just need to be more patient with myself and give myself time to evolve into thinking and knowing what I do or will.

What you really fear is the loss of the known.[9]
Anthony DeMello

July 21, 1980

I've never felt so hopeless in my life. I have lost all of my optimism. I'm afraid I'm going to do something horrible to myself. What's even worse is that I question whether or not this drama is not my way of getting attention from Chris. I've pumped myself with more drugs and alcohol than seems practical or imaginable and I still feel miserable. What's even worse is feeling like nothing will ever make me feel better. The only thing in the world right now that gives me a will to live is Chris and I see that even he could not make me feel happy.

I don't understand what horrible thing is happening to me. If there is a God in Heaven—like I once believed there was—I beg Him to make me feel good once again. This pain is killing me.

The inwardness of the coming generation can lead either to a higher level of hypocrisy or to the discovery of the reality of the unseen which can make for a new world.[10]

Henri J. M. Nouwen

July 30, 1980

There's still a part of me that can't give up. That gives me hope.

August 4, 1980

Things are suddenly starting to seem better. Just when I think that I'm flipping out for good and absolutely losing my mind, I realize that pain and confusion are a part of learning and redefining who I am.

Your pain is the breaking of the shell that encloses your understanding.[11]

Kahlil Gibran

September 26, 1980

I remember a little girl on her third birthday. Her smile was bright and her dreams were real. She didn't know a lot of things that she knows now, but she's still the same little girl. I'm still the same little girl.

I've got to see myself in this light so I can start loving myself. I've cried and cried lately for the little girl I never got to be. It feels good because I have never really cried about that before. Now the big girl doesn't feel quite so lost.

I've always loved people who don't love me in return; except me.

During this period, Chris made it clear that we were only friends and then I started "dating" a young man named Terry who I met at the restaurant where I worked. He was a guy who said that I was beautiful instead of just saying that I had a "pretty face." Knowing that I did not care for him in a romantic way, yet being grateful that someone wanted me, I allowed him to move in with me.

October 19, 1980

It's so terrible when I get the feeling that I don't know what I want out of life. I cannot understand why I sometimes want to get Terry out of the picture and be alone instead.

A cloud does not know why it moves in such a direction and at such a speed.
It feels an impulsion ... this is the place to go now.
But the sky knows the reasons and the patterns behind all clouds,
and you will know, too,
when you lift yourself high enough to see beyond horizons.[12]
Richard Bach

December 3, 1980

I feel terrible right now. I'm so confused and there's a part of me that bitterly hates the other part of me. Everyone says that I have become nicer and more loving lately, but that's totally contrary to how I feel. I think that I'm more mean and horrible than I've ever been. It's just that now I direct all of my rage at Terry. It hurts so much to treat someone I care for so badly. I wish that he would leave me.

I hate the mean, cruel side of myself and that probably helps it thrive. Sometimes I think that I have a split personality or something.

There is no such thing as a problem without a gift in its hands.[13]
Richard Bach

December 14, 1980

My meanness towards Terry comes from deep resentment because I'm playing a game with myself. I'm not happy and what makes me even more miserable is that I'm living a lie. I care about Terry, but I know that he will never be right for me. Sometimes I think that if he went to school and changed, he would be right, but I can't change him into what I want him or need him to be.

To want something from another
is to utterly misunderstand their role in our happiness.
Other people are our opportunity to extend what we are.[14]
Hugh Prather

January 20, 1981

I started college last week. I'm getting excited about the future. The only problem with this excitement is that it makes me dissatisfied with Terry because it seems so unrealistic to imagine him in my future. He's more of a brother to me than anything else. I wish we could end our "relationship" and continue our "friendship."

January 29, 1981

I don't understand what it is that overtakes me and causes me to lose my temper for no reason. Nothing ever seems to be good enough. Dissatisfaction is one of my worst enemies.

When I made my first efforts to be true to myself,
I felt trapped in a self I didn't like.[15]
Hugh Prather

March 6, 1981

All good things in moderation, Paige.

I've been doing too much acid. I almost had everything analyzed and figured out to the point of confusion. I have a funny way of doing that.

My ego's been popping up lately because I've let the weight loss go to my head **(Shortly after Terry moved in, I became bulimic and started throwing up every time I ate)**. It's so weird to all-of-a-sudden transform into a seemingly different person. It's like I expect the compliments and then feel embarrassed when they are offered. Sounds like false modesty to me.

The attention I give
to what I wear, the length of my hair, how much I weigh, etc.,
is designed to control what people will think.[16]
Hugh Prather

August 15, 1981

It seems that the thinner I get, the less I have to say. I find it hard to be myself these days. I guess it's because I'm starting to have a whole new perception of myself. I really don't like it because I feel and sometimes act like a big shot. I've got to learn to be friendly and nice towards everyone rather than being so quick to size people up in comparison to me. I've always wanted to be beautiful, but now that I am, I don't always like the way I act. What's even worse is that usually rather than changing my attitude, I choose to take the stand that I don't care if some people think I'm a royal jerk. I do care! I want everyone to like me. I always have.

It seems that lately I've been overlooking the qualities that life is all about because I've been concentrating on worldly pursuits. I wish I could be like Shannon **(my younger sister)**. She's beautiful *and* kind. At least I'm thinking about it for a change. I just wish that another creative spurt would hit me because lately I feel insipid and shallow. Life on an even keel is sometimes very dull.

When my self-esteem is a veneer, that is, when it stands on superficialities such as body, dress, glibness, reputation,
I am less sensitive to other people as people,
as living, laughing, hurting human beings.
I stop seeing people directly and only watch others for their reactions to me.[17]
Hugh Prather

December 30, 1981

Chris died early this morning in a car wreck. I've never experienced anything like this before. It hurts worse than I could have imagined. This sort of thing affirms my belief that there just absolutely cannot be a loving God. Chris didn't care about the world; he only cared about people.

Many of the young are afflicted by doubt.
They are unable to place their confidence in God, to believe,
since they have not found confidence
in those to whom life had entrusted them.[18]
Mother Teresa

January 16, 1982

We recently found out that I was twenty weeks pregnant. I guess I didn't know sooner because throwing up makes me feel sick at my stomach and keeps me from gaining weight. Mom and Dad put a lot of pressure on me so I had an abortion. I just can't believe that I had an abortion! It's something that I *never* wanted to happen; especially as an adult and when I'm in a committed relationship with someone I care about. I am very depressed.

I had been feeling so much better lately that I had kind of forgotten about depression, but it's sort of like riding a bike; once you learn, you *never* forget. Anyway, I made the decision so I might as well stick to my justifications for it and not dwell on it.

We don't want to look, because if we do, we may change.[19]
Anthony DeMello

April 29, 1982

Terry and I are getting married on May 22! I'm excited, but I'm also apprehensive. I guess I sort of regret not dating around and seeing who was out there, but life's short so I don't need to throw away what I have for what could be.

I'm excited about the wedding, but I'm also scared. Getting married has a lot of commitments that come along with it. I guess I'm ready to make commitments. I've never liked being alone anyway so I'm sure it will be okay.

This odd trait of mind and emotion,
this perverse wish to hide a bad motive underneath a good one,
permeates human affairs from top to bottom.[20]
Twelve Steps and Twelve Traditions

July 19, 1982

Whew! The cycles go on! I got so full of myself with the wedding and the weight loss that I had a big crash. I'm back to square one emotionally, with Terry trying to pull me back into the swing of things.

Sometimes, I live my life so backwards; striving for the tangible while pushing away all truth and intangibility. Love is more important than money and inner beauty is more important than the way I look. I've got to uncover the inside me once again and let the sun shine within my soul.

I'm nothing more than a human being; equal to all and above no one. I have the capability to love, laugh, share, dream, and fulfill all that is good, but I must let go of the hypocrisies I've made into me. I've got to care about other people regardless of how they feel about me. I've got to put the word "unconditional" back into my vocabulary. I must mold for myself a tranquil life rather than a stormy sea of worry and uncertainty. I cannot forget what I've always known to be true - love conquers all.

They say I should be "realistic"
But who is "they" and what is reality?

Perceptions of physicality create the norm that I should follow
But who's to say what's right and wrong for me?
They say I should believe in God
But what or who is God without goodness?
They say I should and shouldn't
Until I believe in anything except me.
When will love open the mind of society?

July 23, 1982

I *do* believe that God exists because when I deny Him, my life seems to block itself from understanding. I've evaluated everything and reset my goals, but the anxiety and depression won't go away. Maybe I expect too much too soon. I've spent a lot of time denying my needs—physically, emotionally, and spiritually. I guess it will take time to mend. I've got to stop losing myself all the time or someday I might not be able to find me again.

Eat right, exercise, no marijuana, pray, be nice, work hard, alcohol in moderation: I always set the same goals, but they never seem to materialize. Why am I such a self-defeatist?

For what I am doing, I do not understand.
For what I will to do, that I do not practice; but what I hate, that I do.
Romans 7:15

October 18, 1982

I haven't been sticking to my goals very well. Mom talked me into seeing her psychiatrist and he wants me to take medication. I believe that I can work out my emotional problems without some bizarre, mind-altering drug like Lithium to do it for me. The day I lose confidence in my ability to cope with life is the day I might as well give up.

I'm less than the epitome of self control, but I'm no crazy fool either. I just need to behave myself **(I was using and selling a lot of marijuana)** so that I can feel good about my life instead of anxious about it.

Life is a banquet. And the tragedy is that most people are starving to death.[21]
Anthony DeMello

October 24, 1982

The past couple of months are a fine example of how one has to hit rock bottom before beginning a new ascension. I ended up losing all hope and before I knew it, I was minus my job, my home, and nearly my own well-being. However, I guess things really do work out for the best, but when you're in a trough, it's hard to remember peaking glory.

Terry and I have been making new friends while relinquishing old ones. I never could understand how Dad could have ex-friends, but now I realize that things move on.

November 30, 1982

Happy Birthday to me ... My paternal grandmother, Maw, died on November 18 and we buried her two days ago. It's so hard to believe. I'll miss her sparkling eyes and cheerful attitude towards everything and everyone. She was one of the few people I've ever known who was totally unselfish and who really knew what life was all about.

I love you, Maw. I'll miss you forever!

And ever has it been that love knows not its own depth
until the hour of separation.[22]
Kahlil Gibran

.2. falling down

February 3, 1983 – October 28, 1986

He who walks in darkness does not know where he is going.
John 12:35

February 3, 1983

I am so ashamed of myself. I had an affair with Dean **(a friend of Terry's from work).** Shannon says that I'll learn from it. I hope she's right. I do not understand why I have to shred my life to pieces.

> *The alcoholic is like a tornado roaring his way through the lives of others.*[23]
> **Alcoholics Anonymous**

February 5, 1983

I can't get Dean off of my mind.

February 8, 1983

I found this quote in *Notes on Love and Courage* that says a lot about the way I have been feeling about myself; "*I feel: That which loves is me. And when the impulse is to hurt and I follow that, I feel like a betrayer, and the I has gone out of me.*"[24]

I have always thought that life gets tougher as you get older, but now I think I'm learning that it's only as hard as you make it. Maybe things seem so stormy to me now because I'm just now really learning who I am in perspective to the world around me.

I don't have to stand out in a crowd in order to experience the beauty that life has to offer. All I have to do is take the time to see the beauty around me. I guess that rather I realize it or not, I am learning from my experiences.

Nothing that is worth knowing can be taught.[25]
Oscar Wilde

March 26, 1983

Life goes on and I'm trying to change into someone I can respect. I'm finally having the courage to make my own decisions and then to weather the consequences. Terry is gone and the marriage is over. It's hard to say goodbye to someone that you care about, but there comes a time when you have to have enough sense to know when the relationship is no longer beneficial to personal growth.

I'm anxious, scared, and sad, but my therapist helped me to realize that these feelings are just a road to the new feelings that will come. I just have to revel in my real, adult feelings and not worry.

I see that I was depending on Terry for security and comfort, but that I never really loved him or believed that we could have a life together. I just didn't have the courage to let go. I let the pain of feeling sorry for him prevent me from doing what is best for me. I can't sacrifice my goals and happiness out of pity for him. People don't make other people happy and they don't hurt other people. People choose to be happy and they choose to be hurt. As cruel as it may sound, how Terry chooses to feel at this time has just got to be his problem; just like how I choose to feel is mine.

Individual growth can't take precedence over relationships;
it can't because it ceases to be growth in the attempt.[26]
Hugh Prather

April 25, 1983

Dean and I moved in together. I am so in love with him.

May 21, 1983

Dean is moving out. He believes that our relationship will endure if I grow up and learn to stand on my own two feet. He's right. No matter how much it scares me, it's about time that I quit making excuses for my insecurity and do something about it.

I really love Dean and even admire him for standing up for what is right. It's definitely not what is easiest or most comfortable, but it's necessary.

Comfort: that stealthy thing that enters the house a guest,
and then becomes a host, and then a master.[27]
Kahlil Gibran

June 5, 1983

Dean is moving away to go to college. I still love him. I'll always love him.

June 13, 1983

Today I said goodbye to Dean; literally and emotionally. I will survive and be happy and I will never revolve my life around a man again.

I love the feeling of being in love, but it's time I quit trying to make a future out of it. I loved what Dean and I had, but I didn't love who I was with him.

You are never in love with anyone.
You're only in love with your prejudiced and hopeful idea of that person.[28]
Anthony DeMello

August 2, 1983

Just when I thought things were finished and I was getting over him, Dean sent me a very encouraging letter. Even though I am probably setting myself up for emotional destruction again, the prospect of working things out with him fills me with anticipation because I really do love him.

I'm so proud of myself for the way I've matured through all of this. I hope that Dean will see the changes in me and be proud also.

August 9, 1983

I'm going to see Dean in a couple of weeks. He better understand that even though this has been a good learning experience for me, I will not be his emotional toy again. I'm not the same love-sick idiot that I was two months ago.

August 15, 1983

I haven't drunk alcohol, overeaten, or thrown up all week. For me, that's excellent self-control.

Most people are asleep. They are having a nightmare.[29]
Anthony DeMello

The visit with Dean was a romantic whirlwind.

September 25, 1983

Dean moved home! We're *so* in love.

You cannot step twice into the same river.[30]
Plato

September 30, 1983

I'm anxious about plunging into a commitment with Dean. I can really feel my independence fighting my emotions of love.

I live from one tentative conclusion to the next, thinking each one is final.
The only thing I know for sure is that I am confused.[31]
Hugh Prather

November 25, 1983

I've been throwing up entirely too much again. That needs to stop because it's bad for me and Dean hates it.

December 29, 1983

Dean broke off the relationship again. I guess deep inside I knew it was coming. I'd like to say that I can't handle going through this again, but I'm not ready to throw in the towel on my life. I'm a survivor.

January 3, 1984

I am very lonely, but I know that everything is going to be all right in the long run. It's just waiting for the long run that's killing me.

Loneliness is not cured by human company.
Loneliness is cured by contact with reality.[32]
Anthony DeMello

January 11, 1984

I see things now that I never saw before. When I left Terry, I thought that it was *him* that was making me unhappy. I thought that Dean would make all the difference in the world because I passionately loved him. Now I see that it wasn't Terry or Dean who were responsible for my happiness; I am responsible for my happiness.

I see now that I have confused being dependent on a person with being in love with them. I have also tended to put too much importance on sex because I have thought of it as an indicator that someone cares about me. Furthermore, I am insecure and sometimes put my own faults on others. This is the truth.

I still believe in love, but all of this with Dean is making me cynical. He says that the Dean I love is the stupid, idiot, child Dean. I know that this is true, but it sort of makes me sad to consider that making something significant out of my life may require sacrificing the part of me that sees beauty in simple things.

Growing up is exciting because it's interesting when things finally start making some sense. It's also painful because it means giving up so much.

And what is it but fragments of your own self you would discard
that you may become free?[33]
Kahlil Gibran

January 16, 1984

I think that God may be working in my life. I prayed and something seems different. My mind is open and clear.

Being made in His image we have within us the capacity to know Him.
In our sins we lack only the power.[34]
A.W. Tozer

January 22, 1984

My new friend from work, Peter, is letting himself care way too much about me way too soon. He's a very nice person, but I'm just not interested in getting involved in any more heavy relationships until I get over Dean. I don't need men; I know I don't.

January 27, 1984

Dean's sorry he broke up with me. I forgave him. Peter says he loves me. I like him a lot, but I like Dean more. Besides, Dean wants Peter out of the picture. I'm just a fool for Dean's love. I wish I didn't know either of them. Sometimes I think I'll never learn.

February 3, 1984

I called Peter and we're still going to be friends. I must be out of my mind! I don't know what I'm doing. I just know that I like them both in different ways and I am a different person with each of them.

A double-minded man is unstable in all his ways.
James 1:8

February 21, 1984

I think I love Peter.

February 29, 1984

Help! I need my head examined. It's still not final, but I think Dean and I are going to get married in three weeks.

March 7, 1984

I couldn't let go of Peter. Dean's sick of me. I can't say that I blame him.

He who moves not forward, goes backward.[35]
Johann Wolfgang Von Goethe

March 17, 1984

I think it's time for me to start doing more constructive things with my life than being in love. I've always known that I need to be alone, but rather than actively do something about it, I just act like a royal jerk so that men will leave me. I've got to quit living by the old Shakespearean line "*all the world's a stage*" because I can actually see myself acting in some highly emotional situations. Mind games are crazy—even though I am pretty good at them. I've got to start being more honest with myself about the way I feel about things and then be more firm about standing up for these feelings.

Whenever a human being becomes the battleground for the instincts, there can be no peace.[36]
Twelve Steps and Twelve Traditions

April 24, 1984

I've been feeling very, very sick lately. I'm afraid that my bulimic act is catching up with me.

Peter was a much heavier drinker than I had ever been, but as they say, ***Water seeks its own level.*** **When I became "friends" with him, I began to drink and use drugs much more heavily than before. Although Peter could be extremely charming and charismatic, he was also violent and abusive when drinking; which was continuously.**

April 28, 1984

Peter and I both know that we'd be better off without each other, but we're also both scared to death of the kind of pain that a break-up would entail. But there's no denying that things just haven't been the same since his big blow-up a few weeks ago **(we got drunk and he beat me up).** He's too cautious and I'm too nervous. Now I get frightened when he drinks too much or loses his temper.

When am I going to open my eyes and face the fact that I have all of these continuous relationship problems because I don't need to be in a serious relationship for a while?

May 9, 1984

Peter and I are engaged!

Whenever we had to choose between character and comfort, the character-building was lost in the dust of our chase after what we thought was happiness.[37]
Twelve Steps and Twelve Traditions

May 17, 1984

I'm having severe second thoughts about this stuff with Peter. He is an alcoholic and I just don't think I have what it takes to deal with his problems. I asked him to cut back on his drinking, but he denies that he even has a problem. I think it's unfair for me to try to change him into the stable man that I need, but it's also unfair to me to try to tolerate all of the chaos around him.

You are always a slave to what you are not aware of.[38]
Anthony DeMello

May 25, 1984

Peter and I broke up. I don't know if all the violence has made me not love him or made me realize that I never did. I feel bad to have to hurt him by refusing to marry him, but I can't ever marry again out of pity and I have begun to feel nothing but pity for him.

May 30, 1984

I've been single for a week. I've been having a blast, but I haven't been taking very good care of myself. Life in the fast lane sure does make you lose your mind!

The great power of sin is that it blinds us so that we do not recognize its true character.[39]
Andrew Murray

June 7, 1984

Things are kind of hectic living alone. I can't remember the last time I was alone. Between Peter, Dean (they're back in the picture), and some new buddies; I hardly ever have a moment to myself. Life's just crazy right now.

Our troubles are of our own making.[40]
Alcoholics Anonymous

June 8, 1984

I don't know what I want anymore. I guess I'm depressed today because I feel like I'm in a mega-rut. I'm having that *let's shake my life to pieces to make it more interesting* urge (again). The day I learn not to make split-second decisions is when I'm going to be heading toward being a more stable adult.

June 9, 1984

Today Peter accused me of using him and I hung up on him, but when I really think about it, I guess he's sort of right. I use him as my emotional security blanket and run home to him when I feel like my other boyfriends have kicked sand in my face. I guess it's not really fair to pretend that I love him when I know that I don't.

June 16, 1984

Today Peter and I said a very melodramatic "goodbye forever," but it ended up being so painful that I fled into his arms. I should be a romance novelist.

My head is in an absolute daze. I snorted about ten lines of coke last night and then only slept three hours before I drank beer and snorted more. As much fun as I have sometimes, I do not approve of this lifestyle I have chosen for myself. All I hardly ever write about is how much I need to straighten my life up, but I still don't do it. Sometimes I don't understand the destructive forces that motivate my behavior. I am such an insecure person.

There are two basic types of people: those led by desire and those led by discipline. Desire will destroy you. Discipline will build you.[41]

James P. Gillis M.D.

August 22, 1984

I'm dying to settle down and have a normal life, but I'm going to have to earn that by nurturing stability within myself. Peter and I could never have a happy life together. He is the sort of person that I *am now*—not the sort of person that I *want to be*. I'm just as mixed up as he is, but I at least admit my confusion and have a desire to change. I want more than reckless, meaningless living. I want to be happy, fulfilled, and mutually in love with a normal man. I've got some problems that I need to straighten out—*alone!*

Our reach must exceed our grasp.[42]

Oswald Chambers

October 13, 1984

I'm through having no credibility—especially with myself.

December 22, 1984

I know exactly what I want for the eventual outcome of my life; my own career, independence, and a stable, happy family (something I've never had), but I've got so many little bridges to cross before I come to the final big one. Sometimes the reality of how long it takes to achieve something worthwhile is agonizing for me. I've never been a patient person, but I'm finally realizing that if I don't start learning to be, I'm going to always experience my life as "not quite fulfilling enough."

It is better to light a single candle than to curse the darkness.[43]
Motto of the Christophers

Even though I knew there was no future with Peter, I continued to see him while Dean moved away from the vortex that was my life.

February 10, 1985

Crash! I don't know where to start. You think you know yourself so well and then you do something completely out of left field that you never thought you'd do. I had another abortion. All I can say is that I will be very careful about never getting pregnant again unless I'm absolutely sure that I am perfectly ready. I feel terrible about what I have done, but I had to. I've learned.

Life's going to change drastically whether I want it to or not. I'm alone and I want to live.

Abortion destroys two lives, the life of the child and the conscience of the mother.[44]
Mother Teresa

February 18, 1985

I feel very sad about what I did, but I know that I will eventually feel good again—or at least better.

Peter and I continued to drink, fight, break-up, and get back together over the next several months. In the meantime, I began working at an exclu-

sive French restaurant where my career started taking precedence over my romances. One Sunday afternoon, I met a new victim in the bar where I drank. Meeting him finally transitioned me away from Peter.

Insanity: doing the same thing over and over again and expecting different results.[45]
Albert Einstein

December 1, 1985

Yesterday was my birthday. I'm back on the love merry-go-round again. I've met a man who I'm getting pretty involved with. His name is Ben. The relationship's nice because I don't expect too much from it. I've just got to accept the fact that no matter how good things go in my life, there will never be constant exhilaration.

March 26, 1986

I've been straightening out my life pretty well, but there are still a few excesses that will be my undoing if I don't watch out. I've just about got the bulimia under control. Every once in a while I feel a compulsive urge to binge and purge, but it's always triggered by either a horrendous hangover or a serious emotional upheaval. The emotional crises are far and few between compared to past history, but the hangovers are way too frequent. I'm on another one of my attempts to stay on the wagon, but I must admit it becomes very hard for me at times.

Ben has stretched, pushed, changed, and molded me so much that sometimes I don't even know if I'm coming or going. This relationship is like nothing before. We lead our separate lives, but we still have a life together; even though we really don't have anything in common. He's definitely dimming my idealistic viewpoint of life.

I feel that he is good for me. I don't know if there's really a future for us because I'm not positive that he's truly capable of loving anyone other than himself, but then again, maybe in the past I have been too convinced that unselfish love is good love. You've got to be a little selfish in order to merely self-preserve. Is that true?

We do not see things as they are; we see things as we are.[46]
Talmud

July 4, 1986

I must be full of it if I want anyone to dim my idealistic view of life and love. I don't want to believe that true love doesn't exist.

Face it baby; he isn't the guy for you! That's why it isn't working.

In the last few months, I've gotten loaded and laid into Ben about how I *really* feel. He left me. We're still seeing each other, though. Tonight when I was having my hysterics about how I don't want us to be separated, I almost told him (admitted) that he is my live-in security blanket and if I can't have that, I don't want anything from him. We have nothing in common. Being alone will be good.

Sin establishes itself in the sinner and takes its toll.[47]
Oswald Chambers

August 12, 1986

The being alone bit is progressing. I like it. The desire to remain idealistic is going away however. Ben and I had a talk tonight about not expecting life to live up to our childhood expectations. I'm realizing a lot of things that I never expected or wanted to realize. Just the same, what I'm realizing is actual reality and not a bunch of fairy tales.

I'm not as good a person as I thought I was. I'm not even sure if "good people" really exist in the sense that I thought they did. I look around me and realize that almost everyone I know is selfish. The one's that aren't are lonely and unhappy.

Am I crazy for having these thoughts? Sad, but true; the world's just not a giving place. You're born alone and you die alone. In between, you find ways to divert yourself from being lonely.

September 5, 1986

The soul-searching continues:
Constant attempts,
Constant failures,
Blaming anyone, but me.
Refusing to believe it's a game of my creation.
Potential for success,

yet settling for less
than I deserve.
Hope swept away
into voids of mediocrity.
Too lazy to change.
It's just too hard to rearrange
a cluttered mess.
I hate my life!
I hate all that has caused this!
Too stubborn to see
the one to blame
is me.
But, I want to live.

October 28, 1986

I think I need to move away in order to be able to stay sober. I've got so many goals that I don't think can materialize in this town. I want to bury my past. I hope to find a whole new world out there. I want to be a better person. I want new realities.

My eve was in truth my dawn.[48]
Kahlil Gibran

.3. came to believe

December 26, 1986 – May 6, 1987

When we became alcoholics, crushed by a self-imposed crisis we could not postpone or evade, we had to fearlessly face the proposition that either God is everything or else He is nothing.[49]
Alcoholics Anonymous

I remember it like it was yesterday. I was sitting in the office of my place of employment, counting the money and jiggling the books in my favor, when that dreaded voice of conviction swept over me, *One of these days, you're going to have to stop stealing. One of these days you're going to have to stop sleeping around. One of these days you're going to have to stop drinking and drugging. One of these days you're going to have to stop throwing up everything you eat. One of these days*… And then the stark realization: *That day will never come.*

By this period of my life, my daily routine was torturous. I started each morning with six beers in order to get moving toward the office. By noon, I began to feel the headache and nausea from the deterioration of both my body and mind. As a remedy, I crept down to the kitchen of the restaurant for lunch and a few stolen beers. After eating, I went into the bathroom and vomited the food before guzzling the beers. I then hid the beer bottles at the bottom of the trash. Next, I returned upstairs and waded through the bookwork until 3:00.

I then went home for a short break in order to prepare for the evening shift. As I ironed my blouse, I drank two bottles of White Zinfandel straight from the bottle. Then I went to the restaurant and waited tables while drinking wine throughout the shift.

After work, I went straight to my favorite bar where I drank screwdrivers until midnight and then switched to straight vodka. When the bar closed, I went home with the "boyfriend" of the evening and drank whatever stolen liquor was stashed in my fridge. We did whatever drugs were available, and each other, until we passed out. When I came-to in the morning, it began again. Day after day I lived this existence until my only goal was to stay one step ahead of the ominous feelings of impending doom that lurked deep within me.

On the evening before Thanksgiving of 1986, I got to the bar early because the restaurant was closed. I met up with another "boyfriend" and we went from one bar to another. We got back to my small duplex around 3:00 A.M. and proceeded to do what I had done so many times with so many different men. As we rolled in the bed, removing each other's clothing, I experienced an unexpected moment of vivid clarity. I had the sensation that I was standing next to the bed, observing what was happening in front of me. One dominant thought rang through my head, *Who is that drunken slob in my bed with that man?* Immediately, I realized that it was me! In that instant, the full impact of what I had become crashed into my awareness. At that moment, I knew beyond the shadow of a doubt that I could no longer continue to live this "moral-less life," as my mother had so often labeled it.

I immediately arose from the bed and ordered the man to leave. I sat on the couch in utter despondency. I knew that I could no longer continue in the destructive pattern that had gutted its way into my being, but I also knew that it was impossible for me to escape. As I sat there, I looked down at the coffee table and gazed at a mirror that was on top of it. On the mirror were white powder and a razor blade. I then knew what I must do; I would cut my wrists.

The thought occurred to me that, since I would be dead, I needed to let my mother know that I would not be in Dallas for Thanksgiving Day. I left my duplex and traveled to the restaurant in order to use the telephone. The expense of a drug addicted and alcoholic lifestyle left no extra money for things such as telephones. I arrived at the empty restaurant around 9:00 A.M. The shelves of liquor were already beckoning me. I called my mother and told her that I would not be attending her Thanksgiving luncheon. She began to weep and to convince me to attend.

Addicts and alcoholics are like small children who stand in the middle of the room with their hands covering their eyes. Since they can't see, they believe that they are invisible. My deteriorated life was definitely visible to my mother. Her pleas were successful and I agreed to come to Dallas.

After I hung up the receiver, the liquor's attraction grew stronger. I thrashed with indecision. I had been convicted the previous evening that I could no longer live with alcohol, but I couldn't live without it either. As I reached into my pocket for my car keys, I discovered a piece of paper that I had never seen before. On it, in my Grandmother Ruthie's handwriting, was the telephone number for a local Alcoholics Anonymous group. It had apparently been placed there during one of the many drunken cries for help that I had wailed in my grandparent's living room.

I picked up the phone once again and called A.A. I spoke to a nice lady who agreed to meet me the following day at noon for my first meeting. I hung up and left the restaurant without taking a drink. At lunchtime, I drove to Dallas to "celebrate" both Thanksgiving and Shannon's engagement to her long-time boyfriend. I was already tired and depressed, but there was one thing that made me even more miserable than myself; the happiness of those I envied.

When I arrived at Mom's house, I told her that I had made a call to A.A. She informed me that she had been there herself and gave me the textbook that went with the program. It was a blue book entitled *Alcoholics Anonymous*.

I opened it and looked at one of the pages. After many years of self-abuse my reading comprehension was somewhat impaired, but I definitely recognized one word that jumped off the page at me—GOD! Experiencing another period in my life of disbelief, my first thought was, *Is God inescapable?* My second thought was one of utter hopelessness, *If A.A. is about God, then A.A. will not work for me because I don't believe in God.*

I made it through the day and was finally able to retire to a back bedroom where I could isolate myself from the excitement of Shannon's engagement. I had always been jealous of her because she had a wonderful life while mine was a dismal failure. It never once occurred to me that the reason for our dichotomy was that she was a praying girl who strived for a life of righteousness while I was most definitely not. The understanding of things such as the consequences that result from various choices I make would not come to me for many years.

As I tried to fall asleep in the back room of my mother's house, I experienced a desperation and hopelessness beyond any before. I tossed. I turned. I cried. I felt sorry for myself. Finally, I did something that I had never humbly done before, I prayed. It was a simple prayer, *God, I don't believe in You, but if*

You're there, please help me. Nothing seemed to happen, but I was able to fall asleep.

The next day, I returned to Fort Worth and attended my first meeting of Alcoholics Anonymous. I don't remember anything particularly impressive about it other than the observation that there was only one guy who looked attractive to me. I left the meeting feeling upbeat because I had finally done it—I had gone to A.A. and quit drinking.

It was now Friday and my father was taking Shannon, Kelly (my youngest sister), and me out for a fancy dinner to celebrate Shannon's and my birthdays. With the bravado of two days away from alcohol, I ventured to the mall to buy a new outfit for the occasion. I purchased satin parachute pants, a velvet hat, and red lipstick. I was back in the game! The delusional belief system of addicts and alcoholics makes it possible to be suicidal one day and out buying a new hat the next. As they say, *Ignorance is bliss* ... when it's not misery.

That evening, I went to dinner with Dad. Although I had lived with him as an adolescent, Mom was more aware of what was going on in my life. By the evening of this dinner, Dad's perception of me was that I was successful because I had a good job at a prestigious restaurant and I was thin compared to what I had been growing up. After dinner, he asked me to dance. I remember him whispering in my ear how proud he was of me. At that moment, the cocky bravado shattered and a sickeningly familiar thought crossed my mind, *If he only knew the truth.*

Two days later, November 30, 1986, was my twenty-fifth birthday. Miraculously, I was still alcohol free. I woke up around 6:30 A.M.; which was a stark contrast to my usual hung over "coming-to." As I sat in my bed, alone, I experienced a sense of well-being that was deeper than the false bravado of believing that I had conquered alcohol forever. I looked out the window and noticed how beautiful the pink sky was in the early morning. It was one of the first mornings in years that I was awake at sunrise without having been up all night. Suddenly, a startling thought resounded in my mind,

> "You are loved. It's not too late to change the path you're on, but you must turn around and go the other way. But do not be afraid; for I am with you always—even until the end of time."

I was shocked! *Oh my God, it's God!* I thought. I began to search for a logical explanation. *God would not talk to me within myself,* I reasoned.

> "Paige, you don't listen to anyone else,"

was the reply.

I then knew without a doubt that God was real and alive—and that He loved me. In the days to follow, I began to receive what would be the first of many direct revelations from Him.

December 26, 1986

Where do I begin to tell the sweetest love story of my God? The wisdom that passes understanding is inside of me. I am aware that He literally wants to save the world; in us—through us.

The call has been received; the judgment is coming. It will be favorable. Life is God. He's here.

> *The kingdom of God does not come with observation; nor will they say, "See here!" or "See there!" For indeed, the kingdom of God is within you.*
> **Luke 17:20 – 21**

December 29, 1986

I am alive and, dear God, does it feel wonderful! I am in absolute awe over the reality that is dawning on me. God is real and He lives inside of us. So few of us are willing to believe this—or to search for the light that is tucked deep within the darkness of ourselves. Peace will be achieved through the reconciliation and balance of this contradiction.

There is *no such thing* as an ordinary person because this is an *extraordinary* world. God is everything and everywhere—and He is calling us together for an open forum. He desires reconciliation; and the peace of the world depends on it. The closer we grow to Him; our innocence will be reborn to introduce a new form of wisdom.

Life is a constant flow of God that ends only in reception of Himself.

> *The light has come into the world, and men loved darkness rather than light.*
> **John 3:19**

January 5, 1987

Well, needless to say, I made a few resolutions for the New Year. When one first receives the Spirit into one's life, one can possibly lose it for a while. I sort of went overboard, but I'm back in tune with material reality now. I am amazed at the world that I never knew existed. It's hard to believe that I could have been so out of tune—so out of control. Thank God I finally woke up.

As we awaken in spirit, God begins to draw back some of the "veils" of misperception that have, until now, blinded our spiritual eyes to the truth.[50]
John of the Cross

February 1, 1987

I am a child delivered through the storm
to bring hope to those who fear that tradition has died.

February 2, 1987

I learn more every day. Breaking through is wild! All this life I felt that there was something special going on, but I never thought much further past what I was going to do after I "straightened out my life." The possibilities are limitless. God keeps telling me that I am destined to be a leader in the future. However, where I will lead will be within. This is the journey Home and it is a long and sometimes seemingly dangerous one, yet it cannot be measured by distance or time. This is the journey deep into the heart because that is where Home is.

We all have great responsibility; the responsibility of being used for the salvation of the world. I've never wanted real responsibility—or blame. However, I know one thing for sure, I can run, but I can't hide from the Truth.

We have a mission—to save the world through the power of love.[51]
Marianne Williamson

Prior to this period, Ben and I had no contact with each other until I started leaving notes at his apartment. I missed him and wanted to share my spiritual experience with him. Late one evening, he appeared at my doorstep; intoxicated. I ended up going home with him and he passed out while I slept next to him. Ben was a graduate medical student whose sole aim in life was his PhD. and the consequent fame that he believed it would bring to him. Therefore, he was adamant about not having unprotected sex. However, on this evening I was awakened by him as he professed his love for me in his sleep. He began to make love to me and was awakened by his own climax. I knew immediately that a child had been conceived and that it was a gift from God. Ben chalked my spiritual experience off to mental illness and continued with our separation. I was led back to Alcoholics Anonymous.

February 18, 1987

I'm going to have a baby! I've sort of spilled my marbles all over the path the past few weeks, but I'm slowly but surely picking them up so that I (now we) may continue our journey. The hardest thing for me to learn is that Rome was not built in a day. Silly me; to think the entire transformation could occur overnight.

There is a long period of reconstruction ahead.[52]
Alcoholics Anonymous

March 14, 1987

I'm living with Aunt Billie and not working. I have changed so much that I don't even recognize myself anymore. I have changed for the better. My faith is stronger now than ever. God has proved to me in many ways that following the path is worthwhile.

Now, I'm just waiting patiently for the growth and birth of my child. No one's ever called me "Mom" before.

March 16, 1987

I have been depressed. I miss Ben and I am lonely. Sometimes I get the temptation to just wallow in aching misery, yet I know that to give up is to be defeated. I must go through with this pregnancy even though I am so uncertain of what the future will bring. It is my greatest hope that it will be good. I'm trying to believe that.

I've never given my life over to God's will before and it's scary, but I know that learning to trust Him is vitally important. I am learning now by doing what I believe to be "right." It was so much easier to take short cuts.

Not working is very strange for me. Taking financial pressure off of me is putting a lot more pressure on my emotional and spiritual growth. There is no way that I can hide from myself with this much time on my hands. I need strength to fight the temptation to throw it all away. Just getting through this pregnancy without making myself miserable is proving to be one of the most difficult jobs I have ever undertaken.

I've come to the conclusion that deep inside I fear that I'm not as creative and capable of giving as I want to believe I am. This is becoming a period of time when I have to prove a lot of things to myself. The desire to "show them" is going away because "they" don't exist anymore. I am now my own antagonist. Growing is a strange experience.

We must enter into the center of our existence and become familiar with the complexities of our inner lives.[53]
Henri J.M. Nouwen

March 21, 1987

Spring has sprung, the weather is glorious, and I'm lonelier than hell.

April 12, 1987

The time has come to let go of Ben and to live by the will of God; not by my plan of what I think I want. I saw a great quote on a picture at the doctor's office today, *"Life is not a puzzle to solve. It is a mystery to explore."* I'm ready for the exploration.

A journey of a thousand miles begins with a single step.[54]
Lao-Tzu

April 4, 1987

The longer I progress into recovery, the more aware I become of exactly how sick I have been. It is a long, long road and sometimes I feel as though I'm not tough enough to survive the journey.

I realize that I've been using dreams of reconciliation with Ben to cover up that I am very sexually driven. When I'm not thinking about him, I'm thinking about Jake **(a friend from A.A.)**. I'm a very insecure person. It's no wonder I procrastinate doing Step Four (the fearless moral inventory). It's like surgery without anesthesia.

Why do I always feel such urgency about life's situations? Who taught me that I have to be in a hurry or I'll miss my chance? Who said that it's now or never? It's when it's supposed to be and, for some reason, that's hard for me to accept. When can I start being me and not always worrying about how this "me" seems to others?

This life truly is a mystery. The further I go, the less I know for sure. Everywhere I turn is a paradox. Every step I take leads me toward the unknown and away from familiarity. I don't want my faith to shake yet it is hard not to be afraid that I am being led astray. I went from the merry-go-round to a runaway-mine-train. When will I truly know the conductor?

How can I begin unless I see where I am starting from?[55]
Hugh Prather

April 8, 1987

I'm noticing some pertinent changes in my acceptance towards my situation with Ben. I remember him as warm and kind when, in reality, he's usually cruel and offensive. I wish he were my dream Ben. Maybe the baby will be.

Jake's a nice person. My lust for him helped me to learn some things about myself. He's a good enough friend not to take advantage of me. He says he loves me too much to fool around with me. Is that possible?

Well, I guess the program works. The winds are changing.

The one who would be constant in happiness must frequently change.[56]
Confucius

April 12, 1987

Ben is interested in getting to know me now that I have changed. No comment on what I *want* to happen.

One thing I've realized is that no man is worth my feeling inadequate over. I watched Ben sleep off an obnoxious drunk the other night and realized that he's just a little boy that needs to be loved—just like I do. I can't believe the enormous power I had given to such a little boy. I see in him the parts of myself that cry so desperately for love and security.

Life never ceases to amaze me these days. I'm at a point where I believe that anything is possible. I now understand the concepts of faith and grace. My conscious contact is strong. I love God and I love life. That's all that matters.

Compassion is born when we discover in the center of our own existence
not only that God is God and man is man,
but also that our neighbor is really our fellow man.[57]
Henri J. M. Nouwen

From the beginning of our relationship, Ben told me that he never wanted to marry or to have a family. I foolishly believed that he didn't mean what he said. Rather than accept the truth, I continued to hang on to the idea that he would change. Therefore, when I started seeing him again, I was continually disappointed because my fantasy of him was inconsistent with reality. This is called "delusion."

April 21, 1987

Change and acceptance seem to go hand in hand. I got drunk last Saturday in a last ditch effort to deny change (growth). I have to accept a lot of things that I don't want to; one being that I am sometimes a very selfish and immature person. The time has come to accept the passing of my childish youth and progress into honest-to-God adulthood. It doesn't mean that I must relinquish my inherent innocence and predisposition to love; yet it does mean that I must accept responsibility for my actions and dedicate time into the evolution of who I am destined to become.

Unfortunately, I must do it alone; with the help of and through the grace of God. No other person can do it for me or replace my need to do it. I owe it to myself and to this child who will look to me alone for guidance. I must exert one hundred percent effort to obtain this growth that leads to recovery and peace of mind. Through the grace of God, I will succeed.

The best thing about the future is that it comes one day at a time.[58]
Abraham Lincoln

April 23, 1987

I saw Ben tonight and realized that, at last, I am working this program for myself and for God—no one else. I don't care if he thinks I'm unattractive pregnant. I don't care if he thinks I'm ruining my life. I'm not ruining his. I have to do what I feel to be right no matter what he thinks or does. I can't change him. All I can do is be myself and love him for who he is. I'm happy to say, I expect nothing from him. I have faith in God.

Faith must be tested
because it can only become your intimate possession
through conflict.[59]
Oswald Chambers

May 1, 1987

I am in great pain today. I want a drink or a joint or a valium or a line of coke or a gun: something to relieve this horrible, unbearable feeling that I have, but I know that the true solution is to live one day at a time and pray for a better tomorrow. Why does living hurt so much sometimes? I don't want to lose faith, but I am just not accustomed to dealing with pain like this. It seems like everything is going to hell today—including my attitude. I feel so negative!

I finally just surrendered and came home to pray, read my A.A. book, and search for serenity.

Being without a mate hurts big time! I know I have to really love myself and help myself (with God doing the major part of the work, of course) before I can truly love someone else. It's just so hard sometimes. But if God wants me alone then alone I will be; whatever it takes to free me from my ego that isolates me from the whole. Egomania is not God's will. At tonight's meeting, a man said that self-centeredness is true hell—when your puny little problems seem important. I don't want to live in hell. This is tough, but like I've heard in the meetings, "Surrender!" I know that if I am patient, good things will happen and I will most likely end up in a nice, healthy relationship, but it doesn't keep me from feeling lonely.

Pain is the touchstone of all spiritual progress.[60]
Twelve Steps and Twelve Traditions

May 4, 1987

I had a bad day yesterday because of a dispute with my sister, Kelly. How do I make amends for a lifetime of misunderstanding? I sometimes find myself resenting both of my sisters for things that are out of their control. I am jealous of them because they have good lives and I don't, but it was my choice to self-destruct for all of those years. They simply made better choices than me. I shouldn't be jealous—but I am. I suppose the time has come to let go of the resentment and accept the facts; whether I like them or not.

They say that God doesn't give you situations that you can't handle. I guess I was cut out to be able to handle more than them; or maybe I'm just a fool. Regardless, I can only blame God or myself, but why bother to blame at all? It's all over now. I am an alcoholic and the most I will ever have is a daily reprieve from alcoholism that is contingent upon the maintenance of my spiritual condition. I guess that means I'll never be "normal."

This obsession of mine towards a relationship with the opposite sex is getting a little tiring. Since Ben is really only a friend, I keep obsessing on Jake. I want to let go. Do you hear me, God? Please take this from me! I'm making a mess! I want to be free.

I've been having irrational fears that something bad is going to happen. I'm just not accustomed to life being good rather than tragic. This concept of expecting good things is alien to me, but I like the story line much better. I guess it's the difference between the authors.

However, with this new story line, it's starting to seem doubtful that I'll ever be famous (**When I was a young girl, I had a vision of myself on a stage in front of a mass of people that convinced me that I would someday be famous).** Why that ever seemed so utterly important to me in the first place isn't very clear. I guess it was because I was always acting rather than living so I felt that I needed an audience or approval to make it worthwhile. Now that I'm actually living my life, the moments of inner peace seem sufficient. It's so hard to believe that true joy is so simple. After so many years of analyzing everything, it seems ironic that the analysis itself was the cause of so much pain.

Maybe there's something to be said about just trusting the general order of things.[61]
Hugh Prather

May 6, 1987

I've been drifting dangerously into fantasies of Ben and me becoming serious again. I guess it's all right to have these dreams as long as I accept that it may not be what is meant to be. I don't like to think about the possibility of him moving back East without me, but I don't want fear to stop me from exploring possibilities.

I really want to make a conscious effort in noting my tendencies toward self-centeredness. There's a girl at the group who is very self-centered. I know that her obnoxiously loud voice is a signal for me to quiet down and that her rudely impatient behavior is a signal for me to relax. She has so many of the qualities that I find unacceptable in my own behavior. She is sometimes the person that I want to stop being.

Look upon every person that annoys you as a means of grace to humble you.[62]
Andrew Murray

.4.

slipping away

May 10, 1987 – December 29, 1987

We thought we could find an easier, softer way.
Some of us have tried to hold on to our old ideas and the result was nil until we let go absolutely.[63]
Alcoholics Anonymous

May 10, 1987

Today is yet another new sobriety date for me. I've been letting that powerfully baffling and cunning drug called alcohol deceive me into thinking that I can use it occasionally without losing my sanity again. How can I forget how disgusted I was with life back in November? How can I forget how wonderfully different my life is when I have conscious contact with God? How can I forget that the contact will fade more and more with each drink or drug? A clear mind is the price I must pay to enable myself to hear instructions and to accept life on life's terms. How can I forget that, without spiritual aid, I might as well be dead (or go back to the living dead as I was before)? I can't forget. Remembering is the only thing that can keep me alive.

The alcoholic at certain times has no effective mental defense against the first drink. His defense must come from a Higher Power.[64]
Alcoholics Anonymous

May 18, 1987

A revelation occurred over the weekend. I think it was the maternal part of me giving birth to itself. I have a strange sensation as if the two opposing parts of me have joined with this maternal aspect and become closer to the whole than before. The realization of what is happening to me is finally sinking in, yet causing no panic. It's a strange sort of peace; so accepting. I realize that in four months I am to meet one of the most significant people in my life; my son or daughter. All-of-a-sudden, a lot of the stuff that was eating my lunch before doesn't seem to matter. The thing that matters is getting through the next four months with good mental, physical, and spiritual health so that this great event may occur in my life. I am beginning to love my baby in a way as never before.

May 22, 1987

I simply must admit that I am powerless over alcohol or my life will become unmanageable once again. I've been "drinking normally" and it's causing deep inner turmoil. I know that if I keep it up, the control will become more limited. I cannot take the risk of allowing that to happen. I've got to get a grip on this situation and ask God to help me to really work a program. I've got to! It's too late in the pregnancy for me to start pulling these stunts!

This is the baffling feature of alcoholism as we know it—
this utter inability to leave it alone,
no matter how great the necessity or the wish.[65]
Alcoholics Anonymous

June 1, 1987

I had a bad slip last night. Today, I felt almost as bad as I did on Thanksgiving. Maybe this is finally the bottom. I hope so. I just don't have the stamina for too much more. I need help. I surrender.

I saw Ben tonight. I love him, but I don't like him. He is rude and insulting. The sooner I accept the fact that he is not going to miraculously fall in love with me, the better.

Today I have felt very powerless over alcohol and everything else. I just want to get through this pain alive. I'll be so relieved when the nightmare is finally over. I'm becoming fearful that I'm not going to make it through while, at the same time, I know that I must.

I'm going to get professional help. I don't know much anymore, but I know that I'm an alcoholic and that I want to feel better. I once wrote a poem that ended with the line *I need belief to keep me sane.* I believe that God will help me. I believe. I hope. I pray.

Many people suffer because of the false supposition on which they have based their lives. That supposition is that there should be no fear or loneliness, no confusion or doubt.[66]
Henri J. M. Nouwen

June 2, 1987

Today has been an eye-opening day. I've accepted some things (or at least am willing to accept) that I have never been able to cope with before. I have decided to give psychiatric drug therapy a try; something that I have never been willing to do before. Maybe I truly do have a chemical imbalance that can be controlled. It would be wonderful to discover that these sometimes-tedious bouts with dissatisfaction are abnormal. Maybe the discomfort is unnecessary. I have hope.

I have also realized that now is the time to come to terms with my repetitious cycle of replacing one infatuation with another. I have "serial" relationships; using one man to get over another. I used Peter to get over Dean and Ben to get over Peter. I tried to use Jake to get over Ben, but he wouldn't let me.

Now that I am pregnant, I'm stuck without a replacement. I just have to ride this one out. Getting over Ben is hard. Maybe he is just the culmination of all the emotional build-up of my "romances."

I find that I am more willing than ever to be responsible for my own happiness. Something wonderful is happening. It's hard to let it all just happen without trying to exert control over other people, places, and things, but I feel encouraged about the "letting go and letting God" part of A.A. I want this program! I am ready to see what real living is.

June 6, 1987

Last night, a lot of stuff about motives came to mind. When I examine my past motives, I see how truly manipulative I was. I tried to control everything. Control is an illusion.

Most people try to live by self-propulsion.

Each person is like an actor who wants to run the whole show.[67]
Alcoholics Anonymous

June 8, 1987

Dad's mad at me because I can't make my car payment. He's always disappointed in me for some reason or another. I don't believe it's good to blame others for my problems, but I do blame him for mine. I'm trying to take responsibility for the moral and spiritual sides of my life, but it would be easier if there had been someone to teach me the difference between right and wrong when I was growing up.

I know my grandfather's early death and neglect of Dad just passed down the line, but enough is enough. When is this family going to finally have enough guts to open its eyes and see the influence we have in each other's lives; especially our children's? The buck stops here.

When one of you falls down he falls for those behind him,
a caution against the stumbling stone.
And he falls for those ahead of him,
who though faster and surer of foot, yet removed not the stumbling stone.[68]
Kahlil Gibran

June 9, 1987

Ben has been calling a lot, but I don't know why. All I care about is the baby and the program and those are the two subjects that he doesn't want to discuss.

June 17, 1987

I have felt very hostile the last couple of days. I think that I am bored. Nothing great has happened, but nothing terrible has happened either. It's times like these when I see what a true crisis junkie I am. I feel like sabotaging my program just so I'll have a mess to clean up.

There is plenty wrong with us alcoholics about which plenty will have to be done if we are to expect sobriety, progress, and any real ability to cope with life.[69]
Twelve Steps and Twelve Traditions

June 22, 1987

I approached Ben on the subject of coaching me through Lamaze. He thinks that Shannon is the wise decision since she will always be a part of my life. I want him to do it.

He was affectionate towards me for the first time since our reconciliation. I am very confused. Being with him makes me realize that my heart will probably break if he really does just turn and walk away, leaving the baby and me behind as a memory.

I have faith that God will direct the situation.

I used to believe that trusting God's goodness meant I would not be hurt. But having been hurt quite a bit, I know God's goodness goes deeper than all pleasure and pain—it embraces them both. [70]

Gerald May

June 29, 1987

Ben says that he is considering settling down with me and the baby. I think that he's starting to love me, but I also think that his feelings for me repel him from me as much as they draw him to me. I know this whole deal is hard on him too. These are life-altering decisions. At least my choice is made. I am going to be a mother—with or without Ben.

June 30, 1987

Tomorrow I pick up my thirty day chip. I'm very grateful. The whole world seems different to me and yet I realize that the only thing that has really changed is my perspective on a world that has always been in flux. I like what I see.

Everything becomes beautiful when you change. [71]

Anthony DeMello

July 7, 1987

Ben and I went to Austin for the fourth of July. We had a wonderful time. I'm in love with him. At this time I can see the similarities between joy and pain. I love him so much that it hurts because I keep allowing myself to become fearful that it's all going to slip away.

Is not dread of thirst when your well is full, the thirst of the unquenchable? [72]

Kahlil Gibran

July 12, 1987

I've been spending a lot of time with Ben and allowing myself to genuinely care for and share with him. I can't believe how much work it is to be fair and loving. I am so grateful for this second chance with him.

The fragrance always remains in the hand that gave the rose.[73]
Heda Bejar

July 15, 1987

I didn't see Ben the past few days and I feel depressed and anxious. I don't know how to love without becoming addicted.

July 28, 1987

Ben spoke of marriage again this weekend. My spiritual growth is important to me, but so is Ben.

You shall have no other gods before Me.
Exodus 20:3

August 2, 1987

I got depressed last night and let my thinking get crazy enough to allow myself to believe that a few drinks would help. Needless to say, I'm very remorseful. Right now I feel like I'm going to feel this way forever and that nothing in this world could possibly make me happy or make me feel better. I know that this is not true, though. I know that this too shall pass and that the meaning of life will continue to shine through.

I've got to accept the fact that I'm powerless over alcohol and that only through acceptance of this fact will I be able to endure the changes in my life. My life is less unmanageable than it used to be, but that will not hold true if I continue to poison myself with the first drink.

I've been feeling anxious over Ben. It's hard for me to let things progress at God's speed. I want him to make a decision about our future.

August 4, 1987

I suffered horrible depression the past two days that evolved into an irritable and agitated mood. I feel very negative and self-destructive. I realized today the full extent of my mental illness that I've always casually referred to as "my self-destructive tendencies." I have hope that I will someday lead a normal, happy life, but I also see that it is going to take work and effort and that the spiritual side of my life needs to grow even stronger.

I want to live and I want to be good, but it is very hard not to become very angry and say, *Why me? What did I do to deserve all this?* Anyway, I'm going to endure. I have faith.

For we have been not only mentally and physically ill,
we have been spiritually sick.
When the spiritual malady is overcome,
we straighten out mentally and physically.[74]
Alcoholics Anonymous

August 7, 1987

I am getting a cold, hard look at the way I tend to think negatively rather than positively. It is sickening. I want so much to just relax and let God take care of things. I really do want to believe that everything is going to be all right, but that kind of faith is so foreign to my old way of thinking. I guess because I was raised on rejection and disappointment, I can't believe that God wants good things for me.

Letting go of fear is definitely proving to be my hardest defect to overcome. I sometimes want to break up with Ben so he can't break up with me first, but I'm not going to run away. I'm going to stand and face it. I truly do believe that fear is the root of all evil.

The chances that you will wake up are in direct proportion to the
amount of truth you can take without running away.[75]
Anthony DeMello

August 11, 1987

I went to my first childbirth class last night and it had an overwhelmingly negative effect on me. Ben should have been with me! I got drunk as a skunk. I've got to start putting this baby foremost in my life, but I feel like such a selfish little baby myself. Dear God, hear my cry.

Without a searching and fearless inventory, most of us have found that
the faith which really works in daily living is still out of reach.[76]
Twelve Steps and Twelve Traditions

August 15, 1987

The baby will be here soon! I can't believe it's almost over. I am huge! In a way it's wonderful because I just love it when it wiggles around and kicks inside of me. It really gives me the strange realization that there's going to be another human being in this world and I'm going to be its mother! I still can't picture myself in that role because I have a hard time realizing that I've moved into a new stage of life and have let go of many of my old ways of seeing the world. It's almost funny to look at the immature things that I cling to that I think define who I am and then, one day, just toss them away forever. Life is weird.

Life only makes sense when you perceive it as a mystery.[77]
Anthony DeMello

August 18, 1987

I'm having a hard time refraining from light to moderate drinking. I'm just so bored and restless. I'm through re-establishing in A.A. I know that a few drinks here and there are not good, but they relieve my feelings of boredom and restlessness. I just don't know what to think. I know that God's alive, but I just don't feel very close to Him and the conscious effort to keep in contact just doesn't seem worth it. I'm not saying that I don't love God and I'm not saying that I want my old life back. I just need a little more excitement.

I don't really believe that I'm powerless over alcohol. Maybe I'm just powerless over depression or maybe I'm just fooling myself. I don't know what's going on.

Now, when you think that you are too busy for your daily visit with God,
let me ask you frankly,
what wonderful thing are you doing that is more important?[78]
Emmet Fox

August 23, 1987

No comment on the last entry. Needless to say, I had an attack of selfishness.

September 16, 1987

Today I realized that Ben may never be able to give when I sometimes need someone to be giving towards me. I cried in front of him because he was complaining about life and saying negative things about the pregnancy. He got mad and said that he couldn't handle emotional outbursts. What about me? Maybe I can't handle stoic indifference.

I say I want to marry him, but do I want a marriage where I walk on eggshells? If I don't cry when I feel like crying, am I growing up or am I not being myself? Am I supposed to change myself for him? My love for him seems almost debilitating.

Any feeling that can make me betray my own heart can have only temporary value.[79]
Hugh Prather

September 24, 1987

Things have been pretty even-keeled the past couple of weeks. I have finally gotten a few days of continuous sobriety under my belt and I feel pretty good about it. I don't want to address the subject too much because when I dwell on my alcoholism, I tend to start rebelling and denying it.

Things with Ben are better. Just being at ease in the relationship is an answer to prayer.

The anticipation of the birth of this child is making every minute seem like an hour. I can't wait.

October 2, 1987

Laurel Shannon Thomas was born at 6:31 P.M. on September 30, 1987. She is beautiful.

Every child comes with the message that God is not yet discouraged of man.[80]
Rabindranath Tagore

October 3, 1987

Laurel and I were released from the hospital today. Overnight, she subtly became the most important thing in my life. She is so precious and has the funniest little personality.

October 20, 1987

My first weeks of motherhood freaked me out, but I'm adjusting better now and feeling more comfortable with the role. I'm getting to know Laurel better so she seems more like a person to me than a little doll that's going to break.

I'm becoming apprehensive about trusting Ben. He's been acting differently.

October 28, 1987

The tension between Ben and I has been mounting. I'm afraid that the responsibility that goes with my life now is too much for him.

The last couple of days have been horrible. I haven't been sleeping and Laurel's sensing my general unrest. I'm withdrawing from alcohol all over again and am becoming very depressed.

I'm so unhappy right now. The responsibility of Laurel is overwhelming me and not drinking is very hard. To be honest, I feel hopeless and suicidal, but I have faith that "this too shall pass." Existing is very difficult today.

In a storm the tree puts down deeper roots into the soil;
through suffering the Father leads us to enter more deeply into the love of Christ.[81]
Andrew Murray

October 29, 1987

Today was a very beautiful day and I felt grateful to be back in A.A. Yesterday, I was suicidal and today I feel exhilarated. No, I don't have a chemical imbalance! There's nothing like being an over-emotional, alcoholic, insane, manic-depressive. A.A. was created for people just like me.

Today I realized that I can choose either to love Ben or not, but that decision must be based on accepting him for who he is; not on who I want him to be. I can't change him.

I once heard someone say to "*Imagine how happy you'd be if you lost everything you had and then got it back.*" Well, I lost A.A. for awhile and, with it, my contact with my Higher Power. It's funny to think that yesterday I wished I were dead. I like looking at life so much better from the non-judgmental, positive side. Just having sunshine, classical violins, Laurel, and A.A. in this world is priceless.

Be thankful for the smallest thing,
and you will be worthy to receive something greater.[82]
Thomas a' Kempis

November 16, 1987

I drank again Friday at Shannon's wedding shower. I felt a little too good and a celebratory glass of champagne seemed reasonable. Then I turned around and drank all day the next day, trying to knock out the hangover. Then I had a few more last night, trying to knock out that all-around horrible feeling. Of course, all of this was in conjunction with overeating and throwing up. I'm telling you, obsessive-compulsive behavior doesn't die from starvation. In one day, I was reliving the hell of last year.

I think that my psychiatric meds may finally be working. I woke up today feeling good for no reason. It's sad to think that all of my life I've been so miserable that I've had to have a reason to feel good.

One thing that is great is this little angel daughter of mine. I'm starting to love her so much. She is the most precious little girl I've ever known. It's still hard for me to express, but something very special is happening between us. She's taken Ben's place in my heart.

What makes you happy or unhappy is not your world or the people around you, but the thinking in your head.[83]

Anthony DeMello

November 19, 1987

I realized tonight that I have never really worked the Steps because I haven't wanted to quit drinking enough to really face what's going on inside of me. I've got to do the work and trust God to guide me through it. Asking Him to remove my character defects without first taking the time to find out what they are just doesn't cut it. I have been working a superficial program.

Every drink is a lie to myself that the outcome won't be the same. I must get honest with myself and humble before God. I must accept defeat. I must let go of the things that make me miserable before God can take them from me. This program is a program of action and I've been sitting on my butt for nine months. No wonder I keep getting drunk.

Almost none of us liked the self-searching, the leveling of our pride, the confession of shortcomings which the process requires for its successful consummation.[84]

Alcoholics Anonymous

November 29, 1987

Tomorrow is my birthday and tonight I got very tempted to drink for celebration's sake, but something important occurred to me that stopped the temptation. I realized that, when I drink, I let negative thinking start up again and then I have to work ten times harder to turn it around. I've been feeling pretty good these past few days because my thinking is not near as negative as it has been lately. Consequently, I'm not depressed, anxious, or worried about things that haven't happened yet. Right thinking is an important thing to pray for.

I got Laurel on a good eating and sleeping schedule. She's so nice to have around. She keeps me motivated. Her needs are simple, but they are also very time-consuming. I love her.

I've started throwing up again. I tell you, if it's not one thing, it's another. I guess I need to get *myself* on a good eating and sleeping schedule. Right now I really don't care because I'm so fat that I'll do anything to get thin. If I get too thin (that'll be the day), I'll worry.

What you give up violently you are forever bound to.[85]
Anthony DeMello

December 5, 1987

I had a long talk with Ben last night. I got some insight into him and saw that his parents made him feel undeserving. It made me sad for him because I definitely understand what it means to feel unlovable.

Ben said that our childhoods are over and we should forget about them; he just wants to accomplish his goals. I agree that it's ridiculous to wallow in the past, but when you have deep-rooted pain, it seems like you need to identify it in order to resolve it. I think it's important to look back.

There can be no knowledge until knowing reaches the hidden reasons.[86]
Meister Eckhart

December 10, 1987

I drank again last weekend because I did some diet pills that made me feel bad and then rationalized that some drinks might take the edge off. *Stinking Thinking!* Then a couple of days later, I figured *what the hell* and had a few beers. I feel very remorseful about it because I really don't want to drink, but I like the speed right now because it keeps me from eating. That's a justification, though. I know that I shouldn't be doing anything that affects me from the neck up.

I haven't been to a meeting in a week.

There was always the curious phenomenon that
parallel with our sound reasoning
there inevitably ran some insanely trivial excuse.[87]
Alcoholics Anonymous

December 20, 1987

I'm very confused about my relationship with Ben. He graduated with his Master's Degree yesterday and didn't even tell me. When I confronted him about it, he was cruel and hateful. I just can't let go of the dream that God's going to zap him like He did me, but I'm beginning to see that it's only a dream.

The object of your attachment had the power to thrill you when you attained it, to make you anxious lest you be deprived of it, and miserable when you lost it.[88]

Anthony DeMello

December 26, 1987

Shannon got married tonight. It was beautiful, but I feel lonely. I didn't have a date so it was kind of uncomfortable. Shannon does everything so perfectly and I do everything so backwards.

December 27, 1987

Today I went to visit a friend and just dreaded coming home. I'm so lonely. I know that I'm not supposed to feel alone with God in my life, but I do. I guess I just have growing pains.

And could you keep your heart in wonder at the daily miracles of your life,
your pain would not seem less wondrous than your joy;
and you would accept the seasons of your heart,
even as you have always accepted the seasons that pass over your fields.
And you would watch with serenity through the winters of your grief.[89]

Kahlil Gibran

December 29, 1987

I love motherhood. The person that I am with Laurel is the best person that I've ever been—the person I enjoy being. The love I feel for Laurel affirms greater faith in God and new love for myself. One look at her and I *know* that there's a God.

As you lay your head to rest,
cradled in the nest of my bosom,
I wonder with awe at the miracle I see

as regal splendor blossoms in eternity.
While bathing in your precious smile,
filled with joy I get charmed for awhile
as my prayer is affirmed
that man is not lost forever.
With a gentle stroke to your tiny face,
I catch a glimpse of myself
that helps to erase
the hopelessness I'd come to know
for I love you so.
How God must love His children even more.
O, precious, infant child of mine,
you're all that's gracious and divine.
You've the light of the world in those sparkling eyes.
You're one of God's angels in disguise.

.5. dogged rebellion

January 1, 1988 – July 17, 1988

A whole lifetime geared to self-centeredness
cannot be set in reverse all at once.
Rebellion dogs our every step.[90]
Twelve Steps and Twelve Traditions

January 1, 1988

The main thing I learned this past year is to be careful what you pray for—because you just might get it. I think I would have been better off if Ben had not come back into the picture. It seems like our relationship is just one disappointment after another. Maybe he genuinely cares for me, but I doubt it.

When I am concerned with what you are thinking about me,
I am not even thinking about you.[91]
Hugh Prather

January 3, 1988

I've been making myself miserable over Ben. It occurred to me the other day that before I can begin to be happy, I must *stop* being miserable. I'm a spoiled brat and it's time for me to grow up! I make myself miserable worrying about things that don't happen. Even if they did happen, the reality of my worries probably wouldn't be as gruesome as the worry itself. I'm sick of being such a child! Do you hear me, God? Help! I must have faith that God will do for me what I cannot do for myself. It was so much easier to walk around with my head up my butt.

God does not give us overcoming life—He gives us life as we overcome.[92]
Oswald Chambers

January 14, 1988

I've been drinking. I'll be so glad when the surrender is complete. I know that absolute sobriety is the inevitable outcome that my life will take, but I just can't seem to get it together and go for it. I keep postponing and delaying the process.

I went to my first therapy session at the mental health clinic. I'm excited about the person I am becoming. According to the therapist, the estimated time of arrival for my authentic self is 1992 – 1993. Learning to be true to myself is forcing me to face the painful reality that my relationship with Ben is far from healthy. I keep praying that God will zap Ben, but I have to keep growing—with or without him. The therapist said I am "codependent."

Being real is very hard and painstaking work for me.

Codependents tend to ignore problems or pretend they aren't happening, pretend circumstances are not as bad as they are, believe lies, look for happiness outside of themselves, seek love from people who are incapable of loving, center their lives around other people, worry other people will leave them, and tolerate abuse to keep people loving them.[93]
Melody Beattie

January 16, 1988

I did some crank and drank some drinks, but they didn't work. I prayed a minute ago because I keep thinking about suicide; even though I know with every fiber of my being that I cannot kill myself. I must live for Laurel if nothing else. She's so beautiful and I love her so much.

I believe (hope) that this is just the beginning of an upward slope. I have to take it one day at a time because if I try to go much farther than that, I panic. My hopes and dreams for my life seem very far out of reach. I want an education, a home of our own for Laurel and I, a decent career so that I can take care of her, a healthy and loving relationship with a man (hopefully Ben), and most importantly, the ability to love and care for myself and to enjoy being the person that I am. I really believe that all of this will materialize as soon as I stop feeling lonely, depressed, and sorry for myself and start taking the steps necessary to get the mega-load of work accomplished that a dream like this requires.

I've always tried the softer, easier route, but I just can't do that anymore because it won't take me to the same place. Richard Bach says that "*You are never given a wish without also being given the power to make it true.*"[94] I believe that.

Tonight I spent a lot of time wishing that I could settle for so much less, but I can't. For today, I know what I want so I guess it's what I deserve to have. I am determined to grow—in spite of myself. Someday, I'll be happy. I know I will. I believe in God with all my heart and I believe that my dreams are there for a reason. The prayers I said are working. I'm feeling better.

You may have to work for it, however.[95]
Richard Bach

Later same evening

Ben called right after I wrote the last entry. He said that he doesn't love me, but it is possible that he will someday. I cried and he told me that I must have been hiding that truth from myself. I liked that because I already knew that he didn't love me yet, but I let myself fall right back into the pattern of crying and being hurt because, after all, isn't a girl *supposed* to be hurt when her boyfriend says he doesn't love her? In reality, it's no big deal. All we can do is keep getting to know one another and see what happens.

It's going to take a lot of awareness for you to understand that perhaps this thing called "I" is simply a conglomeration of your past experiences, of your conditioning and programming.[96]
Anthony DeMello

January 19, 1988

Ben's moving back to New York. I hate it, but I know that it will make me a stronger person. I know that it is meant to happen or it wouldn't be happening. Someday, I will understand all of this.

January 21, 1988

I feel terrible. I can't stay sober and that only adds to the already misery that I am experiencing. I just can't get caught up in this awful trap of melodrama and self-pity. I've got to create a program and stick to it. I've got to walk through this like a mature adult.

Step by step, let whatever happens happen.[97]
Anthony DeMello

January 23, 1988

I'm going to have to accept the fact that this situation is very painful for me and that I can't hide from the pain. I decided that a little crank would lift my spirits, but all it did was increase my anxiety and paranoia.

I took Laurel to a drug house and I feel very ashamed about it. I don't know how low I've got to go before I finally start climbing out of all of this. I hope I'm at the bottom because all of this is frazzling me. I feel so lost. I keep praying and praying, but I just don't feel like God is hearing my prayers. All I want is to handle Ben's departure without a panic-stricken urgency to react. I can't kill myself and I can't kill Ben.

Where I stand right now, *I* can't even love me the way I want to be loved; much less expect someone else to do it. I see that I've still got so much growing to do. I don't know how to do any of this changing stuff. If I've ever needed a miracle, it's now. I've been so sick for such a long time. I know that I'm trying to get well in my own weak way, but I must admit that I feel kind of hopeless. I really would kill myself if I didn't love Laurel so much and if I didn't at least want to believe those people in A.A. when they say it works. I just have to *work it!*

What I really ought to be praying for is gratitude. I'm feeling sorry for myself because this irresponsible jerk is abandoning me when I've still got a beautiful and healthy daughter, a free place to live, food to eat, a free car to drive, clothes to wear, a support group with people that care, a therapist, a family that loves me, the ability to write, beauty, intelligence, and a whole joyful life ahead of me just waiting to be lived if I will just stop feeling sorry for myself and thinking I've got it all so bad because I'm a single parent. It was my decision. I'm so sick and tired of playing the victim. Please, God, help me to stop. I'm sick and tired of being sick and tired!

The things we try to avoid and fight against—
tribulation, suffering, and persecution—
are the very things that produce abundant joy in us.[98]
Oswald Chambers

January 26, 1988

Ben left yesterday. He said to be optimistic; that it will work out. I don't believe him. All I know is that I must rely on God and start over.

What seemed at first a flimsy reed,
has proved to be the loving and powerful hand of God.[99]
Alcoholics Anonymous

February 2, 1988

I've been realizing a few things the past couple of days. The time has come for me to take care of myself as first priority and then everyone else secondly. It sounds selfish, but until I start providing myself with the love and care that I so desperately need, I'll never find it, be able to give it, or share who I am with others. I've got to get to know who I am and where I stand before I can be in an intimate relationship. I must face the fact that I have to be patient and wait until the time is right. I have faith that eventually that time will come.

I'm feeling better lately because it's finally dawning on me that my thoughts and emotions are but a *part* of me—not who I am. I can control them if I learn how and I think that I am learning.

Life is a mystery,
which means your thinking mind cannot make sense out of it.
For that you've got to wake up and then you'll suddenly realize
that reality is not problematic, you are the problem.[100]
Anthony DeMello

February 7, 1988

Where Ben is concerned, I've given up hope **(he promised to call when he got to New York, but I never heard from him again***)*. How could he talk of *sending for the baby and me and announcing our engagement* and then just walk away? Even worse, why did I believe him? I knew he was lying, but I hid it from myself. My fantasy of Ben gained too much power and control over my willingness to face reality.

February 14, 1988

I must admit that I miss Ben's companionship more than I miss Ben.

February 24, 1988

The meeting tonight was on God's will. I don't know what God's will for me is except to love myself enough to take responsibility for my own happiness and to take the best care of myself that I can. I can see the healing process going into effect. I don't know where I'm going, but I do know that it's time to start walking.

In the depth of winter, I finally learned that
within me there lay an invincible summer.[101]
Albert Camus

March 28, 1988

I've been feeling pretty negative lately. I guess it's because I drank a couple of weeks ago. God, it never fails! One binge and I suffer the consequences for weeks to follow. You'd think that I'd learn the simple lesson that I can't drink. For that matter, I shouldn't do drugs either. I'm so sick and tired of writing and talking about my need to maintain complete sobriety and then turning around and either drinking or smoking a joint. I just want to maintain sobriety *period.*

My faith is pretty much in the toilet right now, but I do keep praying so it's not gone. It's not that I don't believe in God. It's that things aren't going my way and it really irritates me. Some spoiled brat, huh? However, everything I read about God and the things I want to believe about Him give me hope that He has good things in store for me.

What does God say to us? He says:
"I have called you by your name ... you are mine ...
water will not drown you, fire will not burn you ...
I will give up nations for you ... you are precious to me ...
I love you ... even if a mother could forget her child, I will not forget you ...
I have carved you in the palm of my hand."[102]
Mother Teresa

April 9, 1988

I started going to meetings again last Sunday and I realized that one reason why I probably keep messing up is that I don't do the basic things that fundamentally *are* the program—go to meetings, pray on my knees, read the literature, talk with other alcoholics, work the Steps, keep sobriety as my number one priority, and *don't drink or do drugs!* I have to admit that I feel better. I know that the program works if I will work it. It's keeping interested in working it that is the hard part. I tend to isolate myself and get knee deep in my stuff. Right now my goal is to make ninety meetings in ninety days; like any good beginner should.

I have made a decision to turn my life and my will over to the care of God whom I still don't understand, but whom I trust and have faith in. I don't think I've really made that decision before now. I really am realizing that my problem is *me* and that the only way to solve my problem is to change and that the only way to change is to surrender to God and that the only way to successfully surrender is to stay out of God's way! I've spent an entire year backsliding and frankly, I give up. I guess giving up is the beginning.

We decided to turn our will and our life over to God as we understood Him.
Just what do we mean by that and just what do we do?
The first requirement is that we be convinced
that any life run on self-will can hardly be a success . . .
We had to quit playing God.[103]
Alcoholics Anonymous

April 27, 1988

I'm trying so hard to break bad habits and replace them with new ones; especially to turn this bulimia thing over to God and let Him keep it. I am the epitome of an obsessive-compulsive disordered person. Food is my drug of choice now.

My life has been such a mess for such a long time that it is taking a tremendous amount of work to clean it all up. I am determined to persevere until self-discipline becomes a permanent and automatic characteristic of my demeanor. I can *hardly* stand myself when I'm throwing up and sleeping late. I don't know how I *ever* tolerated myself when I was throwing up, sleeping late, having promiscuous sex, abusing drugs, keeping a sloppy house, *never* exercising, lying, cheating, stealing, and drinking like a pig! I guess that's what I was escaping from—the realization that I was a loser.

Hey, just as I was writing this I had a realization of the presence of God! I see now that I have finally reached a point in my life where I am not running from myself anymore. Here I am! I don't like certain things about myself, but rather than hating myself and running away, God is giving me the courage to look at the truth. Wow! The program really works!

Though everything is a mess, all is well.[104]
Anthony DeMello

May 3, 1988

It's early in the morning and I feel at peace. God is doing for me what I cannot do for myself. My prayer for today is that my sobriety and my Twelve Step program will stay *at least* as important to me as they are right now. I don't want to compulsively overeat, drink alcohol, or use drugs again. I think that I'm just about ready for complete surrender and to pray only for God's will and the power to carry that out.

Today I have thirty days.

May 8, 1988

I had a one-night-stand with a stranger last night and I feel sick over it. I don't want the old behavior to rear its ugly head. I guess I've got to realize that I'm just beginning my program and that I can't expect to be perfect, but I still *do not feel good about it*. It really makes me see that sex messes me up—regardless of who it's with. When I have sex with someone I don't care about, it repulses me and when I have sex with someone that I do care about, I automatically start hoping and expecting a serious relationship to develop. I must accept the fact that I need to add sex to the long list of things I can't handle. Before I can learn to behave differently in sexual relationships, I've got to abstain and give myself time to change.

Even though I've been feebly trying to work the Steps in order to take some action **(without a sponsor)**, I realize that I'm right back at Step One. I'm powerless and my life is unmanageable. Only God can restore me to sanity. I see that the restoration will be a life-long process. I have made the decision to turn my will and my life over to the care of God, but that doesn't mean that I'm successful at it. Last night, I got right back in the way and followed the lead of my lower nature rather than my higher nature.

I know that I'm changing because there was a time when I thought that one-night-stands were fun and exciting. How disgusting. One thing's for sure; the path definitely grows narrower.

We must accept finite disappointment, but never lose infinite hope.[105]
Martin Luther King Jr.

May 9, 1988

I threw up today and felt as if the downward spiral was taking control. Then I prayed and went to two meetings; one on "expectations" and another on "self-acceptance and unconditional love." All of this really helped and now I feel much better.

The thought occurred to me that the process of practicing spiritual principles is sort of like gymnastics. When you fall off the balancing beam, you have to jump right on up there again—not lie on the floor and feel like it's the end of the world because you fell. There's such a fine line between self-discipline and beating myself up. I have mercilessly punished myself lately for my misbehavior. In reality, the misbehaving act was the punishment itself.

I think I'm getting past Ben.

How shall you punish those whose remorse is already greater than their misdeeds?[106]
Kahlil Gibran

May 11, 1988

I have an eating disorder and it is scaring me. I go on a binge without even realizing what is going on. I don't know what's going on inside of me. I realize that I am very out of touch with my feelings. It seems to me, though, that I am way too hard on myself. I've made my program so strict that I don't even feel grateful because I'm too busy feeling like a failure. It's a real dilemma because I know that all I should concern myself with right now is not drinking or drugging, but it's also important to me that I exercise and stay on a diet. I hate being overweight. I want so badly to be thin again, but I want to do it the old-fashioned way—not throwing up everything I eat. I disgust myself when I do that. I pray that God will remove my overwhelming compulsion to eat. Please, God.

I know that I'm striving so hard for perfection that I'm not even noticing my true progress, but I *don't know how to stop*. Maybe my obsession with my diet is another device I have for running away from my problems, but I don't know. Eating is a crutch for me, but I still can't figure out what is hurting that eating soothes. *Please* help me, God! I can't do it without You.

May 13, 1988

Right now I feel like I don't know anything about life. Everyone talks about how they had to face reality once they got in the program and sobered up. What *is* reality? Either it's passed right over my head or I haven't started facing it yet. I do realize that the things I want out of life are going to require hard work, but I still believe in miracles and dreams come true. I won't give up—ever.

I want to know if you can live with failure, yours and mine,
and still stand at the edge of the lake and shout to the silver of the moon, "Yes!" [107]
Oriah Mountain Dreamer

May 15, 1988

What I wish for from God …

The ability to help others
The desire to help others
Joy
Complete freedom
Peace
Love
An understanding of God
God's will in my life
To be able to live my life responsibly
Self-esteem
Ego deflation
To be a good mother
To be able to have a decent relationship with a man
To find my soul mate
To accept life on life's terms
My miracle

Everything comes to us that belongs to us if we create the capacity to receive it. [108]
Rabindranath Tagore

May 20, 1988

I've been feeling sorry for myself lately and have been in a bad place until tonight. I was at a restaurant with a group of people from A.A. and saw Peter smashed out of his mind. It made me realize just how good I've got it. But for the grace of God, there go I. He was pitiful and I really did feel sorry for him, but I wouldn't want to trade places with him for all the tea in China. That life seems like a million years ago and I want to keep it that way.

I've been feeling some pain. I guess it's good. I suspect that it's about Ben; maybe I'm not totally over him. The thing that's hard for me to accept is that I shouldn't have any emotional involvements for at least a year. That seems like an eternity. I'm sure that if I follow that guideline, the pay-off will be tremendous, but I don't *want* to. I know that at this time I don't know how to do serious relationships except in sick ways, but I still keep trying. I considered letting Peter spend the night with me even though every fiber of my being was yelling, "No!" I think I have a learning disability. I just don't seem to learn from my mistakes.

To be without some of the things you want is an indispensable part of happiness.[109]

Ralph Waldo Emerson

May 28, 1988

I don't feel like I'm growing. I'm still as negative as ever and stay irritated at people, places, and things a lot of the time. Today Jake told me that only weeds grow fast. I don't want to accept that.

Today's one of those days when not having a relationship for a year seems like a very long time. I'll be so glad when this part of my life is over. Being a single mom is lonely and scary. I love Laurel, but being her mother requires such a sacrifice. She's worth it, but this is hard. I have so many rules now when once I had none. I don't understand why I had men galore when I was wild and now that I'm doing all of this work, I have none. I guess I'm just getting prepped up for the right man, but like I said, I don't know anything except that as time goes by, I am facing more and more responsibility; which is pretty scary for a basically reckless and irresponsible person. One of the things I've learned in the program that made me feel better tonight is that "*This too shall pass.*"

Count it all joy when you fall into various trials,
knowing that the testing of your faith produces patience.

James 1:2–3

May 31, 1988

I saw my therapist today for the first time in a while. I found myself crying my eyes out over the pain of being teased all of my life about being fat. I feel like today was some sort of breakthrough. God, it hurts so badly, but at least I understand where it's coming from. I've always felt like I wasn't good enough to fit in with my peers so I drank, drugged, and sought out my social inferiors. I'm scared to death about not being accepted because somewhere along the way it was ingrained in me that being overweight is totally unacceptable. I feel so sorry for the child that I once was. It was real hell living through that humiliation and shame. Anyway, I hope that this will be the beginning of me learning to love and nurture my child inside and teach her that she is a worthwhile and cherished person. My therapist told me to write her a letter:

Dear Child Paige,

I am so sorry that you had to endure the pain and humiliation of being outcast by your peers. If only I had understood, I would have never let your weight get so out-of-control, but I didn't understand and the pain of being separated from Mom was just too much. My only comfort was food. It seemed to be my only friend. I want you to know that I think you're beautiful—inside and out. You've got so much to offer other people and the people that you let in really love and care for you. I love and care for you too. I just wish that I could hold you in my arms and assure you that everything is going to be all right because it is. It's never too late to start over. You've got all the time in the world. Relax, take your time, enjoy yourself, and know that you are loved—by me and by God.

Love, Paige

I want to know if you can sit with pain, mine or your own, without moving to hide it or fade it or fix it.[110]
Oriah Mountain Dreamer

June 9, 1988

Well, I've been in the total pits. Last Friday I seriously contemplated suicide and Mom had to come over and hold my hand. I don't know what it's going to take to get myself off of my own back. I've always operated on the "too much too soon" motto and now I'm trying to do it in my recovery. I'm expecting too much growth in too little time and then kicking myself for not meeting up to my expectations. Who fired God and put me in charge?

The only difference between codependents and the rest of the world is that the other people don't pick on themselves for being who they are.[111]
Melody Beattie

July 2, 1988

Tomorrow makes three months of not drinking. It all feels sort of anti-climatic. I'm still not feeling much better. I threw up tonight and it made me feel horrible with a bad headache on my right side. Sometimes, I get worried that I am going to die soon. I hope it's just me being paranoid and not some sort of premonition. I pick some crazy things to think about. I really miss Ben.

July 17, 1988

I'm still depressed, but it occurred to me that I have let my program go. I've slacked off on meetings, quit praying on my knees, don't have a sponsor, and never read the A.A. literature. Maybe all of this has something to do with the way I've been feeling.

It seems like by now it would be obvious to me that my way doesn't work, but I just keep on hanging in there and persistently trying to do the same old things over and over, expecting different results. One of my character defects is that I am very hard-headed.

Another thing I've got to stop doing is feeling sorry for myself. I've been on my pity pot and it's getting old. Basically, I'm getting sick and tired of this "poor me" routine. If I want to get my life into action, I'm going to have to *do something*. I've just been lying in bed dreaming that my life will get better.

I've been having suicidal thoughts. I think it all boils down to the fact that I'm unhappy with the realization that where I am (point A) and where I want to be (point B) are very far apart with a mountain in the way. I hope that I choose life and stop being miserable and feeling like a loser.

There must be another way to go through life
besides being pulled through it kicking and screaming.[112]
Hugh Prather

.6. dark valley

August 1, 1988 – August 28, 1989

Prepare the way of the Lord; make straight in the desert a highway for our God. Every valley shall be exalted and every mountain and hill brought low; the crooked places shall be made straight and the rough places smooth.
Isaiah 40:3–4

The following four chapters cover a three year period during which I continuously rode the roller coaster of drug addiction, alcoholism, and sexual promiscuity; as well as had a major spiritual experience without proper spiritual direction. I hope that these chapters will educate you concerning the nature of addiction, the principles of the Twelve Step Recovery process, and the perils of traveling alone on our walk with God.

As a minister, I have come to regard the Twelve Steps as a highly effective process of sanctification that parallels the Biblical account of the Israelite's exodus out of Egypt, through the Desert, and into the Promised Land. Steps One through Three prepare a person for the deliverance from bondage, but it is the submissively obedient process of Steps Four through Nine that truly accomplishes transformation. In Steps Ten through Twelve, a person learns to incorporate the Biblical principles of all the Steps into their daily lives; which facilitates spiritual maturity. It is at this level that one is adequately prepared to effectively carry the message of hope to others who suffer.

The foundational directions for working a program that have made Alco-

holics Anonymous extremely successful are known in the recovery communities as the "Five Alive." They are:

1. **Pray in the morning and ask God to keep you clean and sober.**
2. **Attend meetings on a daily basis.**
3. **Read the program literature.**
4. **Call a sponsor (whose job is to provide accountability and to direct the process of taking the Steps).**
5. **Pray in the evening and thank God for your sobriety.**

The A.A. literature says, *Rarely have we seen a person fail who has thoroughly followed our path.*[113] Rarely have I seen a person succeed who didn't follow these simple instructions. As you will see, I held out for three years in both the valley of self-pity and on the mountain of pride until I was brought to a place of true willingness to follow directions.

A.A.'s Twelve Steps are a group of principles, spiritual in their nature, which, if practiced as a way of life, can expel the obsession to drink and enable the sufferer to become happily and usefully whole.[114]
Twelve Steps and Twelve Traditions

The Twelve Steps of Alcoholics Anonymous

1. We admitted we were powerless over alcohol—that our lives had become unmanageable.
2. Came to believe that a Power greater than ourselves could restore us to sanity.
3. Made a decision to turn our will and our lives over to the care of God, as we understood Him.
4. Made a searching and fearless moral inventory of ourselves.
5. Admitted to God, to ourselves, and to another human being the exact nature of our wrongs.
6. Were entirely ready to have God remove all these defects of character.
7. Humbly asked Him to remove our shortcomings.
8. Made a list of all persons we had harmed, and became willing to make amends to them all.

9. Made direct amends wherever possible, except when to do so would injure them or others.
10. Continued to take personal inventory and when we were wrong, promptly admitted it.
11. Sought through prayer and meditation to improve our conscious contact with God as we understood Him, praying only for knowledge of His will for us and the power to carry that out.
12. Having had a spiritual awakening as the result of these steps, we tried to carry this message to alcoholics, and to practice these principles in all our affairs.[115]

August 1, 1988

I didn't quit feeling sorry for myself and I've been drinking and smoking pot again. I just couldn't handle all the pain. I've got to admit that drinking made me feel even worse.

I don't know what's wrong with me. I'm not sure if I'm mentally ill or just a bad person. The storm seems to be darkening. Hopefully, it's darkest before the dawn.

Spiritual darkness is the result of something that I do not intend to obey.[116]
Oswald Chambers

August 22, 1988

Three weeks already! I've been out of the program—out of my mind. I don't know what's going on. I've been learning a few things, but I'm still riding the endless merry-go-round of party-hangover-sometimes lucid moments. I'm slipping back into my old ways. I don't know who I am, I don't know if I'll make it, and I don't feel confident in my actions. I'm lost.

I hope with all of my heart that God is really there and that if I hang on tight, I'll make it through with Him at my side. I can't believe how scary life has become. I need God's help desperately right now, but I don't know exactly how to pray. I just want God's way. I don't want to live or die in hell. I feel as though I'm very familiar with what hell is—no control—self-will run riot. I want so much more.

September 1, 1988

I got a ridiculous brainstorm to do some crank to suppress my appetite. It really messed me up. I haven't slept for two days and I'm depressed. I don't know what to do. I'm plunging ahead when I don't even know who I am or where I'm going. I just don't think that I'm going to make it.

I saw my therapist today and went to the eating disorder group. It's so obvious that I need to quit drinking and doing drugs again, but I don't feel up to it. It's too painful and I just can't handle it. I don't know which is worse—the drug addiction and alcoholism or the eating disorder. All I know is that I'd rather be drunk than fat.

I don't know if I'll ever sober up and fly right. The bulimia has me near death—vomiting blood, bloating, and severe headaches. I don't think that I'm ever going to get it together. The worse part is that I don't even know if I want to. It's just too hard. I feel as though I'm doomed to live in darkness forever.

It's not that we fear the place of darkness,
but that we don't think we are worth the effort to find the place of light.[117]
Hugh Prather

September 18, 1988

I have this feeling that something's missing, but I don't know what it is. I don't ever seem to be satisfied.

Without Me you can do nothing.
John 15:5

October 2, 1988

I'm starting to realize that I'm a flaky failure, but I guess I'll just have to accept it until I get ready to change with the help of the program. I'm scared. I'm two weeks off the booze, but this is my first day off pot. I just pray that the bottom doesn't fall out on my eating again as I start to sober up.

I'm very apprehensive, but unfortunately I don't have that many options. I'm going to remain a mess and a failure until I sober up, endure the pain, and get the sobriety show on the road. I don't have any idea of exactly what God has planned for me, but it's becoming pretty obvious that sobering up is a part of it. I keep ending up in the program even when I'm sure that I'll never go back.

I just wish that I had more hope. Frankly, I don't really see the light at the end of the tunnel, but I've got to convince myself to believe that there is one. If just once I could succeed at something—anything. Maybe it will be sobriety.

We can easily forgive a child who is afraid of the dark.
The real tragedy of life is when men are afraid of the light.[118]
Plato

October 24, 1988

I'm getting blown away because good things are actually happening for a change. I have been letting go of a lot of my worries and God really has been taking care of things. I feel good. I see now that going back to A.A. and N.A. was definitely the right answer.

We found that God does not make too hard terms with those who seek Him.[119]
Alcoholics Anonymous

October 30, 1988

Lately, I can feel Step Three working in my life because I am truly starting to see that my way doesn't work. All it does is lead me around in circles. I'm starting to see that life is happening *now*—not yesterday and not tomorrow. One day at a time, I grow.

November 2, 1988

My self-esteem is finally growing a little and I'm starting to value myself as a person. I have hope.

November 7, 1988

I feel something stirring inside of me for the first time in a long time. I guess I need to take time to be quiet and listen while it tells me things about myself. I'm beginning to become aware of the fact that there are a lot of things that I am not aware of.

Where have I been all of my life?

Deep down in every man, woman, and child, is the fundamental idea of God.[120]
Alcoholics Anonymous

November 15, 1988

I've been so lost lately that I have totally neglected Laurel. I need to start taking care of her myself instead of letting Ruthie do it for me. I hate myself for being so selfish. The issues concerning motherhood have caused me so much pain lately. The way I expected to feel as a mother and the way I actually feel are so different. The one thing blocking the way between my little girl and me is a tremendous amount of selfishness and laziness. Realizing these things hurts so badly, but the pain is cleansing.

November 19, 1988

I started to change jobs yesterday, but I decided against it. It's *me* that needs to change; not my job or where I live or who I date or even how I look. It's very hard for me to accept and understand that.

I want to live from the inside out, not from the outside in.[121]
Hugh Prather

November 22, 1988

I'm a sex addict. I use it as a weapon. I use it to fix me. I use it to mask my loneliness.

I see how much my quest for control and dominance over men has gotten me into lots of trouble. It also got me into motherhood.

November 29, 1988

Laurel has a broken arm and I know deep in my heart that I am the one that broke it when I shook her Friday night because I was angry that she woke me up. To say that I feel terrible is putting it mildly.

God, I just hate the person that I am. I want to change so badly, but I don't even know how. I just pray that the Twelve Steps will do the job.

For the good that I will to do, I do not do;
but the evil I will not to do, that I practice.
O wretched man that I am! Who will deliver me from this body of death?
Romans 7:19,24

November 30, 1988

I chaired the 10:00 meeting at N.A. It was my first time to chair a meeting and I enjoyed it. The topic was "forgiveness" and by the time the meeting was over, I felt forgiveness for myself for hurting Laurel and for Dad for not being there when I was growing up. The thought crossed my mind that we're all just human beings doing the best that we know how.

Forgiveness is only real for him who has discovered the weakness of his friends and the sins of his enemy in his own heart and is willing to call every human being his brother.[122]

Henri J. M. Nouwen

December 17, 1988

I had a pretty rough week. The issues with Laurel are still tearing me apart. The responsibility of taking care of her is just too much for me. As things are now, I only see her on Sundays, Mondays, and Tuesdays and then she goes to Mom's from Wednesday to Sunday. A part of me feels very guilty for not being with her more, but I tried keeping her all week this week and frankly, it was just more than I could handle. I had anxiety all week long. I just wish that I could be a stable mother, but I can't.

I don't feel very good about myself right now. I have little hope that this program will work for me because I'm either too busy with work or too lazy when off work to work it. Trying to balance all of the things in my life is hard.

Those who do not recover are people who cannot or will not completely give themselves to this simple program.[123]

Alcoholics Anonymous

December 18, 1988

Well, I went to the meeting and all I could hear was "work the Steps" and "denial of the disease makes you sicker." I'm in denial so badly right now that, frankly, I can't see the forest for the trees. I feel lost. I just wish that I had the capacity to be honest with myself.

May 25, 1989

I don't really understand my rebellious attitude about the Twelve Step programs. I just don't want to work. It seems like every solution depends on me taking some kind of action and, for some reason, I hate that. My friend, Lon, says that you can't get this deal through osmosis. I guess that's what I try to do.

Anyway, I guess I'll just keep persisting. Maybe God will help me pick up that phone and call a sponsor. Frankly, I just don't see what kind of difference it will make, but I guess I'll never know unless I earnestly try it. Lon says I'm not getting anything out of the program because I'm not putting anything in to it.

There is a principle which is a bar against all information,
which is proof against all arguments
and which cannot fail to keep a man in everlasting ignorance
—that principle is contempt prior to investigation.[124]
Herbert Spencer

June 5, 1989

My program is in the pits. I don't understand what it is about me that makes me unwilling to do the things which *are* the program.

One thing I *have* been doing is looking at some of my resentments. The thing that really eats me alive is my anger towards Dad. All I know is, right or wrong, I blame him for all of my problems.

My childhood is over,
so exactly when will I be old enough
to take responsibility for what I am?[125]
Hugh Prather

July 3, 1989

I need some direction in my life. Sometimes I want to be a drug counselor and other times I don't even know if I want to stay clean myself. I feel like I'm dead—or at least like my spirit is. I beat on myself so much that I can't thrive. Sometimes I think that I'm looking for more meaning in life that there really is. If it weren't for Laurel, I'd blow myself away because the experience of being me is very painful.

We had come to believe in the hopelessness and
futility of life as we had been living it.[126]
Alcoholics Anonymous

July 29, 1989

This week I spent a lot more time with Laurel and it made me realize how much I have plain and simply neglected her. God, I've been carrying around so much guilt about it. I really have been lazy and have not wanted to exert the energy necessary for parenting. I've been lying in bed all day and letting everyone else do my job. That's very painful to accept. I've been blaming all my sleeping on my anti-depressants when it's really because I want to avoid life.

Mom wrote me a letter and told me that Laurel needs me and that the more I just lay around, the more slovenly I will become. It kind of made me angry, but only because it was so true. "Slovenly"—I hate that word, but that is what I have become. I've just been lying around, stuffing my face, and complaining about what a raw deal life has given me. As much as I don't want to admit it, life is just like the program—you get out what you put in. Unfortunately, most of my life I've been a taker and haven't invested any time in cultivating a life for myself. It's sad, but true.

Oh well, I'm not going to beat myself up over who I am. There's bound to be something good about me. I just don't see it at this time in my life. I am truly my own worst enemy.

> *We were having trouble with personal relationships, we couldn't control our emotional natures, we were a prey to misery and depression, we couldn't make a living, we had a feeling of uselessness, we were full of fear, we were unhappy, we couldn't seem to be of real help to other people.*[127]
>
> **Alcoholics Anonymous**

August 11, 1989

The only thing that gives my life the slightest bit of meaning is being Laurel's mother. If it weren't for her, I'd be dead because on those days that I don't want to go on living, her little smile keeps me going. As much as I absolutely hate my life sometimes, I love her more than I've ever loved anyone and I just can't go off and leave her an orphan. She needs me and I need her. I'm beginning to understand why she's in my life—to keep me alive!

My sobriety is suffering pretty badly. I go through periods where I want to drink more than anything. I have that insane desire to drink just a little bit—like I'd be able to stop. I know that taking a drink would be a really stupid thing to do, but I won't be surprised if it happens. I know that I'm setting myself up for a relapse by not going to meetings or working the program, but I can't seem to stop it.

Lack of power, that was our dilemma.[128]
Alcoholics Anonymous

August 14, 1989

I relapsed. That just about says it all. I just took an overdose of anti-depressants to put an end to this miserable existence. I love Laurel so much, but I know that she'd be better off without me. I want to die.

I don't have enough fight left. I'm fat. I'm lost. I'm out of control. Nothing has any meaning for me.

As many live because they are afraid to die, as die because they are afraid to live.[129]
Charles Caleb Colton

August 16, 1989

Well, I didn't die, but I came close. Mom found me unconscious and had an ambulance take me to the emergency room. I can't believe that I did something so stupid and self-destructive! Alcohol is not to be underestimated.

Today I really am just grateful to be alive and to be with Laurel.

Remember we deal with alcohol—cunning, baffling, powerful! Without help it is too much for us. But there is One who has all power—that One is God. May you find Him now![130]
Alcoholics Anonymous

August 17, 1989

I feel terrible right now. I'm so depressed and suicidal again. I need to be in a hospital, but I have my doubts that it will happen. The realization of how sick I am is overwhelming. I am a very sick woman and I don't seem to be getting any better. My relationships don't work because of my mental illness and neither does my life. I know that the Twelve Steps have helped people that were as sick as I am, but I still don't have very much hope. I keep winding down more and more. Once again, I'm caught in the downward spiral. I literally don't want to get out of bed at this point. I can't feel any joy. It seems like the whole world is enjoying life without me.

I wish so much that I hadn't taken that drink, but I've got to admit that I feel so bad that I could do it again. But now I see what they mean—there's no situation so bad that taking a drink won't make it worse. This too shall pass. I need God. I need support. I need professional help. A sick mind does not heal itself.

Those who are well have no need of a physician, but those who are sick.
Matthew 9:12

August 21, 1989

I've got to go job-hunting tomorrow. A restaurant I've always wanted to work at needs a waiter. My confidence is low, but what the heck. Even though I'm scared of being rejected, I'm going to go for it. I know that it's time to go back to work, but there's still a part of me that wishes I could stay home with Laurel. However, I'm never going to love myself until I start taking responsibility for myself and part of that responsibility is being financially independent. Besides, I need the structure that work provides.

I didn't go to a meeting today. I know that I've got to go if I want to stay clean, but I really wish that I didn't have to. I guess I can wish that I wasn't an alcoholic until I'm blue in the face and that I didn't have to go to meetings, but I always will be and will have to. God, grant me the serenity …

Once an alcoholic, always an alcoholic.[131]
Alcoholics Anonymous

August 24, 1989

I'm exhausted. I didn't sleep at all last night because the doctors have been changing my anti-depressants. I got a job and I've done well on my diet all week, but I still feel terrible and empty. I don't know what it's going to take to make me feel better.

Come to Me, all you who labor and are heavy laden, and I will give you rest.
Matthew 11:28

August 28, 1989

I've been anxiety stricken for two days. Give me a job and the first thing I do is become absolutely terrified that I'm going to lose it. I'm so sick.

The chief activator of our defects has been self-centered fear—primarily fear that we would lose something we already possessed or would fail to get something we demanded.[132]
Twelve Steps and Twelve Traditions

I got the job at the restaurant where I wanted to work. It was a nice restaurant with an even "nicer" waiter on staff. I was very infatuated with Mike and

could feel immediately that he was becoming a distraction for me. One day on the way to work, I told God that I knew that three weeks after a suicide attempt was probably not a good time for a relationship so I asked for His will with Mike. When I got to work, Mike told me that he heard I was a member of A.A. and that he needed help. He asked me to take him to a meeting. Of course I agreed so we went after work.

After the meeting, we went back to his house and he told me that he had studied for the ministry during a three year period of his life. He then began to talk to me about the "Word." In that discussion, he looked at me with the most beautiful blue eyes that I had ever seen and said, *Do you know how much God loves you?* At that moment, I felt the power of the Holy Spirit begin to fill me from my finger tips to my toes. My personality was immediately transformed into one of joy and enthusiasm and I effortlessly lost fifty pounds over the next five months. The transformation of my character, however, would be a much more arduous and lengthy process.

.7. if the light in you is darkness

September 30, 1989 – May 19, 1990

Unless a grain of wheat falls into the ground and dies, it remains alone.
Matthew 12:24

September 30, 1989

I've been getting blown away by all of the miracles that have been happening in my life. I feel very close to God at this time. It's so nice to be able to hear His voice again—like I did when I first met Him. I truly believe in my heart that He is calling His children home and that a part of my job is to help.

October 9, 1989

My recent experience with God has finally gotten the message through that I might give the Bible a little consideration in my search for the truth. I am a true believer and a witness to the fact that God is still in business. That gives me hope. The most rewarding experience I have ever had is the realization of the power of prayer. God really was listening! What more could I ask for? I am truly beginning to see that life is a journey—not a destination.

Almost the only scoffers at prayer are those who never tried it enough.[133]
Twelve Steps and Twelve Traditions

October 12, 1989

All I can say is that I have never felt better in my entire life. I am so grateful for all of the wonderful things that are happening. Although I try very hard to cultivate a sense of self-worth, I know deep in my heart that I do not deserve the mercy that God has shown me. One very painful realization for me has been the knowledge of exactly how dark my life was prior to my rebirth. It scares me because it makes me realize that just as strong as my pull towards God and virtue is today, so was my pull towards darkness in the past. I really don't know how to put it in perspective.

I really don't want to utter these words, but there's a part of me that is afraid of Satan. I don't even want to acknowledge that jerks existence and maybe I never will. That's one thing that disturbs me about Christianity—the idea of Satan and of spiritual warfare. I'm much more comfortable just pretending to believe that the only evil that exists is fear and my belief in limitation. Maybe that's a crock. There's so much that I don't know, but I'm learning.

Remember, Rome was not built in a day.

Anyway, I still don't have the foggiest idea of who I am or where I'm going, but I do know that there's a light in my soul that is giving me directions and there's love in my heart that opens my eyes to life's great beauty. I remember a lady at the restaurant who would always toast to the "joy of living." I was so cynical that I thought she was a fool. Today, all I can say is *Cheers to You, God*—my Lord, my Father, my Life.

Put on the whole armor of God,
that you may be able to stand against the wiles of the devil.
Ephesians 6:11

October 16, 1989

For a long time now, I've been praying for God's highest will in my life and I've asked Him to mold me into the person that He would have me be. It's becoming pretty clear to me that He is doing just that—transforming me into a likeness of Him. Now, by no means am I saying that I'm perfect or anything like that, but I am definitely making dramatic progress. I am seeing things in a different light and I know that it is because of God. I have been blowing them away at meetings. Last night, they actually applauded me!

Remember: Self that seeks to serve God is more dangerous than self that refuses to obey God.[134]
Andrew Murray

Mike became disenchanted with what he considered to be my big ego and advised me to ask God to show me myself through His eyes—in order to see what a miserable sinner I was. I prayed the prayer. The next morning, I walked into the bathroom and saw something that I had never seen at depth before—a valuable and worthwhile person who was no greater nor less than anyone else. I looked at myself and said the words, *I love you and I accept you just the way you are.* For the first time after years of attempting to say such "affirmations" in the mirror, I meant it.

October 17, 1989

The realizations keep coming and coming. I am finally breaking through the walls that have kept me isolated for all of my life—the walls I began to construct when I first began to believe that I was unworthy and undeserving of love. I'm finally making friends with the person that I've been waiting all of my life to meet—myself. Guess what? She's not the monster I had believed her to be.

I have been very misguided at times and have done many terrible things, but I am not as worthless as I have led myself to believe. All I know is that the child inside of me has been trapped for years and has been crying miserably for love and nurturing. I realize now that by isolating her, I never intended to hurt her—only to protect her from a world that seemed so unkind.

> **Well, Paige, you can come on out, honey. Nobody is going to hurt you for I will protect you and care for you. You have My permission to be happy.**

All of this is absolutely incredible! God is healing me and making me whole. He keeps telling me that I'm a significant person in the "Big Picture," but who cares? What is ahead of me is really none of my business. If I am indeed supposed to do something important, I will know what to do when the time comes. God is my guide and He is directing me step by step by step. All I know is that, for today, I am to go forth in the world in love and to be true to myself. It's okay to be genuinely real in a phony-baloney world; just a little rare and unusual.

I don't know exactly what my life's work will be for sure, but for today, I know that is my job to be kind to other people, to listen to them, to support them, and to help them to feel better about themselves. Now to what extent this is to be done is none of my business. I am willing to go to any length and God knows that.

Although this is an ending in a way—having *finally* gotten even just a slight glimpse of what I have been searching for *forever*, this is also just the beginning. The healing is occurring miraculously. After the healing, my work begins. Step by step by step, God will reveal His plan.

For I know the thoughts that I think toward you, says the Lord,
thoughts of peace and not of evil, to give you a future and a hope.
Jeremiah 29:11

October 23, 1989

Deep in my heart, I believe that God is establishing His Kingdom on earth and somehow, I have a part in it, but I am through discussing it with people who aren't really into the Jesus Christ thing. I'm convinced now that there is truth in Christianity. I started asking for the truth and here I am, seeing the world through the eyes of love. It's hard work, though, because the world isn't exactly being run on positive energy.

What kills me is that after every meeting, we stand there and recite the Lord's prayer, "*Thy Kingdom come, Thy will be done . . .* " and then if you even so much as insinuate that it might really be happening, everyone goes nuts. If we don't really believe it, why do we bother to say the prayer?

All I know is that every day I become a little more accepting of the fact that I am just now beginning to get even a glimpse of what's really going on. We truly do live in a material world and I have been a material girl.

In the program, they define insanity as doing the same thing over and over, expecting different results. When I was doing that, it felt normal and now, going in a new direction feels foreign. The saner I become, the crazier I seem to those around me. I'm beginning to understand what Mike meant when he said that I would realize that I am in enemy occupied territory.

I guess I just need to shut up and listen to other people for a while and try to help them rather than explaining the meaning of life to them. I'm beginning to realize that most people aren't interested in the meaning of life.

My greatest wish would be that we could all enter the Kingdom simultaneously. Ah, Heaven on earth. Oh well, I'm not going to stop dreaming. Even though I really don't have anyone to talk to right now, I still find great comfort during my quiet time alone with God. I'm beginning to see what the Bible means when it says, "*The Son of Man has nowhere to lay His head."(Matthew 8:20)*

Oh well, I'm sticking to the only good decision I have ever made—the one to turn my will and life over to the care of God as I understand Him. I guess I just need to pipe down and live it for a while and let my life speak for itself.

Do you wish to be great? Then begin by being. Do you desire to construct a vast and lofty fabric? Think first about the foundations of humility. The higher your structure is to be, the deeper must be its foundation.[135]

Saint Augustine

October 25, 1989

Everything is great! Well, everything is exactly like it's always been, but I feel better. I've been leveling out. The magic is intense and exciting, but I think that I can handle the transformation better if it's gradual rather than overnight. I have definitely become a true-blue Christian. I read *Mere Christianity* and it helped me a lot. I have truly been born again and am in the process of allowing Christ to take over and master my life. Thank God! He literally saved me.

We were reborn … We were now at Step Three.[136]
Though our decision was a vital and crucial step,
it could have little permanent effect
unless at once followed by a strenuous effort to face, and be rid of,
the things in ourselves that had been blocking us.
Our liquor was but a symptom.[137]

Alcoholics Anonymous

October 28, 1989

Well, I'm still the new me. Thank God! It's finally sunk in that I have actually gotten a little better and that as long as I maintain my spiritual condition, I don't ever have to go back to my old ways again.

I am being seriously called into the ministry. I don't care if I ever own a thing or have a credit card. All I want is to know my God. It's so ironic that I wrote my college entrance essay on self-understanding. I see now that who I am today is just an evolution of who I have always been. I'm just coming of age.

All of the pain and suffering has been worth it. I've looked at the picture from many angles and where I sit now is definitely the best view I've ever had. The beautiful thing is that we can all sit in the same seat. No one has to move in order for someone else to see.

We have seen what we are not, and what God wants us to be,
but are we willing to be battered into the shape of the vision to be used by God?[138]
Oswald Chambers

October 31, 1989

I need to realize that even though sometimes my way and God's way coincide, that doesn't mean that He's going to grant my every wish. He's my Master—not vice versa.

Don't forget that, Paige.

Let us avoid the fatal mistake of calling Christ "Master"
but not doing what He says.[139]
Andrew Murray

November 28, 1989

One of the biggest things that I need to stop doing is comparing myself to other people. When I was doing poorly, I would compare myself to other people and feel worthless and now that I'm doing so much better, I compare myself to others and feel like top-dog. This is wrong! I am willing to let go of this character defect.

There is only one person with whom you can profitably compare yourself,
and this person is your yesterday self.[140]
Ralph Waldo Emerson

December 12, 1989

Face it, Paige, when you first woke up you felt as though you had it all figured out. You're at the tip of the iceberg, babe.

This life is a school from which I will never graduate as long as I'm alive. The finish line is my last breath. I just need to slow down and stop reacting to other people. I can only work on myself. I can only control my own thoughts and behavior to the best of my ability. I cannot change the world. I can't even change me. All I can do is trust God and do the things which are in front of me to do and keep praying and believing that God will do for me what I cannot do for myself.

December 14, 1989

Lately, I am becoming aware of some major character defects that I have never seen before. I have no respect for other people's boundaries. I just invade as if I'm entitled to do or say anything I please. I guess being aware of these things is the beginning of being able to change.

We now clearly see that we have been making unreasonable demands upon ourselves, upon others, and upon God.[141]
Twelve Steps and Twelve Traditions

December 18, 1989

I truly am one with God and all I have to do is recognize it to be fulfilled. I guess for a while there I felt as if I have to pray constantly for God to be with me. Today I realize that He is with me always and forever—no matter what. I love Him so much. My life is so rich today simply because I asked for help and became willing to accept it.

For if anyone is a hearer of the word and not a doer, he is like a man observing his natural face in a mirror; for he observes himself, goes away, and immediately forgets what kind of man he was.
James 1:23–24

December 21, 1989

I see that I have been very self-righteous about my program. I will never be immune from this disease. I see what they mean when they say I must guard my sobriety with vigilance. I realize that there still lurks something inside of me that wants to shatter my world. That is very scary.

Be sober, be vigilant;
Your adversary the devil walks about like a roaring lion,
seeking whom he may devour.
1 Peter 5:8

December 28, 1989

I've sort of been a fool, but that's okay. I guess the bottom line is that I am realizing that although I am a spiritual being, I am also a human being who, even when I am doing my best, still has room for improvement. I don't have to climb to the top of any ladders to see how beautiful the view is. The beauty is the experience of life itself.

Hey, Paige, I love you and accept you just the way you are.

January 1, 1990

I'll never forget 1989—the year I woke up! I've been learning a lot about life. Lately, I have been complaining that my spirituality is slipping. I think that more than anything, my ego has been deflating. I was getting very arrogant and cocky for a while there.

Self is the root, the branches, the tree, of all the evil of our fallen state.[142]
Andrew Murray

January 15, 1990

Today, Laurel cut her chin and had to get stitches. I was proud of both of us. She was a brave little soldier and I kept it together and handled the situation like an adult. I was able to be there for her and that was a valuable experience. I love her so much and it hurt to see her in pain and fear, but it felt good to be strong enough to be her mother. This morning I was watching her and my eyes filled with tears. I must have done something right to be blessed with such a beautiful and cheerful child. There's just nothing quite as tender as the love I feel for Laurel. Being her mother is such an honor.

We will intuitively know how to handle situations which used to baffle us.[143]
Alcoholics Anonymous

January 20, 1990

Last night, Troy **(my new boyfriend)** and I got into a big fight and I ended up hysterical. The bottom line is that no matter how spiritual I am, I am still alcoholic emotionally. When I go nuts, the only place I can get what I need to feel better is Alcoholics Anonymous.

The delusion that we are like other people,
or presently may be, has to be smashed.[144]
Alcoholics Anonymous

January 22, 1990

My pride has really been in the way lately. I guess my tripped out spiritual experience knocked me way off balance because I actually started believing that I belonged on a pedestal as an example of how to be. I am no longer an example of how *not* to be, but I've got a long way to go and a lot to learn before I will be qualified to be a model human being; especially a model Christian.

I hate admitting all of this, but I know that it's true. I realize, though, that I can't hate myself for being immature. So much of this junk has to do with my addiction, and as they say, "*I'm not responsible for my disease, but I am responsible for my recovery.*" It's not really *all* my fault that I'm so crazy, but it's up to me to be willing to grow up.

I know the grown-up Paige is coming. Sometimes, she makes a sneak preview. However, I don't know how to keep her here at all times; at least I don't know how yet. I am definitely doing the best that I can do—I even think I might be trying too hard. I love myself and I accept myself just the way that I am, yet I am willing to change—more than willing, I *want* to change—on the inside. My goals have always pertained to external things—my income level, my weight, my job, and my possessions. I never once thought about defining goals for the kind of person I want to be; until now. Anyway, once again, I see that my ego blew up and my humility vanished.

Pride and humility are the two master powers,
the two kingdoms in strife for the eternal possession of a person's soul.[145]
Andrew Murray

February 21, 1990

I guess my problem these days is that I don't really have any. Everything is okay and I guess I find that kind of boring. I am painfully aware that I am a major crisis junkie.

The past week or so, the world seems a little grey again. I guess I'm just going through a little ebb with God. I haven't been making as many meetings as I should and I definitely haven't been reading enough. I guess sometimes that I want to pretend that I don't have to do all of the work that the program requires for me to be okay.

It is easy to let up on a spiritual program of action and rest on our laurels.[146]
Alcoholics Anonymous

March 1, 1990

I've realized a few things these past few days. Number one, I have been spending more time with Troy and less time with my program and God. *Wrong!* I have to double-up on meetings so I can keep myself in balance. I let Troy get between God and me rather than keeping God between Troy and me. I give my life to You, God. Do whatever You want. You know what's best for me. I don't know how to do anything but destroy myself.

But seek first the kingdom of God and His righteousness,
and all these things shall be added to you.
Matthew 6:33

March 2, 1990

Troy and I are taking a break. I've been doing well under the circumstances. I'm experiencing enormous amounts of pain with no real relief except prayer, but I'm walking through my first really big storm—and staying sober and abstinent. I hate the pain, but I recognize that it is an enormous opportunity for growth. This experience will help me. It's in God's hands.

We could never learn to be brave and patient, if there were only joy in the world.[147]
Helen Keller

March 14, 1990

Troy and I don't have anything in common, but I still keep seeing him. I know deep in my heart that he is *not* my mate. I pray with all my heart that there really is someone out there who belongs at my side. I long for my soul mate—my true love who will be my husband for the rest of my life. The bride is almost ready. I know that when the time is right, we will meet. I'm just so tired of waiting, waiting, waiting. I want to go home. My home is at the side of my soul mate. Where is he?

March 22, 1990

Lately, I find myself having a lot of negative thoughts about people. I realize that they are showing me the things about myself that need to change; things I've never seen before. I'm such a hypocrite. I get so upset when other people talk about me, but I talk about other people all the time. I need to change my attitude.

Dear Father, please help me.

In whatever you judge another you condemn yourself;
for you who judge practice the same things.
Romans 2:1

March 23, 1990

I am angry with myself because I know that I am supposed to stay away from Troy, but I have been too weak to do it. We break up every other day. This is ridiculous! Father, please help me to *stay* broken up!

Don't pray that God's on our side; pray that we're on His side.[148]
Abraham Lincoln

March 27, 1990

I told Troy that I am going to see other people and do whatever I want. To be honest, I think that my strongest attraction to Troy is that he seems like he could use my help. Am I codependent or what?

Anyway, that's not what I want to write about. I want to write about what's happening in my program. I ended up being the Sunday speaker at my A.A. home group this past weekend. What a trip! It went great. Everyone mobbed me and told me that I ought to go on the circuit. I was elated.

Therefore let him who thinks he stands take heed lest he fall.
1 Corinthians 10:12

March 28, 1990

Earth to Paige! Earth to Paige! It occurred to me that if indeed I do become an emerging voice in the recovery scene, I need to clean up my act. My manicurist who was at the speaker meeting pointed out to me that, although my talk was great and I could definitely be a circuit speaker, I did not set a very good Christian example by standing up there with a cross around my neck saying the "f" word. I told her that I wasn't trying to be an example, but she said that whether I was trying or not, I am an example when I am on the platform. She's right. If I'm going to understand and talk spirituality, I need to *live* spirituality. That's kind of heavy.

Also, I've started feeling bad because of my deal with men and sex. I've been being promiscuous and it is messing me up. Who am I fooling? I can't do it. I just can't give myself permission to be promiscuous.

What you do speaks so loudly that I cannot hear what you say.[149]
Ralph Waldo Emerson

April 5, 1990

I read *Women Who Love Too Much.* It's all about me—the kind of woman who falls for a man who she can help. It's noble and altruistic. It's also sick. It really explained to me how I keep trying to resolve my deal with Dad by attracting the same type of men that he is—emotionally unavailable—and then trying to win their approval. It can't be done. I just have to overcome the need through acceptance.

I also realize that I can strive for total surrender and bliss, but that doesn't mean that I'm not going to have bad days that *hurt.* I've been happy and I share that in meetings, but I also realize that I need to be willing to share my pain. Number One, because I need the support and number two, because I need to keep myself off of the pedestal that I am so afraid of getting on as I climb on top of it. I need the humility that hurting and needing support from others gives me. This balance deal is tough.

April 10, 1990

I've been a little confused lately. I guess it's because I sometimes have this arrogant attitude that I've got the greatest program in the world and then everything changes and I realize that I am a spiritual becoming—not being. That's the deal—everything changes—constantly.

Troy said that what I'm looking for in a relationship is a fairy tale. I've never seen what I want modeled so maybe there really is no such thing. What I've got to accept is that those intense relationships that I yearn for are temporary and unhealthy. Sometimes I think that I feel so uncomfortable with Troy because *unhealthy* is what feels *comfortable* to me. Troy is the kind of guy I've always fantasized about being with, but I'm unhappy with him.

There's something very scary about getting what you want—it takes away your excuse for being dissatisfied.

Never was there enough of what we thought we wanted.[150]
Twelve Steps and Twelve Traditions

April 17, 1990

The other day a friend of mine told me that she fears that I laugh at her behind her back. I said that I would *never* do that and then I had the sickening realization that I *do it* all the time. I'm not a very good friend sometimes. I assassinate the character of the people that I am supposed to love the most. That realization is very painful for me, but I also realize that the realization itself is progress.

Is he not, even in his best moments,
a producer of confusion rather than harmony?[151]
Alcoholics Anonymous

May 5, 1990

I think that the thing that attracts me to Troy is the impossible challenge of trying to win someone over who can't be won.

Face it, babe, what you have with Troy is ADDICTION.

Troy is my new drug of choice and once again my addiction to my drug of choice is going to destroy me it I don't abstain from using it. Please God, help me let go.

Paige!!!! Troy is not the one.
Troy's NOT the one! Troy is NOT THE ONE!!!!

I see now that back in October I realized that I was a valuable and worthwhile person. I saw the good side of myself. However, I got such a charge that I began to deny the bad side that I once believed was all there was. Lately, I've been taking a look at the not so good things about Paige, and it hurts. Basically, I'm a self-centered, untrustworthy, obnoxious, game-playing, controlling, manipulative, and trouble-making big mouth. I just hate that. However, I know that there is hope because the real progress is that I *see* it. Until now, I have hidden this truth from myself forever. I just drank, drugged, ate, and had sex like crazy so that I wouldn't have to face these things.

For a while, my life was deep-seeded awareness of the bad in me with no awareness of the good. Then, it was newfound awareness of the good with denial of the bad. Now, it's reality; all of me—the good and the bad of Paige. I am definitely willing to let go of these character defects. I am willing to change.

I guess it's back to the drawing board. I am not as bad as I used to think I was, but I am also not as great as I thought I was. I'm just a struggling spiritual being trying to maintain my balance in this human experience.

In actual practice, we usually find a solitary self-appraisal insufficient.[152]
Alcoholics Anonymous

May 19, 1990

I cheated on Troy. This whole situation has definitely made me realize that I am far from being the person I want to be. I can't change by self-will any more than I can quit drinking by self-will. I have definitely realized that in sobriety, the sin *is* the punishment. I have never regretted anything so bad in my life as telling Troy about my indiscretion. I guess I shouldn't have even done it either, but at least I learned a valuable lesson about emotional binds. It gives me a lot of insight about what happened in my past relationships. I never resolved *any* of them.

DENIAL
Don't Even Notice I Am Lying
A.A. Phrase

.8. shadowed peak

May 29, 1990 - December 10, 1990

Whoever exalts himself will be humbled.
Matthew 23:12

May 29, 1990

Troy's and my problems were huge before this affair deal. Now, we're both pretending that *it's* the problem. The real problem is that we have nothing in common. This is the point that I need to get through my thick head. I must accept this.

June 15, 1990

These codependency issues are killing me. I'm beginning to realize that my sobriety could actually be at stake. I get crazy enough over Troy that I could end up drinking. I don't want to drink, but I go nuts when he won't do what I want—and I don't want him to be with other girls.

I don't want him, but I don't want anyone else to have him either. I know that's not fair.

Driven by a hundred forms of fear, self-delusion, self-seeking, and self-pity, we step on the toes of our fellows and they retaliate.[153]
Alcoholics Anonymous

June 22, 1990

I want this ego of mine deflated! I want to do everything I can to bring in God's Kingdom on earth, yet I also want more than anything for my desire for recognition to fade. Trying to get noticed gets in the way of what I'm supposed to be doing.

Sure, there's a part of me that would like to be really great and someday have the entire world applaud my greatness, but that's the little girl in me who desires to be the center of attention. I know today that no matter how hard I try, I can't make everyone like me and appreciate me. This deal is not about being loved. It's about *loving.*

The promises of God are of no value to us until, through obedience, we come to understand the nature of God.[154]
Oswald Chambers

June 23, 1990

It's time for me to get a sponsor to go through the Steps. I can see that I am getting to some core issues and I need help. I've been rationalizing that it's okay to go to bars and communicate with practicing alcoholics because I'm helping them when, in reality, I only go to bars to cruise guys and to try to run into Troy. On an even deeper level, I may be going to bars because my alcoholism is trying to get me drunk.

Paige, you do not have permission to go to bars or clubs any more! Got it?

Father, I need peace. I'm tired of being a crisis junkie. Help me, please.

Going it alone in spiritual matters is dangerous.[155]
Twelve Steps and Twelve Traditions

June 26, 1990

I have anxiety this morning. We found out that Granddaddy has cancer. The doctors gave him six months. I dread watching him suffer. I pray that he dies before the pain gets too bad; for his sake and ours. I love life today, but it certainly hasn't gotten easier. To the contrary, it seems more difficult.

I know that everything is going to be all right. I just have to watch as God reveals His Plan in His Time. I trust God. Sometimes it's just my self that I don't trust. I've been going to the bar too much—and enjoying it. No matter how exciting and fun it sometimes is in there (and no matter how much attention I get from men), I have no business being in that scene. It is dangerous because alcohol is cunning, baffling, and powerful. I am not immune from the first drink. My business is to work on myself, cultivate my soul, and help people who need it, want it, and *ask* for it.

Paige, it is not your job to capture practicing alcoholics and bring them into recovery. Stay out of the bars!

Please, Father, don't let my desire for fun and excitement destroy me. Help me to delay gratification.

But each one is tempted when he is drawn away by his own desires and enticed.
James 1:14

July 1, 1990

Paige,
If you don't stop doing the bar scene and hanging out with using people, you're going to be very sorry. Get your medicine refilled and do the right things that are in front of you to do. I Love you.

Father,
Please hear my prayer. I've been walking on the edge and I'm scared.

You are that one's slave, whom you obey,
whether of sin leading to death, or of obedience leading to righteousness.
Romans 6:16

July 7, 1990

I know that the reason that I do not have a boyfriend at this time is because *I am not supposed to.* What I am supposed to be doing is what I was doing in September and October before I got distracted by my sick relationship with Troy; studying my books and putting everything I've got into my relationship with God.

I know that, for today, I am exactly as I should be at this time and I don't need to worry about where I'm going or who I'm becoming. I also know that I haven't been studying like I would really like to because I've been too busy obsessing on men. I just need to put first things first and realize that my whole-hearted search and study of God will result in life beyond my wildest dreams. I must remember that I am on the journey, not at the destination. My time has not yet come. The Plan for my life is still in the embryonic stages.

You cannot transmit something you haven't got.[156]
Alcoholics Anonymous

August 8, 1990

If I really am in training as a future Leader/Messenger, then I am definitely just in pre-school. I'm still very immature and foolish, but I'm definitely light years from where I was.

All of God's revealed truths are sealed
until they are opened to us through obedience.[157]
Oswald Chambers

August 10, 1990

I realized that if I choose to go an extra mile rather than settling for mediocrity, it is just that—my choice. It's not for me to sound the trumpet as I over-achieve or for me to expect one hundred percent from other people. I can only gently nudge myself to do the best I can do and to be the best I can be. I always have to remember that none of us are less than spiritual beings, yet, at the same time, none of us are more than human beings. One has to find that fine line where expecting a miracle and expecting nothing meet. This has been a period of major realization about balance. There's a lot of gray area between the black and the white, yet through the gray is the color. When man attempts to blend all the colors, he gets black. When God does it, the result is white ... like light.

I judged myself by my intentions, while the world was judging me by my actions.[158]
Alcoholics Anonymous

August 19, 1990

I have really been going through some heavy opposition and persecution, which is depressing me. Blessed are those who are persecuted for righteousness sake? God, I hope all of this is for the sake of righteousness. Dad said I'm on an "ego trip." I hope that's not true.

Also, Granddaddy's fading fast. It's heartbreaking. It's so hard sometimes to keep in mind that what's going on outside of me isn't really what's going on.

But everyone who hears these sayings of Mine, and does not do them,
will be like a foolish man who built his house on the sand:
and the rain descended, the floods came,
and the winds blew and beat on that house; and it fell.
And great was its fall.
Matthew 7:26–27

August 26, 1990

Yesterday I got in touch with some low self-esteem. I felt upset because a guy that I casually messed around with very gentlemanly walked another girl to her car. I got indignant and thought *What makes him think that he can treat me like a piece of 'A'?* Then I realized that I do—because he can—because I let him. The difference between her and me is that I'm easy and she's not. Bottom line, it's time for me to keep my clothes on and try to abstain from sex.

I also realized that I've been a cocky jerk lately; full of pride over my "mighty recovery." I've been acting like I am well and everybody else is weak for not being equally well. I've just got to admit that I'm not as well as I would like to believe. If I were okay, I wouldn't be acting out sexually and my eating wouldn't be slipping. What happened to my patience, tolerance, and compassion?

Dad was right—I've been on an ego trip lately. I've been hanging out in the bar so I can be separate and unique rather than just one sober member of A.A. God!!! Relieve me of the bondage of self!

We could wish to be moral, we could wish to be philosophically comforted, in fact, we could will these things with all our might, but the needed power wasn't there.[159]
Alcoholics Anonymous

September 7, 1990

I had my first A.A. birthday night and it was a little disappointing. It was really no big deal. Sometimes that fact that there are no big deals is kind of disappointing in itself.

My serenity is inversely proportional to my expectations.[160]
Alcoholics Anonymous

September 16, 1990

I have a terminal, killer disease called addiction that wants to destroy me and I cannot fight it alone. This guy said tonight that it's a "we" disease. I see. I've had a great time sharing in meetings, but I am not cured. I am still sick. I need the program and fellowship of Alcoholics Anonymous to stay alive. I am not beyond hearing things that I need to hear.

I know that I'm growing because I'm changing again. Forget circuit speaking, twenty-first century Messenger, world-wide fame, and recognition. I want to focus on program maintenance, being a good mother, doing Twelve Step work, trying to get out of debt, learning how to have a decent relationship, and having a nice family. I just want to learn how to be a plain old human being. Besides all of that big stuff is like point Z. I'm probably at about point C (and that's being generous). You can't get to point Z without going through A … B … C … D … E … F … G … etc. There's no way out but through.

Face it; you've just now learned that you were running the wrong way. Now, do the next right thing and stop over-thinking. If anything of greatness is supposed to happen to your life, it will be in spite of your wheeling and dealing. Your life is none of your business so keep your nose out of it. Do the footwork and leave the results up to Me. Got it?

He hungers for the goal but not for the struggle.[161]
Hugh Prather

September 22, 1990

I had casual sex the night before last and I felt awful yesterday. We had a meeting on sex last night and I realized a few things. I have always started with sex and then (maybe) proceeded into love. Love needs to come first. Anytime I act out with no love, I feel terrible. In the meeting people were talking about other people getting hurt as a consequence of thoughtless sex. The person I hurt is me! Sometimes what "feels good" on my outsides shreds my insides to pieces.

Stretch the bow to the very full, and you will wish you had stopped in time.[162]
Lao-Tzu

October 8, 1990

I think I'm pregnant. I've got all the symptoms. Needless to say, abortion is out of the question.

October 16, 1990

I'm definitely pregnant and I'm having a hard time deciding what to do. My head says abortion and my heart says to have it. I know good and well that God doesn't speak through my head. I have a plaque on my wall that says "*A child is God's decision that the world must go on.*" I don't even know why I bought that thing. I think it's trying to tell me something. I have made life difficult for myself.

Within each of us is an enemy—self.
He must be expelled from our soul by violence. [163]
A.W. Tozer

October 29, 1990

I had an abortion and felt okay about it. As a matter of fact, I felt great about it (too great). I ended up running into one of last summer's flings and going home with him and having sex! I am totally angry at myself. I just cannot believe that I would sabotage myself like that.

I am powerless and my life has become unmanageable. I have come to believe that a power greater than myself will restore me to sanity. I need belief to keep me sane.

If you want to enter into life, keep the commandments.
Matthew 19:17

November 6, 1990

I had an encounter with Troy that made me so angry that I ended up smoking some pot. I was depressed about it yesterday, but I also hated the way it made me feel so hopefully I won't do it again. I know in my heart that I was born to be sober.

Granddaddy's going down fast. They're putting him on morphine today. They don't think he'll make it another three days. I feel numb about the whole deal. I vacillate between being angry and depressed. He is terrified.

If an alcoholic failed to perfect and enlarge his spiritual life through work and self-sacrifice for others, he could not survive the certain trials and low spots ahead. [164]
Alcoholics Anonymous

November 7, 1990

4:07 A.M.

Granddaddy died about twelve hours ago. We were all here at the end for him. I remember when death once frightened me, but it wasn't frightening; just poignant. One thing I know in my heart is that he is going to be okay. We're all going to miss him, but I can see that this whole thing is nothing but a circle; a cycle of beginnings and endings. The pain of it all brings many tears, but what would life be without it?

Goodbye Granddaddy … until we meet again … God bless you always.

November 15, 1990

They tossed all of Granddaddy's prescriptions, which freaked me out. I've been using a lot of his Valium, muscle relaxers, sleeping pills, and pain pills to sleep. My program has been very strained. I'm grateful that I have not taken a drink, but that's about all I haven't done. There's no point in beating myself up, though.

I feel kind of numb these days. Sometimes I think I know it all and other times I'm back to asking what it's all about. I just want to be happy and at peace.

Have we skimped on the cement put into the foundation?
Have we tried to make mortar without sand?[165]
Alcoholics Anonymous

November 19, 1990

I smoked pot all weekend. Today, it occurred to me that I should pray for the desire to not smoke. That should help.

Not everyone who says to Me, "Lord, Lord," shall enter the kingdom of heaven,
but he who does the will of My Father in heaven.
Matthew 7:21

December 10, 1990

Needless to say, I finally drank. It seemed to me that the only way to get myself out of half-measure's land was to go all the way out so I could go back in (re-establish a new sobriety date). I see now that was stupid, but at least I did re-establish. I also now see that my participation in A.A. is really a matter of life and death for me spiritually. I almost broke my neck falling off of that pedestal, but it feels good to be back down to earth with the common folk. I hope I have learned my lesson about spiritual pride. Being a guru can be very dangerous. I spent my whole life being "less than." Then, I spent a year being "better than." Now I want to be a part of the whole.

The fact was we really hadn't cleaned house
so that the grace of God could enter us
and expel the obsession to drink. [166]
Twelve Steps and Twelve Traditions

.9. broken

December 18, 1990 – May 22, 1991

The stone which the builders rejected has become the chief cornerstone.
Psalm 118:22

And whoever falls on this stone will be broken;
but on whomever it falls, it will grind him to powder.
Matthew 21:44

When I took my first drink after a year of continuous sobriety, it seemed like no big deal. The experiment went so well that I tried it again the following weekend. For many consecutive weeks afterward, I drank two glasses of wine on Friday and Saturday night. There were no major consequences and I became convinced that my period of uncontrollable drinking had been nothing but a phase. Shortly thereafter, I felt the desire to drink a 12-pack of beer on a Sunday morning. I had no mental defense against the thought. Once I became drunk, the compulsion to drink took over my life.

> *Our drinking careers have been characterized by countless vain attempts to prove that we could drink like other people. The idea that somehow, someday he will control and enjoy his drinking is the great obsession of every abnormal drinker. The persistence of the illusion is astonishing.*[167]
>
> Alcoholics Anonymous

December 18, 1990

I may have learned my lesson about spiritual pride, but I didn't learn my lesson about powerlessness over alcohol. Today is my third day sober after a miserable five-day drunk; complete with blackouts, hangovers, and utterly embarrassing and humiliating behavior. When I went to bed two nights ago and thanked God for my day of sobriety, I meant it. I have realized that I don't know how to stay sober. Once my binge started, I couldn't stop drinking even though I wanted to.

I've always looked at the strict A.A. members as if they were fools, but I was the fool. Deep spiritual thought may be great, but that's Step Eleven! I'm on Step One.

I just went back to a miserable trip to the past where I was nothing but a hateful drunk. I really am grateful for who I am today because I realized that it *really isn't me.* Paige with God and Paige alone are two very different characters. I'm so glad to be back. I was becoming homesick.

Now that I'm sober, I have to pick up where I left off two months ago; grieving Granddaddy's death, the failure of my relationship with Troy, and the abortion. God, it's beginning to seem that a part of my soul died in that abortion clinic. I'm really sorry that I did that.

I think I'm finally beginning to see that anything in this life that I truly desire will never be mine until I stop trying to make it happen. Sounds like powerlessness to me. I have no control in this world.

For us, the process of gaining a new perspective was unbelievably painful.[168]
Twelve Steps and Twelve Traditions

January 17, 1991

Last Thursday I ended up drunk again and had another miserable weekend.

No other kind of bankruptcy is like this one.[169]
Twelve Steps and Twelve Traditions

January 28, 1991

I realize that if I want lofty heights, I better make sure I have a sturdy foundation. Before, I tried to build a skyscraper on top of a card table. Even though the last few months have been anything but fun, I must admit that I have learned some priceless lessons. I pray with all my heart that one of them is that

I am powerless over drugs and alcohol. I mean *powerless.* There is One who has all power and that One is God. May I find Him now!

The beginning is the most important part of the work.[170]
Plato

February 7, 1991

Troy and I were getting along and I couldn't stand the peace and harmony so I called another guy. I ended up drunk (as usual). Anyway, Troy really blew his stack and said that I am unwilling to do the things necessary to stay sober. He's right in a way. I definitely have not been willing to go to any length.

I've been looking at all of this and questioning what it is about me that causes me to ruin all chances of my dreams coming true. I think it's because all of my dreams pertain to something happening that's never happened before. However, when something new happens, I start getting uncomfortable because of the unfamiliarity—so I start manipulating to put my circumstances back to familiar ways that I *am* comfortable with. The problem is that what I am comfortable with is intense pain and heartache where I can somehow manage to be a victim of circumstance. But I am not a victim and I do not have to live in pain and turmoil.

I'm really starting to understand what drives me: the need to control—to be the best—to be in unchanging circumstances—to be the center of attention—to sabotage my own success so that I can justify myself as a failure rather than give myself permission to succeed. These are character defects and I am willing to let go of them. As a matter of fact, I pray with all my heart that God takes them from me because they are blocking me from His plan for my life. I also see that the people I most resent are those who see the truth about me when I am unwilling to see it myself. Basically, they're the people who are my teachers when I am in an unteachable state of mind.

More than anything, I pray that I somehow find the middle road of humility; which I heard is between pride and guilt. That really makes sense to me. I tend to either be on a one-way ego trip or beating myself mercilessly for being imperfect. It's time to understand that I'm just the way God made me right now this very minute. There's always room for improvement, but right now is where I am and this person writing is who I am today and she's valuable, worthwhile, and beautiful just as she is. She's just not finished yet!

I guess I'm lucky that I didn't die from the last ordeal. I certainly contemplated suicide last Wednesday because I was so appalled by my behavior. This whole thing scares the hell out of me. I hope so because the "hell" in me is what destroys me.

Where humility had formerly stood for a forced feeding on humble pie,
it now begins to mean the nourishing ingredient which can give us serenity.[171]
Twelve Steps and Twelve Traditions

February 15, 1991

I really like Unity Church, but I think that the belief in Jesus as a mere Way-Shower might be inadequate. I think I'm beginning to believe in Him as Savior. I'm willing at least, which is something.

There is only one key, and it is called willingness.
Once unlocked by willingness, the door opens almost of itself,
and looking through it, we shall see a pathway beside which is an inscription.
It reads: "This is the way to faith that works."[172]
Twelve Steps and Twelve Traditions

February 23, 1991

I've been reading a lot of Codependency books this week and boy have my eyes opened (I've been dreading this). Those books give me a lot of compassion for Troy and they help me understand his behavior better, but there is no denying that, even though there is a therapeutic explanation for what is going on between us, this relationship is not good for me.

This above all: to thine own self be true.[173]
William Shakespeare

February 26, 1991

I'm definitely in a new phase of the process. My understanding is increasing and I believe that I might be obtaining a small pinch of wisdom. I'm really getting a feel for what they mean when they say "look at yourself." It never truly occurred to me that when I'm resentful, there's something *inside of me* that's causing it. Now, it doesn't mean that the person I resent doesn't play a part, but it's not my job to figure out their motives and then try to explain to them why they are the way they are. It's my job to do that to myself! I can't believe it's taken this long to understand this.

When I sit in judgment of other people, I deprive myself of the joy of experiencing them as they are. Underneath all of that, the truth is that when

I am passing judgment on other people, it's really the way I feel about myself. Everyone out there is me and every horrible thought I have about them is what I'm thinking about myself. When I look out there and see the beauty in each and every person, then I can be sure that all is well in my world because my world is inside of me.

Thank you, God, for saving me once again.

There is a God and, fortunately, it's not me or we really would be in a mess!

It is a spiritual axiom that every time we are disturbed, no matter what the cause, there is something wrong with us.[174]

Twelve Steps and Twelve Traditions

March 9, 1991

Today I got another one-month chip. My ego says "big whoop," but after that relapse ordeal, I see that even just one month is a miracle. One day is a miracle.

I've been in horrible pain over Troy. To put it mildly, I have a very hard time letting go of the dream that we're going to live happily ever after. The only way that will ever happen is if it's God's will and I know that it is *not* God's will for me to mess around with men who aren't in recovery. I must go with God and follow my appointed path. I'm so sad. I'm so powerless. This really is God's deal and I don't know what's going to happen. All I know is that I trust God.

A tragic mistake that is often made is to assume that the will of God is bound to be something very dull and uninviting, if not positively unpleasant... The truth is that the will of God for us always means greater freedom, greater self-expression, newer and brighter experience, wider opportunity for service to others—life more abundant.[175]

Emmet Fox

March 20, 1991

I made the mistake of stepping on the scales at the gym. I was feeling okay about my appearance until then. I've been gaining weight, but I know that it is because I have spent the last month sitting on my butt. I know that I need to let it go, take right action, and pray to eat the right quantities of the right foods. Maybe I ought to go eat some cake first.

Nothing's really going on. I guess everything is smooth and normal. I'm not high or low, yet I have a sense of peace within myself and all is well in my world. Of course, my first impulse is to stir up some excitement, but I guess that that's another one of those character defects. I need to get used to the middle so I don't fall off the edge again.

It is only by accepting and solving our problems
that we can begin to get right with ourselves and with the world about us,
and with Him who presides over all of us.[176]
Twelve Steps and Twelve Traditions

March 24, 1991

Most people who face the kind of difficulty relating to each other that Troy and I do would give up. Not us, though. Either we're really in love or else we're plain addicted to each other and too scared to lose each other. I know it's not either/or. We love each other *and* we're addicted to each other. I will admit that I'm terrified at the idea of us really ever breaking up and I know he is too. God, it's pretty sad when *I Need You Like A Drug* is our song. That's not sad, that's sick!

One thing I just hate about the recovery process is that no matter how much I blame the other person and try to be the victim, when I start looking for solutions, I'm always led right back inside myself to work on my real problem—*me*—bummer in the summer.

I had a real bad sabotage compulsion on Friday and it scared me. I had to lock myself in the house and pray until I fell asleep. I have to work harder at my sobriety than ever. If I don't take a two-hour quiet time every day (at least), my attitude stinks. Also, if I don't work out, my neck kills me. These are great incentives to work out and spend the appropriate amount of time with God, but I'd still feel better about myself if I did these things because I am naturally disciplined and spiritually altruistic. I guess beggars can't be choosers.

The Lord works in mysterious ways. How else do you get someone like me to spend hours a day in prayer and meditation than to have it be a contingency for staying alive? I'm grateful to be chosen to do this work rather I'm dedicated to doing it voluntarily or not. It beats the hell out of the old way of life. Besides, I'm being too hard on myself. I'm not that bad. I'm just not that good either. I'm just a normal old person who had a few blinding spiritual experiences which were kind of on the life-altering side of the balance. What all this means is still unclear to me. It probably doesn't mean anything except that God loves me and wants me to be happy just like He loves everyone and wants them to be happy. Sometimes, it's just hard to get my attention, but leave it to God to figure out a way. He definitely got my attention. All I can say when I focus on Him is, *What a view!*

God loves each of us as if there were only one of us.[177]
Saint Augustine

March 29, 1991

I've been running into my defects a lot this week. I've noticed that I really lash out and behave defensively when I'm wrong. The lady at the mental health clinic asked me about paying my bill and I lashed out at her. I missed an appointment in Irving today and tried to blame the person I had the appointment with. I guess I have a problem with facing the fact that I'm very irresponsible. I like to pretend that I'm not irresponsible, but I'm tired of trying to fool everybody. Maybe I'm just fooling myself. I need God to help me change.

I've also noticed that I tend to expect perfection rather than be grateful for progress. I really need to work on gratitude for what *is* rather than expectations of what will be and I need to work on patience with the process. It's the journey that counts; not the destination.

I'm beginning to see that if I will put the energy I use trying to convince Troy that he needs to change into doing all of the things that I need to be doing for myself, I will most likely see some changes in myself that will probably ease my perception that Troy needs to change. Denial is a monster because sometimes I really can believe that I'm looking at myself when I'm looking at anything *but* myself. Guess who I'm talking to when I say *You need to change and you need to work harder in the relationship?* I'm talking to myself. It's me. It's all me. This whole life of mine is nothing but a mirror to teach me who I am and what is going on.

Once again, it all boils down to nothing but God. Only He can show me these things. Only He can change me. The only thing that really matters is my relationship with Him. I am powerless. I believe in God. I surrender. Help me honestly inventory myself, Father. Show me the way.

For the wise have always known that no one can make much of his life until self-searching becomes a regular habit, until he is able to admit and accept what he finds, and until he patiently and persistently tries to correct what is wrong.[178]
Twelve Steps and Twelve Traditions

April 5, 1991

Things are so weird right now because I'm not accustomed to absence of emotional turmoil. Troy and I haven't had a single blow up this week. I'm beginning to believe that all of the fighting really has been a result of my fits when I don't get my way.

I've been thinking about the other relationships. I've always wanted my men dependent on me so I could have control (or let's say the "illusion" of control). Letting go of that illusion is one of the hardest things I've ever tried to do.

My biggest complaint about the relationship with Troy is that we don't do things t*he way I want,* but the other relationships were the way I thought I wanted them and they didn't work. I always knew that the "living together" thing was a mistake, but I never had the discipline to delay gratification nor the emotional maturity to be solo and entertain myself so that I did not require constant companionship to distract me.

I guess I should be grateful for the progress. I'm definitely a lot more comfortable with being alone than I used to be, but the discipline thing is surely lacking and delay of gratification is being imposed on me. If I had my way, Troy and I would be married. Thank God, I don't have my way. God is definitely doing for me what I can't do for myself.

It is necessary that we extricate from an examination of our personal relations every bit of information about ourselves and our fundamental difficulties that we can.[179]

Twelve Steps and Twelve Traditions

April 10, 1991

My attitude towards Dad is changing a lot. That's what trips me out about recovery—you dream of all of these things that would require miracles to happen and then realize that what's really required is a change in yourself in order to accept life on life's terms. Guess what? Life on life's terms is a miracle.

The truth is that life is good and everything is okay the way it is. Now, to get to a state of mind where you can *see that* is a miracle. I never dreamed in a million years that beyond forgiving Dad, I would realize that I was wrong in blaming him. I'm grateful for all of this because it's giving me something that I've needed for a long time, respect for Dad.

My prayers really are being answered. My faith is strong right now and my willingness to change is at a very high level. I look forward to these changes because the more I change, the better my life seems to get.

Who needs fame when plain old life turns out to be not so plain? Life really is a gift. Thank you, God.

Don't ask the world to change—you change first.[180]
Anthony DeMello

April 16, 1991

I have really been on an emotional crying jag lately. I get angry and feel sorry for myself because when I need someone to comfort me, Troy can't do it to my satisfaction, but it's not his job to comfort me when I need comfort; it's mine and God's. The problem is that I'm a little teeny girl—in an adult body—who needs a lot of love. I think I'm just having growing pains.

Things are at a point where I don't really have anything to complain about. I'm so addicted to intensity and excitement that the lack of it almost makes me crazy. Obtaining peace in the midst of the storm is nothing to obtaining peace in the midst of the peace. It's me! It's me! It's me! *I'm* my problem.

I guess that I've just been coming out of denial and seeing that I really do need to change. I am irresponsible, immature, and lazy. Basically, I just need to grow up and face the responsibilities of personhood. I want to throw my arms up and retreat with people having to take care of me, but I can't stand myself when I do those things. I just can't get away with self-pity anymore because it irritates me with myself.

I guess what is really going on is that a parent-child relationship within me is developing. I've always resented people telling me what to do, but now I don't have that and I feel that I need it. Guess what? I do have a disciplinarian and He's inside of me. I think that I've always been rebellious of authority because I was in such denial about my need for direction and discipline. Paradoxically, it seems that when I realize that I really need discipline and become willing to accept it, I get it from within. This journey really is about becoming integrated into one whole, healthy, human being.

I finally met up with my wounded child. She's about ten years old, in a lot of pain, and lashing out with anger. This is a trip.

The bottom line is that I am beginning to change from the inside out. I may not want to grow up, but I need to. I am beginning to want what I need rather than need what I want. Thy will, not mine, be done.

We begin to see that all people, including ourselves,

are to some extent emotionally ill as well as frequently wrong,
and then we approach true tolerance
and see what real love for our fellows actually means.[181]
Twelve Steps and Twelve Traditions

April 25, 1991

I'm in a lot of turmoil today because I am beginning to once again question whether or not Troy and I are compatible. I don't know if I'm feeling this way because I'm finally facing reality or because I'm creating a crisis!

April 27, 1991

I broke up with Troy for the first time in our relationship's history. I miss him and I hurt, but I feel good about my program today. I really am being given the courage to change the things I can. The A.A. literature says that *lack of power is our dilemma.* Yesterday, the 24-Hour book said that we are given power when we need it to take right action. I see that. I understand now why at some times I'm a seemingly powerful person and at others, I'm a sniveling coward. I especially see why Troy cannot see the power of God in my life; because I have not taken right action in this relationship.

I'm not desperate and insecure today. Even if we end up permanently split, at least he will see what I'm capable of doing. He will really see my program in action. My sponsor says that I am beginning to command respect in my life.

May 5, 1991

I've been actually experiencing some peace. It's totally still and silent; like nothing with everything contained within. All spiritual books say that the silence is where the most profound contact with God exists. It's all new to me, though, because I've always been a person of many words.

Sometimes, I miss the intensity of euphoric highs, but I see now that I was really wasting a lot of energy making noise. God seems to be rewiring the energy these days, which enables me to do some things which would have once been impossible—like break up with Troy.

I've been in pain about the split, but the more I evaluate the situation, the less I want to reconcile. I really don't want to be in a relationship with someone who's not actively seeking spiritual growth.

Last night, this guy was talking about the reconciliation of good and evil within oneself which, to me, seems similar to inner-child discovery work. I don't think I wrote about my experience a few weeks ago where I seemed to meet up with my wounded inner child (or at least one of them). She was that pig-tailed fatty who had to wear regular clothes her first day at private school because her jumbo uniforms hadn't come in yet. I reached out to her and explained that she didn't have to hate in retaliation to her pain. I gave her permission to feel those feelings—and did we ever feel them. Anyway, I've noticed a lot of empowerment as a result of that. She really is a remarkable child—so smart and creative; so lonely.

Thank God I don't have to feel lonely any more! I can honestly say that one of my favorite past times is being alone. I really like to just sit and be (more amazing progress).

Be still, and know that I am God.
Psalm 46:10

May 14, 1991

I had a miserable weekend. I got into so much pain that I finally called Troy and had a big argument with him. I started raging. Sunday, I drank to ease the rage and all that happened was I blacked out and went totally insane! I made death threats to Troy—death threats! The real messed up thing is that I really felt homicidal.

I feel pretty sad because that stunt really opened my eyes to some hard, cold facts. The reality of the situation is that the relationship never existed. Troy and I have nothing but an addictive, dysfunctional bond. It has become as toxic to me as drugs and alcohol.

I'm very grateful that I didn't end up on a three or four day spree. I just tried an experiment to see if alcohol would kill the pain. I also tried a desperate attempt to get Troy's attention. I got it all right, but not in the way I had in mind. I became willing to fall in order for him to pick me up. Instead, he turned away.

I'm a lot sicker than I was willing to own up to. I'm ready to work on my codependency and adult-child issues. Why do I choose such emotionally unavailable men?

But with the alcoholic,
whose hope is the maintenance and growth of a spiritual experience,
this business of resentment is infinitely grave.
We found that it was fatal.[182]
Alcoholics Anonymous

May 15, 1991

I think I'm making Troy's acceptance of me the foundation for my acceptance of myself. I need to get into self-acceptance and I don't mean the way I look. I am powerless over myself. Only my willingness to change and to leave myself alone can allow God to change me.

I guess I don't love myself as much as I thought I did. If I did, I wouldn't judge others so harshly in order to make myself feel superior to them. I guess the real truth is that I really do believe that if people find out who I really am, they won't care about me.

Why *shouldn't* I feel that way? Maybe it is a self-fulfilling prophecy, but how do I keep people from finding out how crazy I really am? I was so mad at Troy for making me out to be a *Fatal Attraction* girlfriend and, in reality, that's exactly what I am! I'm so sick that I can't even let go of a man who I *know* is not right for me.

I guess that this is Step Two—believing in God to restore me to sanity. I'm just going to give this whole mess to You, Father. Take all of it and do whatever You want. I am miserable today because of the pain and hopelessness, but I know that this too shall pass. I don't want to relapse any more because I know that recovery is my only lifeline. I don't want to die because Laurel needs me. Please give me the courage to keep putting one foot in front of the other. Please take away my attraction to the things of this world.

I am a person who has always said that I don't care what other people think. What a lie! I care *too much.* Show me the truth, Father. Show me reality that I may face it square in the face. I'm ready to let go of my old ideas completely. Show me myself through Your eyes, Father.

My grace is sufficient for you, for My strength is made perfect in weakness.
2 Corinthians 12:9

May 22, 1991

Friday I decided that a trip into the party world would be fun and would distract me from the pain of detaching from Troy. Wrong! I ended up using a lot of cocaine and it was very hard on me physically and psychologically. Both of these experiences the past two weeks have shown me how mentally uneasy drugs and alcohol make me. Without sobriety, I have a diseased mind!

I was thinking the other night about what an emotional wreck I was becoming in the relationship with Troy. Even after two relapses, I'm better now than I was then. I've always known that being alone for a while was inevitable, but I guess I used to think that I'd have a choice. I realize now that I don't have a choice. I see that when God is ready for me to face something, I have to face it. I can't escape.

Drugs and alcohol don't even work any more. It takes me a week to recover from one drunk. Food doesn't work any more either and I can't stand cigarettes. As for other men, forget them. Three weeks ago I played kissy-face with a guy at work and I felt horrible about it. There's nowhere to turn but to God!

I just don't know what's going to happen with Troy. He's afraid of me after the death threats. Maybe he should be. I'm trying not to be too hard on myself about all of this. I've just been trying to pick myself back up and keep on keeping on. Like the motto says, *"To try and fail is hopeful."* I haven't given up yet. I never do.

I truly believe that everything that happens is a part of God's divine plan. At this point, I'd kind of enjoy an encouraging telegram from Him telling me what I have to look forward to, but I believe that whatever it is, it will be better than I can imagine. I've seen dark days before and they passed. Usually they even developed into shiny new beginnings. I believe that it's darkest before the dawn. I just hope that the sun starts shining soon. I feel a little shaky and insecure, but I still have hope that the best is yet to come. I thank God for the painful lessons because I know that this deal with Troy will really help me to grow. I thank God for the privilege of being alive.

Eye has not seen, nor ear heard,
nor have entered into the heart of man
the things which God has prepared for those who love Him.
Isaiah 64:4

On May 25, 1991, I began my day with a case of beer by the pool. In the evening, I invited one of my flings from the summer over and we drank a fifth of gin, smoked marijuana, snorted cocaine, and had sex. By 3:00 A.M., I craved more drugs so I left Laurel at my grandmother's apartment, alone, while I drove around town in my nightgown to see if I could score. I returned home in a black-out and passed out.

The next morning, I came-to with a horrible headache and suicidal depression. In a matter of minutes, I began to shake uncontrollably and to throw up. I felt as if there were bugs crawling all over me and I hallucinated that there were spiders covering the walls. Suddenly, I had a vision as if I were lying in a casket with the lid closed. With the sensation of dark coffin ruffles

in my face, a thought shattered my mind, *I am going to die from this disease!* The next thought came immediately, *But I want to live!*

To date, I have never taken another drink of alcohol.

It was only by repeated humiliations
that we were forced to learn something about humility.[183]
Twelve Steps and Twelve Traditions

.10. climbing up

May 28, 1991 – September 25, 1991

If, when you honestly want to, you find that you cannot quit entirely, or if when drinking, you have little control over the amount you take, you are probably alcoholic.[184]
Alcoholics Anonymous

We had to fully concede to our innermost selves that we were alcoholics. This is the first step in recovery.[185]
Alcoholics Anonymous

May 28, 1991

The world is scary to me today. I had a three-day drunk that was worse than anything I can remember. I was sick both mentally and physically. All I know is that I have lost all respect for and good feelings about myself.

I'm scared. Last night, I literally got on my knees and surrendered. I don't know how to live. I'm real shaky today because on top of everything, I haven't been sleeping well at all. My thinking has been trying to revert to old ways. I have a disease that tells me I don't have one. I am an alcoholic!

I need help. I need You, Lord.

Half measures availed us nothing.[186]
Alcoholics Anonymous

May 29, 1991

I feel like myself again today. Thank You, God! Last night I talked to Troy and he told me to forget about him and start worrying about myself. He told me that I had put so much of myself into the relationship with him that I was gone. He's right. Yesterday, I saw a very mature and self-disciplined person in Troy. In the long run, Troy's pushing me away has been the best thing for me. I was presumptuous to think that he would bottom out and seek recovery if I left him. It was the other way around. I was talking about myself.

Today, I'm willing to go to any length which, for me, means to *follow directions.* The directions are: a meeting every day, a tough sponsor, thorough working of the Steps, no relationships (or sex) for a year, no relationships with non-recovering people, new group, new weekly therapist, no sugar, daily exercise, healthy diet, and most importantly—put God first! ~~OLD PLAYMATES, OLD PLAYPENS, OLD PLAY THINGS.~~

If you have decided that you want what we have
and are willing to go to any length to get it—
then you are ready to take certain steps.
At some of these we balked.
We thought we could find an easier, softer way.
But we could not.[187]
Alcoholics Anonymous

May 30, 1991

I see that I only love myself when I am aware of God's presence within me. I am not a precious child of God unless I am focused on Him. Now I see what Jesus meant when He said, "*He who is not with Me is against Me.*" (Matthew 12:30) Righteousness is right thinking. Once again, I understand "think God." This time around, I think I'll try to walk it instead of talk it.

Preach the Gospel at all times and when necessary use words.[188]
Saint Francis of Assisi

June 1, 1991

Well, it's Saturday and I'm sober. That's a good sign. I don't ever want to forget exactly how powerless I am over alcohol. I'm really beginning to believe that to drink is to die (it's about time).

Yesterday was my first day back in the world after my latest resolutions and I totally blew my commitment to the Lord. I want so much to behave in a respectable manner, but instead I was bouncing off the walls and behaving inappropriately. I remember hearing that if you resolve to change, you will get immediate resistance. I like to think that our egos resist change or maybe God tests the resolutions, but some say that Satan is the tempter (the Bible says that). I'm beginning to believe that. Even though that idea scares me, it keeps me clinging closer to God. Being protected from me doesn't seem near as scary as being protected from Satan. My sponsor said that the closer the pull to God, the harder the resistance from Satan. Man, is that ever the truth.

One thing that has been great about this week is that I'm pretty focused on myself again; which sets me free to live my life. I really have a good life. I realize how truly blessed I am to get back to this state of awareness so quickly after I was foolish enough to trash everything that means anything to me. I truly believe that I am here for a Divine Purpose or else He wouldn't keep saving me. I am supposed to be alive and the only way that I can live is sober and focused on God. I know that. I still think that I'm supposed to be a minister, but I've definitely got a lot of calming down and growing up to do before that will be possible.

I give myself to You, Father. In the name of the Lord, I pray that You keep me close to You and focused on Christ-like behavior. I'm ready. I pray for Your peace and spiritual discernment.

God's work can be done only in God's strength, by God Himself working in us.[189]

Andrew Murray

June 3, 1991

I had a good weekend; a sober weekend. I feel pretty good. I'm comfortable with myself. There are a whole lot of things that need to change, but I have faith that they will. I'm just sort of taking it one character defect at a time.

I realized that Troy mirrors the negative things I believe about myself and that my new friends mirror the more healthy things I believe about myself. I guess what I'm waiting for is for Troy to mirror the new beliefs, but that's approval seeking and I'm learning that I never get approval from others until I stop seeking it.

There are so many paradoxes. When you desire something and pray for it, if you believe that you receive it, you'll get it, but it seems to me that it's *only* when you become willing to not have it—or even better yet, when you don't have the desire for it anymore. I guess it's because you have to be okay with where you are and what you already have before you can get something new or different.

Only God can fix me; with my cooperation.

Your Father knows the things you have need of before you ask Him.
Matthew 6:8

June 5, 1991

It dawned on me that rather than trying to be spiritual, I should just relax and be who I am. I'm already spiritual so I just need to let the evolutionary process unfold. Sometimes, I try too hard.

June 20, 1991

Sunday night I had a dinner party for Dad. I was disappointed because he was withdrawn and unobservant of my environment and me. Once again I could see myself jumping up and down screaming, *Look at me Daddy! Look at me!!!*

I was also in a lot of pain because I've been reading more about codependency. For the first time, I really understand what the shame core is all about. It was almost sickening to realize that the horrible feelings of anger, pain, fear, and shame that I've been carrying around all of my life probably aren't even *my* feelings, but the feelings of my major caretakers who either were in denial about their feelings or irresponsible with them during some sort of abusive act towards me and, believe me, there were a lot of them if you take into account that abuse can be defined as something as seemingly minor as failure to appropriately give physical and emotional nurturing. I still haven't fully inventoried the abuse history, but I've begun the process and it hurts.

I had almost forgotten about these feelings because of the joy that recovery sometimes offers. Just like a guy said yesterday, "*In recovery even fifteen minutes of joy can turn twenty-three hours and forty-five minutes of misery into a good day.*" There was no joy before recovery.

I can honestly say that at this moment right now, whether or not I have a romantic love interest in my life is not important to me. Unbelievable! My focus really is on God and myself! I have really passed through a barrier that has been blocking me for a long time—the one of "falling in love" with every man that gets close to me.

A thorn can only be extracted if you know where it is.[190]
Rabindranath Tagore

July 5, 1991

It dawned on me that the idea that the romance between Troy and me can work out is just as crazy as the idea that I can drink normally. When I get into even a little acceptance that the romance is over, I am a lot happier. I need spiritual aid to do this.

Happiness cannot be defined. What can be defined is misery.
Drop unhappiness and you will know.[191]
Anthony DeMello

July 16, 1991

I know in my heart I have a spiritual calling to do work for God in the form of being of service to other people. I keep forgetting that if God hadn't literally saved my butt (on more than one occasion), I'd be dead. I'm here to do what He wants me to do; not any and every thing that I want.

I also keep forgetting that my "*pain is the breaking of the shell that encloses my understanding.*"[192] I should be grateful for this horrendous pain! It is very difficult to maintain that perspective.

I realized the other day that I can have all of the knowledge in the world of what to do and how to do it, but that doesn't mean anything without the power to carry it out. And guess what? I am utterly powerless. I hate that! Guess where I get that power? God! Oh yeah. I forgot. I have a teflon brain!

I guess I'm really beginning to see that I am not that vital or important to anyone except me. A.A. gets along just fine without me. Troy seems to be doing just fine without me. The only person that really needs me—besides me—is Laurel. I guess that's the way it's supposed to be. A lady said today that thriving to be needed by other people is sick! I guess that giving and expecting nothing in return except for the person to be dependent on you is not giving at all; it's control and manipulation.

I guess I thought that Troy needed me. Troy needs Troy. I need Paige to cooperate with God and help me. I am not the center of the Universe!

Face it Paige! You don't run your life well at all! I do a better job of being God than you do. Recovery is a process! Surrender is a process! Humility is a process!

Talk about a never-ending journey! The journey continues …

It is only when we forget all our learning that we begin to know.[193]
Henry David Thoreau

July 19, 1991

I finished a thorough inventory Wednesday night and then did my Fifth Step with my sponsor. I can't say that it was a peak spiritual experience, but I did experience lack of turmoil when I was finished. I woke up this morning and had a flood of memories from my childhood. That was interesting. I started remembering a lot of spankings for stupid stuff that's pretty normal for a small child. If I whipped Laurel for the things that I got spanked with a belt for, the kid would be black and blue. I let go of a lot of pain in the Fifth Step so it doesn't hurt so badly, but I still feel pretty nauseated and anxious. I'm starting to understand why I was so terrified all of the time; my punishments were too severe for the behavior.

I feel good about my recovery right now. I really have been fooling myself about those Steps. This is the first real inventory I have ever shared with another human being.

Face it, Paige, you never got willing to go to any length until this year.

It's really kind of hard to believe that my spiritual experiences could have been so overwhelming without the Steps. I guess that's why I couldn't handle them. I've probably got the same level of spirituality now (if not more), but it doesn't seem so intense because I have more balance. I still feel like I have important spiritual work to do, but the trumpet blowing days are over. I can tell that I have a lot more humility than I ever have before.

Basically, the further I go, I see just how much I am incapable of managing my own life; drunk or sober. Also, that inventory really let me see the futility of holding onto the dream of resolution with Troy. From the very beginning I believed that I was there to rescue him. I always believed that he needed rescuing. In other words, I did not accept him how he was. I'm not sure if I have ever even looked objectively at who he actually is.

There are a thousand hacking at the branches of evil
to one who is striking at the root.[194]
Henry David Thoreau

July 24, 1991

Yesterday, I went on a real sabotage thought-train. Peace is very unusual for me. I realize that I still don't know anything about "living." I've practiced a few principles which have helped me to solve some problems and to overcome some obstacles, but I always destroy my path as soon as God gets it clear. Yesterday I thought, "*What's the use of going on? Wonder if my life really gets good and I don't'like it? What then? I might as well just drink.*" Stinking thinking, huh?

Above all, take the shield of faith
with which you will be able to quench all the fiery darts of the wicked one.
Ephesians 6:16

July 31, 1991

Whew! The guy I spent my last drunk with called me tonight. I went to the bar to meet him and he asked me to come home with him. I started to, but *for once*, I listened to that inner voice which said

"Don't do this."

I ended up coming home and just writing him a really nice note instead. I did the right thing and I feel good about it. My program is working. God is with me.

It occurred to me that I have just been through one of the worst periods of my life: no job, no money, I gained all of my weight back, I relapsed, I went through a very painful breakup with someone I love, etc. You know what, though? I don't really even look at it that way. It made me realize that there's really nothing to be afraid of. I've been afraid of things ever becoming like they were the summer of '89, but they *were* like that again and I didn't even notice because I knew that it would pass. I knew that God was with me. I knew that the best was coming.

I'm real grateful for where I am with my recovery today. I can see the progress. Today, I know for sure, though, that as long as I'm walking this earth, I have not arrived.

The spiritual life is not a theory. We have to live it.[195]
Alcoholics Anonymous

August 8, 1991

I got angry tonight at Troy ... at myself ... at the world. Finally, I realized that I'm mad because this grieving process over Troy is taking a lot longer than I believed it would. Even though I'm grateful to be at a recovery point where

I'm at least willing to grieve, I can't say it's fun. Sometimes the pain tempts me to return to the lies; to the illusions of love. However, the love I yearn so desperately to experience lies beyond me; not behind me. The only way to get there is to keep putting one foot in front of the other.

People don't really want to be cured.
What they want is relief; a cure is painful.[196]
Anthony DeMello

August 22, 1991

I had an excellent evening at my home group tonight. I could really feel God's presence, and therefore my spirituality, flowing through my veins. The words that I spoke in the 6:00 meeting were powerful and Spirit-filled. It seemed like old times.

A few guys and I took some time after the meeting to try to help a really bottomed out indigent. It was an incredible experience in gratitude. This dude was at the bottom! All we could do was get him arrested by the police, but at least it got him a roof over his head with some supervision in case of DTs or convulsions. God bless his soul; he was pitiful. It made me so grateful to be sober that I couldn't believe it. Today I had my first true realization of what it means for my primary purpose to be sober and to help other alcoholics to achieve sobriety.

Blessed be the Father of mercies and God of all comfort,
who comforts us in all our tribulation,
that we may be able to comfort those who are in any trouble,
with the comfort with which we ourselves are comforted by God.
2 Corinthians 1:3–4

August 26, 1991

Life is good right now. Every day I learn a little more about myself. The Lord's gotten real good about taking the wind out of my sails when I start getting too cocky. I'm very grateful for the December fall because it really did teach me a lot of things about the tendencies of my ego. I really have to watch myself and keep myself from bragging about how spiritual I am. I think it was a Scott Peck book that pointed out to me that people who have big-time spiritual experiences are people who *need* big-time spiritual experiences. I am learning that I may actually be more spiritual when I can see the light without being blinded by it. I was really off my rocker last year. I let my journey become an ego trip.

Today I was looking at my photo album and just about cried my eyes out because of that beautiful little girl of mine. She is so sweet and innocent. I almost hate to see her grow up. We have real power struggles these days, but I still love being her mother. Having her is the second best thing that ever happened to me. Believing in God is the best. A lot of great things have happened to me. It's a wonderful life in sobriety.

It is your Father's good pleasure to give you the kingdom.
Luke 12:32

September 6, 1991

Today has been very spiritually rewarding. Last night, when I was going to sleep, I was thinking about the new happiness and freedom that the program offers. I remember last year when I thought it was a cool deal that I didn't have to drink or drug, but that's just the beginning. Last year my ego told me that I was so smart that I couldn't possibly be at the beginning. I had to be evolved not only past the beginning, but also past the point of any other person; probably almost as much as Jesus. That's some true humility, huh? Anyway, it's real exciting to realize that there are horizons beyond my past "highest" horizons.

I'm really enjoying myself these days. The most serious problem I have is lack of rest because I'm too busy living a wonderful life and having a good time. Simple solution—take a nap. It's so funny how simple it all really is. All I really have to do is be. What an order!

Yesterday it dawned on me that practicing these principles in all of my affairs is for *me* and for my serenity. I always thought it was for me to look good and to gain approval. That's ridiculous, but true.

I'm realizing that there's freedom in being a fallible human being. When Jake used to ask me if I wanted to be right or happy I didn't know what he was talking about. Right, of course! Now I understand better. It's okay to be wrong. It's okay to make mistakes. It's even okay to not be okay. Today, I don't have to be right, to be the best, to explain, or to make excuses. I guess I'm getting better at owning my reality. The hardest thing to do sometimes is to be present to the moment, but God is teaching me.

The ever-present now is the mystery and the glory of eternity.[197]
Andrew Murray

September 16, 1991

I watched *Steel Magnolias* and it stirred up some grief. I cried over Troy, over my relationship with Dad, over Granddaddy, and over just how much I love Laurel.

Your joy is your sorrow unmasked.[198]
Kahlil Gibran

September 20, 1991

I had a big emotional upheaval over Dad this week. I did something wrong and he's angry and I felt all of those feelings like I'm a total failure, like I'm worthless, and like I'll never be good enough. Who told me that I wasn't supposed to make mistakes? It's more of that letting go of my old ideas thing. It's okay to be wrong. It's okay to be imperfect. It's okay to be me.

I realize that growing up, I was told in words that I was better than everyone else, but because of actions toward me, I felt worthless. That's very confusing. I need to remember more things from my childhood. One thing I know for sure: I am not the person whom I have been told that I am. I still have to have arguments with myself to convince me that I'm not a bad person. I must realize that it is not being wrong that does the damage, but being *unaware* that I am wrong. All of these new tapes are so different.

I also realize that I have grown up believing that I am unworthy of forgiveness.

There are only two choices:
integration and acceptance of our whole life story, or despair.[199]
Eric Erikson

September 25, 1991

A member of our A.A. group committed suicide last Friday night. It has really given me a reality blast about the seriousness of the disease.

But for the grace of God there go I.

.11. uncharted waters

October 3, 1991 – April 14, 1992

You cannot discover new oceans
until you have the courage to lose sight of the shore.[200]
Anonymous

October 3, 1991

I've been going through a lot of struggle and turmoil the last few days because Troy has been having emotional outbursts; the first ones I've ever seen him go through. He's been calling me and telling me that I'm the woman he loves and that he's realized that he's been in denial about his feelings. Needless to say, I've been in shock. God only knows how long I've prayed for that guy to wake up and how long I've dreamed of him coming back to me and expressing those sorts of feelings.

The funny thing is that when I dreamed of his coming back, I thought I'd be gloating with self-satisfaction. That wasn't the case at all. To hear Troy cry broke my heart and to have him reach out to me caused every good feeling that I've ever had about the man to whirl like a tornado through my heart. I've been very confused. My heart cries for Troy, but my head tells me to get over it and not to believe a word the guy says. God only knows who'll win. I told him that my terms were still the same; recovery and marriage. I told him it would take some major action on his part to convince me. He went to his first therapy session today.

I'm real proud of him, but I'm trying not to project into the future with expectations. I don't even know what I want to happen because I've been so happy with my recovery. I keep trying to remind myself that I am not my feelings, but that my feelings are a part of me. Love is not a feeling, but a decision and a commitment.

At this point I've been maintaining my balance pretty well. I haven't passed the test *yet* because I still entertain thoughts of going back to Troy, but I haven't taken any action on them. I'm real grateful because I can see my recovery in action. There would have been a day when I would have jumped right into bed with Troy the minute he admitted missing me. I wouldn't have given a second thought to the consequences of my actions. This time I thought it through. I opted not to sabotage.

Way to go, Paige!

When I have listened to my mistakes, I have grown.[201]
Hugh Prather

October 9, 1991

Yesterday was the most tumultuous day of my life. Troy broke down emotionally and begged me to come back to him. He was so over-wrought that I just couldn't refuse. On top of that, my heart longed for him so I went to him. However, I knew immediately that it was a mistake.

Before all the drama, Troy and I had the most beautiful conversation about wisdom; the combination of love and intelligence; the balance between the head and the heart. He has just broken open like an oyster. I'm so proud of him.

It seems so strange to see Troy cry. I know it's good for him, though. I cried every day for years. I cried a million tears yesterday. Troy will always be a very special person in my life. Last night, I finally identified the kind of love I feel for him. It's *maternal* love. I love Troy the same way I love Laurel.

Some of my friends made comments that all of this must have been good for my ego and that I must have felt real powerful. Judging from all fantasies I've ever had about this sort of thing, I would have thought the same, but that wasn't the case at all. I felt terrible. It hurt to see Troy cry over me. It caused me pain to hurt him. That was an interesting thing to learn about myself; that I really don't want to see Troy hurt the way I've hurt; that I want him to be happy with or without me.

I think I'm growing up. Today, I see beauty within myself.

To lose the self is to suddenly realize that
you are something other than what you thought you were.[202]
Anthony DeMello

October 11, 1991

Well, that last decision wasn't final. I decided to go for the dream with Troy, but I must admit that sometimes it scares me. I've had a few second thoughts, but I know it's just fear motivating me not to take any risks. My hope and faith tell me to dare to believe in dreams come true.

October 13, 1991

Yesterday, Troy proposed to me. I am having a hard time grasping the reality of all this. I have fantasized and romanticized about that moment forever and yet it was nothing like I had imagined; it was better.

Seeing Troy this way is one of the most dramatic miracles that I have ever witnessed. His transformation is as dramatic as mine has been. He is much more witty, personable, sensitive, kind, and intelligent than I ever gave him credit for being. I feel like I have won first prize in the game of life.

All of this is so extraordinarily unbelievable that I can hardly identify my feelings. Sometimes I feel fear because a part of me, the negative, self-defeating part of me, tells me that this is too good to be true and that it's a cruel joke that life is playing on me. Thank God that I don't have to buy into that junk anymore. I'm just blown away with joy. I feel like the most blessed person in the world because the story of my life has become a touching, poignant, deep, romantic comedy. It's the kind of life that everyone dreams of—even me.

My dream came true!

In this world there are only two tragedies.
One is not getting what one wants and the other is getting it.[203]
Oscar Wilde

October 14, 1991

I'm having so much fun with my new fiancé. I put the finishing touches on "our" apartment last night and I love the way it turned out. This place has a very peaceful feel to it. Troy said last night that he was so excited to come home that he felt like a little boy going home to his toys.

We officially set the date for February 14. I'm still blown away. Each day goes by and the fear just slips away. I can't believe that this is my life. You just don't get from the pain and agony that I've known to this point without spiritual aid. I am so grateful! After this, I truly believe that nothing is impossible in God's world—nothing. And I still believe that the best is yet to come!

The new covenant is in danger of being abused—
by seeking our own happiness or holiness
more than the honor of God or the deliverance of men.[204]
Andrew Murray

October 21, 1991

This has been a very confusing week. Troy has been great, but I feel lost and isolated to my life and myself. For some reason, I just can't be myself when I am with Troy. I miss my life. I don't want a limited world for two.

I feel like such a fool! I guess I just don't trust Troy. I feel as though I'm being lured into a trap. I keep waiting for his old insensitive behavior to rear its ugly head. I'm always on edge and I feel like a stranger in my own home. God, what a mess!

I guess that I thought moving in with Troy would be the point of no return, but there is apparently no such thing. It's never too late. I love Troy very much, but I feel drained by him. I guess I feel that he's doing all of these things to keep from losing me and not because he genuinely wants recovery. I just don't know what to do.

This is so hard because I care about Troy, but my own program is beginning to slip. I'm losing my enthusiasm. I'm losing myself.

Show me the way Lord.

We cannot learn without pain.
Aristotle

October 22, 1991

I found myself lying on the floor crying because I don't want to grow up. That's what a lot of this fear is all about; taking responsibility for my life and being a mature adult. Those are the things I simply don't know how to do. This week of staying home and keeping house and being a mother to my child and a mate to my future husband have shown me just how much I really have been avoiding life in the name of recovery.

We are nudged to grow whether we want to or not.[205]
Hugh Prather

November 4, 1991

A lot of stuff has been going on inside of me. My defects of character have been sprouting up like weeds. There's nothing like a little decision to get married to trigger all of my adult-child issues and more. Honestly, I don't know which way is up or down. I've been in a lot of fear lately; fear of people, fear of rejection, fear of being terminally ill, and fear of my disease destroying me. I can tell that my self-esteem is pretty low.

Fear was an evil and corroding thread.
We asked ourselves why we had fear.
Wasn't it because self-reliance failed us?[206]
Alcoholics Anonymous

November 13, 1991

It is very obvious that I have taken a nosedive since the day I went back to Troy. I don't have strong enough boundaries to be in this sort of relationship. I left him.

I've been in a lot of pain and have wanted to blame him and to be a victim, but I have to take responsibility for my decisions. With the help of my sponsor, I can see that the big bait that hooked me was the security of a home and a family for Laurel and me.

This has been a painful learning experience, but I am grateful for it because I feel close to God and *that's* my favorite feeling.

Those who seldom make mistakes seldom make discoveries.[207]
John M. Templeton

November 19, 1991

Well, I think that I'm finally in a place where I can write the truth rather than what I want to be the truth. The truth is I don't know what's going to happen; that I don't even know what I *want* to happen.

I realize that so many bad situations in my life stem from me not taking care of myself. I guess that I get desperately afraid that if I don't let other people enmesh with me, I'll lose them. I set enmeshment traps. I use my charm and sexuality and spirituality to lure them in and get them so involved in my process that they need me to help them define themselves. That is very sick and twisted.

I guess seeing this is the process to getting closer to God. It figures that when self-examination becomes sickening, you're on the right path. It was more fun to look at myself and see glorious perfection. What a lie, though! I was using God as a public relations mode to promote myself. No wonder I fell on my butt.

Today, what I see when I look at myself is a lovable, valuable, imperfect, mixed up child of God. I like the kid, though. She's real sweet and nutty.

Where I stand today is alone. I'll just take care of myself and more will be revealed.

Thy will be done, Father.

Self-searching is the means by which we bring new vision, action, and grace to bear upon the dark and negative side of our natures. It is a step in the development of that kind of humility that makes it possible for us to receive God's help.[208]

Twelve Steps and Twelve Traditions

December 16, 1991

I haven't written for a while because my life has been so confusing, but the fog finally seems to be clearing away. I am at a place where I *know* that Troy is the man I want to merge my life with. We're going to keep trying.

A lot of this bull has been about my fear of commitment and my unwillingness to grow up and take responsibility for my life. The days of being footloose and fancy-free are over. What I've really been running from is my motherhood. I'm just now learning what it really means to be Laurel's mother. It's hard work.

Work is love made visible.[209]

Kahlil Gibran

January 4, 1992

I think I'm actually growing up. I've really been calming down lately. I woke up this morning and cried with gratitude because my life is so peaceful and lovely. It's just so amazing how much has changed. I'm somewhere that I never even knew existed. To think I thought that I knew it all! That's absurd to me today.

The best and favorite part of the changes is the one concerning my relationship with Troy. I'm really beginning to understand the concept of marriage; two souls united. That man is a part of me. I love him so much and I think that he is wonderful. I didn't even know what love was when I first began my journey. The exciting thing is that I still know nothing compared to what is ahead to learn.

1991 was a very interesting year. I saw a mountain move with Troy that helped me to believe that in God's world, all things are possible. I still believe in my life-long vision of myself before the multitudes. I still believe that I'm here to work for God, but that's God's deal. I also believe that it's none of my business and that He'll take care of it in His time.

It is impossible for anyone to begin to learn that which he thinks he already knows.[210]
Epictetus

January 18, 1992

I have not been writing because I have been experiencing peace and balance in my life. This is the longest I've probably ever gone without creating a crisis and I'd say it's been about ten days.

I realized something the other day that really blows my mind; living doesn't hurt any more. The wounds are healing.

I live in a different world today and I am a different person and I am so grateful for that. Today, I am a person that the old me would have absolutely hated. I'm everything that I always believed that I never wanted to be. I can see now that all of that anger and non-conformity were really masks for my pain from tremendously low self-esteem. Rather than admit that I felt so less-than, I just lashed out and hated everyone and told myself that I didn't want to be a "part of." I'm finally "a part of" my own life.

Maturity is wanting nothing but what we see with the purity of our heart.[211]
Hugh Prather

January 29, 1992

Troy and I are back in the stage of the relationship where I bailed out last time. It's so hard for me not to freak out when the ebb and flow of romance ebbs. The tide is out, but this too shall pass. I need to get out of the fear of uncertainty and just put one foot in front of the other while I see what *where I've never been* and *what I don't know* have to show me. Yet one more example of how important it is to stay in the present moment.

I guess I get into that old fear that if I don't bend over backwards to please Troy, he'll leave me. Then, when my imperfections rear their ugly heads, I immediately want to break up with him before he dumps me. It all boils down to that very simple lesson that I just learned recently; we're all imperfect human beings in an imperfect world. All in all, though, Troy and I are doing well.

I've really been the domestic goddess lately. I've been spending tons of time with Laurel and it's been great! She and I have something that I have always yearned for. Of course, I would prefer to be the child and not the mommy, but what the hell; you can't have everything. The point is that that my yearning for family is being fulfilled with Laurel. I'm beginning to understand the "motherly love" deal. I really love her and I think that she's wonderful.

Somehow, I just don't think that my parents felt that way about me when I was a child because there's still a tiny voice inside of me that say's *nobody thinks I'm wonderful,* but maybe that has nothing to do with my parents. I know I have to cultivate that within myself, but it's still hard not to envy Laurel sometimes. I wish I had a mommy to rock me and tell me that I'm wonderful. I wish I were my own mommy.

Guess what, Paige? You can be.

Whew! All of that mommy stuff stirred up some pain. I wish I knew what that was all about. The other day I remembered being in the first grade and being shamed by the school doctor because he said I was too fat. I remember exactly how I felt—*horrible.* I know that not being accepted because of my weight is probably at the core of all this. I was different than the other kids. I was always different. Thank God I am finally becoming ordinary.

The most useful piece of learning for the use of life is to unlearn what is untrue.[212]

Antisthenes

March 1, 1992

I have a lot to learn about being a supportive mate. We had a small financial setback so Troy worked a lot of extra hours to make up for it. I acted like a spoiled brat and had a tantrum where I cried and said he didn't care about me. It didn't have anything to do with me in the first place. I'm so powerless and apparently God's giving me more time to become fully aware of just exactly what that means. I want to stop being such a brat.

One blatant lesson I have learned recently is that I'm always going to be restless until I get into action and start doing the footwork to accomplish my goal for myself as far as my life's work is concerned. Suzy Homemaker is not who I want to be when I grow up. I've realized that I simply do not have a choice about following my calling. I'm too introspective to ignore its pull.

I'm actually pretty excited and enthusiastic about life these days because I'm so painfully aware that I don't know *anything*, which means that there's a lot to learn and learning is a big thrill for me these days. Anyway, I can see progress. I'm definitely not stuck anymore. I like who I am becoming. Die, old self, die!

God is not attained by a process of addition to anything in the soul, but by a process of subtraction.[213]
Meister Eckhart

March 10, 1992

Troy and I have been in therapy and it's very interesting. The bottom line of so much of our stuff is that I react to certain behaviors of his which cause me to feel that my feelings are not important; in other words, like I'm insignificant. That feeling of being insignificant is like the sickest, darkest hole of pain for me. I've finally made contact with that inner wounded child and I feel so sad for her. Reliving the pain has been unbearable. Every time I feel abandoned, I relive that scary, lonely feeling that I used to associate with Sundays—when Mom would take us back to Dad's after our weekend visit with her.

Tonight, the meeting was on "anger and resentment." We kept talking about anger being our number one offender and the root of all of our ills, but it occurred to me that my anger is nothing more than my pain in a mask. I guess that's why so many neglected children become alcoholics. They're neglected—they hurt like hell—they lash out in anger—the anger scares them—they use something outside themselves to change the way they feel, etc. Only God within me can make all of the hurt go away.

What is not fully understood is not possessed.[214]
Johann Wolfgang Von Goethe

March 20, 1992

I am in a lot of turmoil right now. Troy and I have been having some problems. Troy does things that really hurt my feelings, but I'm not sure whether he needs to change the behavior or if I need to change my reactions. Sometimes I really question whether or not Troy is the person I am supposed to be with. Sometimes I think that I'm not supposed to be with anyone. I'm so upset. Lately, I have been experiencing so much anger that it scares me. All of these hurt feelings are ancient and these situations with Troy trigger them. Sometimes I feel so insignificant. It's like everything with Troy comes before me, but is he supposed to put me first? Do I put him first? Do I even love him? Do I even know what love is?

My anxiety is the tension between my desire to control the world and the recognition that I can't.[215]
Hugh Prather

April 6, 1992

I finally came to some conclusions about what has been happening with Troy. First, his personal growth is none of my business. Second, it's not his job to adjust himself to my liking. My job is to accept him or leave him and I don't want to leave him. Basically, I've been mad because he won't do what I want him to do when I want him to do it.

The other day it occurred to me that other people's inability to own up to their wrong-doing is not about me. It took me twenty years of therapy, five and a half years of A.A., and every mistake imaginable to get me to even begin to own my imperfections so where do I get off expecting others to understand this? Remember, "*Anyone who thinks that all of the fruits ripen at the same time as the strawberries doesn't know anything about grapes.*"[216]

Troy is a grape, Paige. Leave him alone. Live and let live.

I've been realizing a lot of things, which help me understand how I ended up so twisted. Basically, I just didn't get enough attention as a child; which caused emotional neglect. That's all fine and well, but I'm really ready to let go of all of that, pray for Mom and Dad, and begin anew. Regardless of how painful and sad my life has been, God has helped me through it and who I am becoming and where I am today is enough.

Face it, Paige, all of that is behind you. There's absolutely no reason whatsoever to be angry or to feel sorry for yourself anymore. You don't ever have to go back if you don't want to.

The farther I go, the more miraculous my life becomes. God has carried me a long way and I believe that this is just the beginning.

It is pointless to become angry, or to get hurt by people who, like us, are suffering from the pains of growing up.[217]
Twelve Steps and Twelve Traditions

April 14, 1992

I just don't know how many times I have to remind myself that I am responsible for my own reactions. I find myself believing that just because certain behaviors of Troy's triggers old feelings, he should change the behavior. That would be nice, but I'm totally powerless over him. My only range of domain is within myself.

I've really been rocking the boat lately. My self-centeredness is showing. Any time Troy does anything that doesn't pertain to showering me with attention, I throw a fit and take it personally. I've gotten so wrapped up in my wants and demands that I've totally gotten away from the things that I love about him. I've even complained about them.

A judgment of another person is an abstraction that adds qualities which are not there and leaves out what is unique.[218]
Hugh Prather

.12. progress, not perfection

April 23, 1992 – September 21, 1994

Freedom is not worth having if it does not include the freedom to make mistakes.[219]
Mahatma Gandhi

April 23, 1992

I moved back to Ruthie's last weekend because I was frustrated at Troy's. I was blaming it all on his lack of consideration and attention, but I know that the bottom line is I skipped over the taking care of myself part of life and went straight to the relationship. I've got to learn to take care of myself. I keep complaining because I get no respect, but that's because I haven't earned it for myself. I'm beginning to see that.

Though we travel the world over to find the beautiful,
we must carry it with us or we will find it not.[220]
Ralph Waldo Emerson

June 20, 1992

I have hit my core issues lately and frankly, I feel crazier than ever. I can see why I've always run like hell from these feelings. I am in pain—original pain—and it hurts. It all started coming out since I started doing inner child access meditations. I found myself at three. She told me that her mommy didn't love her. I found myself at nine and she was sullen and gloomy. I loved her a lot. Last night, I cried about being separated from Troy and ended up crying about being separated from my parents. I'm finally starting to grieve their divorce. The pain is unbearable, but I've got God (and I've got myself). I'm ready to walk through this. I don't have to lose my mind or myself over this anymore. I feel a lot of fear, though.

July 14, 1992

I'm finally trying to just let go of Troy and let God do whatever needs to be done. Sometimes I feel so hopeless that we'll ever really be able to make it work; especially since we've regressed all the way back to only occasional visits and dating other people. The idea of him being with another woman really kills me, but not enough that I'm willing to recommit. I can't commit to him at this time. I just don't know what I want enough to do that. All I know is that I love Troy very much and that accounts for something. May God's will be done.

Kelly and I have become very close. It's really wonderful. She's my closet friend, but the bond goes way beyond that which I've ever experienced with a "friend." My therapist says that I'm learning what it's like to have a real sister.

Life is pretty good these days. I'm not perfect, but right now this very minute, I can think of a lot of things to be grateful for and that's what really matters—trying to find reasons for being happy rather than excuses for not being happy. I'm so glad that I found A.A. and that God found me. I just keep on changing and changing.

Contentment is not the fulfillment of what you want,
but the realization of how much you already have.[221]
Ralph Waldo Emerson

July 29, 1992

I am in California with Kelly. This trip has really made me appreciate home. Something has happened to me. I don't need turmoil and excitement anymore. I don't need anything that I don't already have. All I need this minute is to *be still.*

I'm beginning to realize what a radical feminist I have become. I never thought I would see the day when I would be so opinionated about women's roles and other social issues, but that's who I am becoming. I'm not a minister; I'm a revolutionary. I yearn to be part of the movement that really starts changing the world.

Paige, you are a part of the movement that is changing the world … it is called "recovery."

We were driving through San Francisco the other day and I saw a homeless man wearing tattered, dirty rags. He was clutching a small animal to his breast. That brought a tear to my eye. That is humanity—to still reach out, to give, and to love even when you're at an all-time low. That image just won't leave my mind. It tore me apart.

Dear God, how far down the scale do we have to go before we open our eyes? I pray for this country. I pray that we all realize that homelessness is everyone's problem. Dear Lord, make me an instrument of Thy peace. My true place is calling. I am going to find my destiny.

Reality eventually forces you to take a second look, and what you see begins to dissolve your selfishness. You see that you are not alone, that your time will not be spent alone, that your life is in fact many lives, and that no matter how determined you are to make it so, your happiness cannot be solitary. What you see is that there is something else as important to you as your own life.[222]

Hugh Prather

August 15, 1992

Things have been terrible with Troy lately. We're back to battling over the same stupid issues even when we barely see each other. This whole ordeal has been so unpleasant and draining that I almost feel relieved that it's probably over. I pray to God that it's over. Of course, letting go of the beautiful dream that our relationship would consummate in marriage makes me sad, but brother, if I can just walk through the pain one last time, I won't have to hurt over Troy ever again.

I've been having some wonderful experiences with God lately. He's been using me to talk to a lot of people. I like that. That's what I'm here for anyway, to work for God; not to play mind games with silly men.

I trust God and I trust the process. Thy will be done.

September 1, 1992

Ever since I started sponsoring people, I haven't needed distractions like other men in my life. I've been growing up a lot lately. It's really dawning on me that everything and anything I desire in this world requires my cooperation and participation. If I want to be thin, I have to eat right and exercise. If I want to be financially independent, I have to work hard. If I want a good relationship with Troy, I have to stay on the beam and not react to him. I play a part, but thank God I don't have to depend on myself. It's so simple just to ask for God's power to do the right thing. It's funny that I never gave much thought to right action before.

That slogan *"happy, joyous, and free"* is taking on a whole new meaning:

Happiness = the product of right living
Joy = unmasked sorrow
Freedom = doing what you are supposed to do because you *want* to

You must be the change you want to see in the world.[223]
Mahatma Gandhi

September 15, 1992

I've really been struggling within myself about getting into action to do the things necessary to take care of myself. I need to act my way into right thinking, but I keep holding back and procrastinating. What am I afraid of? Is it change? Is it independence? I fool myself about being the type of person who embraces change and then I balk at new actions. Hopefully, I'm just fueling up. I believe that there are no mistakes and that everything happens for a reason. I guess I just need to accept my reluctance and allow myself to stand still if that's what I need to do. I guess the problem is that somewhere deep inside I believe that I am a bum and that I'll never amount to anything. Please help me to change my beliefs, Father. It can't be true. No one is inherently a no-good bum. Help me to be willing to take right action. Please remove these barriers which block me from my highest good.

I've noticed that when I am in this sort of place, I try to blame my unhappiness on other people. Other people have nothing to do with my unhappiness. I can see that today. I want to love more than I want to be loved. I believe that it is truly better to give than to receive. There's just so much work that needs to be done in order for me to become the loving person that I long to be.

You cannot cross the sea merely by standing and staring at the water.[224]
Rabindranath Tagore

September 23, 1992

I've started doing a Tenth Step and I feel good about it. Everything boils down to the fact that I need to concentrate on right action, acceptance, trusting God, and being loving. I guess gratitude wouldn't hurt either. I can see why we are supposed to live one day at a time; I can only remember important things I know for about one day. I need a lot of reminding.

God will constantly disclose more to you and to us.[225]
Alcoholics Anonymous

January 14, 1993

I've been becoming quite the recluse lately. My favorite place to be is alone and my favorite person to be with is myself. That's a real change, huh?

I've noticed that the commitments I have the hardest time keeping are the ones I make to myself. I guess that shows me what a people pleaser I am. I try not to let other people down because I want them to like me, but I don't think twice about letting myself down when getting mad at myself is the worst person in the world to have mad at me because I can feel it.

I expect too much from myself and I don't know how to stop. I need to be patient with myself, but there's just so much I want as far as the person I am becoming goes. I am literally driven to become more and more aware. I don't know if that's good or bad. I guess it's neither. I guess I just need to sit back and realize that I'm right where I'm supposed to be. In my meditation today, I heard that I need to stop worrying about where I'm going and to just be where I am. There's nowhere to go—but here.

The rainbow is more beautiful than the pot at the end of it,
because the rainbow is now.
And the pot never turns out to be quite what I expected.[226]
Hugh Prather

January 19, 1993

The last two days have been an emotional tailspin. Yesterday, my stepfather, Jack, died from a massive heart attack. I can't begin to describe the feelings that have been associated with this situation. I've been so upset. I feel terrible because I've always had such a bad attitude towards him. Just writing about him sends gut wrenching pain through me. I am so regretful.

God, how can I possibly think that I am Christ-bound when I still get so tangled up in petty judgments and attitudes? I pray with all my heart that Jack has gotten the message about how dreadfully sorry I am. I guess I've realized that I loved him. I never realized this before he got targeted as being different from me. The bottom line is that *I thought* that *he thought* that I wasn't "good enough." I wanted him to approve of me and I resented him because he didn't seem to. I have no idea how he really felt because I never talked to him. I have been such a selfish brat and it's killing me inside right now.

This has really taught me something about the fragility of life. It's especially opened my eyes about Mom. It's given me the willingness to let go of the past and start treating her like someone I love because I *do* love her.

It's the same theme over and over again. If I am or feel something, I have to *demonstrate it.* All of my ideas have still been seedlings—ideas that have not made their way into manifestation. I pray to change; to start over with Mom.

Most of what we feel and think we conjure up for ourselves in our heads.[227]
Anthony DeMello

January 30, 1993

Jack's death was a real growing experience for me. I think it was the first thing to truly slap me in the face and show me that this human life of ours is fragile. I really have just acted out the dramatic child roles with my parents; trying to win their approval and to prove that I don't need them; that I'm okay without them. Maybe all that is true, but whether or not I need them, I see now that I really love them and want them to be a part of my life. They're fragile and mortal too, and that really scares me.

I'm very grateful for these realizations; especially where Mom is concerned. Jack's death shone a bright light on everything; which illuminated the truth. I'm not mad at Mom anymore. I love my mother and I'm very proud of her. No matter what she knew or didn't know before, she now knows loss. Life's given her one of the hardest chunks to swallow that it has to give—the death of a spouse. She's been very brave and constructive. She's quite a lady. I just see things in her that I never saw before. Right now this minute, I feel proud that she is my mother, and that Dad is my father.

I'm so in love with life right now. Every time I turn around it just keeps getting better. I feel such a deep, peaceful sense of belonging within this earthly family of mine. It seems so ironic that the most blatantly damaging characteristic of my childhood was a lack of family and family values. My, haven't things changed? I know absolutely that all of the changes are the direct action of a more wonderful God than can be humanly imagined. I am so grateful.

Through the Lord's mercies we are not consumed,
because His compassions fail not.
They are new every morning.
Lamentations 3:22 – 23

February 1, 1993

Troy and I agreed last fall that we would make some decisions about our future on February 1. Anyway, that day is here and Troy said that he's not ready so I broke up with him. I'm happier. I promised myself that I'd go on alone today if he wasn't ready to go with me. This is the last thing I wanted, but I promised myself. I'm not hanging around for one more day of this unacceptable relationship.

I'm willing to accept God's will in this situation. I'm willing to be alone. I'm willing to walk through the pain one more time; hopefully the last time. I trust my God and I love myself enough to do what I need to do.

During this period, I returned to the restaurant business as a manager.

February 16, 1993

I've been in too much of a hurry lately and I'm suffering for it spiritually. I need to take the time to connect with God or I just don't really enjoy living. Some of the most positive things are happening in my life right now and I can't even enjoy them because I'm so busy and wrapped up in what I'm doing. I just don't want to be so consumed with work and the discipline of life that I don't have time to stop and smell the roses. I don't want to be oblivious to everyone around me.

Ultimately my character is defined by the quality
of my sensitivity to other people.[228]
Hugh Prather

April 5, 1993

Lately I have been doing some reflecting and came to some startling conclusions. It finally dawned on me that the intense desire to be famous and superior is not an ambition, but rather a character defect which blocks me from God. I went through a period there where I was taking work, position, and material possessions too seriously. I was rationalizing that my year to be a part of "the world out there" had come.

That is true to some extent because I no longer have fear of being with people who aren't in the program, but on the other hand, I have realized that being "great and successful" makes me pretty miserable. There's a part of me that yearns for success and recognition, but I'm finally at a place where I'm willing to be willing to let go of that fantasy. I also realized that if I want to dream of being a celebrity, I must be willing to risk failing and to do a lot of fancy footwork. The most direct way to get from point A to point Z is a straight line directly through the middle points. I realize that I've been sitting at point A and dreaming about Point Z without really considering the action that needs to be taken to get there.

I'm at another one of those stages of my recovery where everything changes. It seems amusing to me that every time I get any sort of humility it is because I finally see how blind and arrogant I have been.

I really am at a stage where I just want to have a humble heart and a willingness to be helpful. I've been pushing myself on a quest to win attention from other people. It's finally dawned on me that all that really gives me fulfillment is the knowledge that at the end of each day I have done the most careful things with myself and others.

Life is fragile and I tend to sometimes treat it like it's indestructible. I pray for a heart that truly loves. I've been trying to believe that I'm a nicer person than I really am. I am willing to be nicer, but I need help with it. I need my God and Lord to help me.

Most people believe that their greatest weakness is their greatest strength.[229]
Hugh Prather

May 22, 1993

I've been going about ninety miles an hour this past week between getting ready to move and then actually moving **(I finally got an apartment of our own for Laurel and me).** Today's what seems like the first time in ages that I've actually sat still and figured out what's going on inside of me. I feel a little sad because Ruthie and I have been together for a long time. It feels scary leaving home for the last time; leaving the only *real* home I've ever known.

I guess I'm just reflective and a little low from the anti-climax of finally achieving something that I've wanted for a long time. Life's funny that way. It really shows me just how much life is *not* about being "successful" in the material sense.

I know that the true meaning of life is love and service: two things that I have a long way to go on. I guess that I've just needed to get the basics like food, clothing, shelter, transportation, and human contact squared away before I could truly begin. Everything up until now has been a preparation to get to the *beginning!* How many times have I thought I was finished only to realize that I was just approaching the starting gate?

It's been a long road of recovering the ground that was lost through drugs and alcohol. Today, I am where I was in '85 and '86—my own place to live, my own car, a good job, and a minimally consistent exercise program. I've achieved sober what I did drunk. The only difference is that today I'm *here* to appreciate it—or take it for granted.

Character-building and spiritual values had to come first.[230]
Twelve Steps and Twelve Traditions

I found out shortly thereafter that I was pregnant and Troy agreed to marry me. After we moved in together, I had a miscarriage, but we decided to go through with the marriage.

August 20, 1993

Troy and I have been getting along better these days than we have in years. God, is that a blessing. I was really afraid that he'd cancel the wedding after the miscarriage. I felt good when he didn't. I have to admit that he would never have married me at this time if I hadn't gotten pregnant, but I have to believe that his reluctance was about fear and financial insecurity—not about not loving me. He needed a shove over the threshold—and he got it.

The most difficult issue for us right now is resolving our conflicts. It can be very frustrating. Our pattern has always been to storm away and break up. This just isn't an option anymore. We live together and our wedding is in four weeks. We can talk big, but talk's cheap. It's hard though because neither one of us are very good at admitting when we're wrong or at saying that we're sorry. We're making progress, though.

October 3, 1993

Well, the wedding is over and I'm glad. Don't get me wrong, it was beautiful, but the stress was killing me. I had really underestimated the power of my alcoholism and the meaning of the slogan "*Easy Does It.*" The whole thing was hard on me. I can *really* understand better about life being a journey and not an event. Events are never what they're cracked up to be. Those expectations will kill you every time.

I kept my awareness of the fact that the wedding wouldn't be like I expected, but I let the fact that other people wouldn't "act" like I expected just slip into my unconscious. It took a week for me to realize that all of my turmoil came from other people "not doing what they were supposed to do." Sometimes I forget that life on life's terms means letting other people be who they are. That issue is very prevalent with Troy, but I need to take a big look at how it applies to *everyone*. Life's so tricky. That's what makes it fun.

I've been really angry at Jake and his girlfriend because they didn't get excited over the wedding, but justifiable anger stinks. I can be so judgmental and snotty sometimes, but I'm willing to change. It all boils down to the fact that I have been being selfish and self-centered about my marriage to Troy.

The most amazing thing on my mind right now is that the biggest deal about the wedding is the lessons I learned from it. I guess I thought it was going to be some sort of spiritual experience. I forgot that you don't get those by wearing fancy clothes or going to Mexico. Spiritual experiences come from quiet prayer and meditation and kindness and love towards others. It's just amazing to me that being nice to people and getting along with them is a "bigger deal" than getting married to the man I love with all my heart. Life's a trip.

I guess I can consider myself lucky because I truly have had the experience of getting just about everything I've ever wanted—and realizing that it doesn't matter. Don't get me wrong, being with my husband matters, but making a big production out of marrying him doesn't.

The whole bottom line is that peace of mind and serenity is what it's all about. You don't get that in the blowing of a trumpet or the beating of a drum, but in the blowing of the wind in the trees and the beating of a tiny heart in a sleeping child.

To those of us who have hitherto known only excitement, depression, or anxiety, this newfound peace is a priceless gift.[231]

Twelve Steps and Twelve Traditions

November 24, 1993

Until recently, I've been all wrapped up with being married and with making money. Seek ye first the Kingdom of God and all else will be added unto it. Why can't I remember that? I think I understand it and then roll right through life until I hit a brick wall and then I remember it all over again. I've almost run out of things to roll through life with. I've just about got everything I've ever wanted that I was really willing to put effort into. I'm sober, I'm learning to be a good mother, I got to marry the man I wanted, and I've got the job I wanted.

I've got it all, but I'm still empty inside without a *lot* of prayer, meditation, and effort toward being a decent person. I wish I could say it comes naturally, but it doesn't. I guess I ought to be grateful that my spirituality takes constant vigilance or I would quickly take it for granted and become complacent about it—just like I tend to do everything else.

My ego is far from being totally surrendered. It still takes a lot of things outside of me to make me feel worthwhile. Where did this inherent sense of worthlessness come from? God only knows. All I know is that I don't need to know. I just need to let go and let life be what it's supposed to be. The hardest thing to get through my thick head is that my life is absolutely none of my business.

In the Fall, the soul refused the rule of the spirit and became flesh,
and the spirit lost its rule and became little more than a dormant power.
It was no longer a ruling principle, but a struggling captive.[232]
Andrew Murray

September 21, 1994

Troy's time seems to truly be coming. For some reason, though, I've been acting like a total idiot ever since he started making a conscious effort to work on himself. My theory is that it is human nature to try to maintain equilibrium and since he's been rocking the boat with new behavior (similar to my usual behavior), I've been reciprocating with *his* usual behavior! Maybe that's bull. Maybe I'm just a crisis junkie who needs turmoil and since he's not causing it, I am. Either way, thank God I have a choice to do things differently. There's no telling how good it could get if we both put a conscious effort into the relationship.

If I had only . . .
forgotten future greatness
and looked at the green things and the buildings
and reached out to those around me
and smelled the air
and ignored the styles and the self-styled obligations
and heard the rain on the roof.[233]
Hugh Prather

.13. soul mate

October 24, 1994 – March 17, 1995

Unless there is someone to whom I can give my gifts, in whose hands I can entrust my dreams, who will forgive me my deformities, my aberrations, to whom I can speak the unspeakable, then I am not human.[234]
Hugh Prather

October 24, 1994

I've moved home to Mother's. No matter how much I love Troy and want it to work out with us, I can't do all the work in the relationship. My issues concerning rejection are just too painful to stay in a relationship where my feelings are discounted. I have no idea what's going to happen. That's probably great news because it leaves me no choice but to let go.

I feel good about my decision to be here. It hurt like hell for a couple of days, but then I immediately began to feel empowered. The pay-off of right action is worth any price. For today, there is *nothing* more important to me than my spirituality.

I'm just so ready to meet my true spiritual mate. The other night, the most overwhelming sense of longing came over me as I lay on the bed and cried for him, *I don't know who you are, but I am so ready to meet you.* Where are you, my love?

October 29, 1994

Right now I'm sincerely trying to close every door that has Troy on the other side. I'm just so ready to move on without him. It's over—I pray! I've been feeling close to God. I know that I'm doing the right thing. I surrender to the Christ within.

November 7, 1994

I'm hurting over Troy. I know that I have to let go and let God, but it still hurts. I haven't talked to him for four days. It's just so hard to believe that it's really over. Every time that I come home and don't have a message that he's called, it seems more real. I know that we'll both eventually find our good and be happy. This is just a devastating disappointment. I feel so sad. I had really convinced myself that we would always be together. I want to cry.

Thy will be done, Father.

When one door of happiness closes, another opens.[235]
Helen Keller

November 14, 1994

This week seems like a quantum week on the journey. I've become acquainted with a man who is very intriguing. We've had some wonderful conversations and I'm *very* attracted to him; which makes me feel too vulnerable. My first reaction to all of this is to hit the trail and disassociate myself from him, but there's something between us that I can't deny. His name is Randy DeHart. I have a feeling I'll be writing more about him in the times to come.

Getting in touch with my fear of him gave me one of those "Aha!" moments. I see that it terrifies me to feel vulnerable. I've opted for rejection over vulnerability my whole life! However, if I don't practice being vulnerable, I'll never truly be close to others.

I saw more of this fear when I shut down as Kelly tried to offer me comfort. It felt so *un*comfortable. Maybe Troy's right—I won't *let* people love me. I just want to love them—or control the love.

We really do "*teach best what we most need to learn.*"[236] I've been telling Randy not to be so hard on himself and then I apologize to my closest friend for being vulnerable. I guess I'm just afraid to let people get close to me. I'll pretend to get close to them, but it's always on my terms. I have to be "in charge"—the master. Wow. Life's a trip.

Well, okay Lord, I see all of this so please take it and do what You will. I've been begging You to teach me how to love. Now will You teach me how to *be* loved? I love You. Thy will be done.

I want to know what you ache for,
and if you dare to dream of meeting your heart's longing.[237]
Oriah Mountain Dreamer

November 21, 1994

What another wild and wonderful week! Those realizations really opened a new door for me and began to break the walls that have enclosed my vulnerability. I've vacillated the past few days between absolute joy and spine tingling fear. It seems that my request to learn to "be loved" is being honored. I love God so much. He takes the most fantastic care of me that I can imagine. My inner skeptic tells me that this joyous adventure called my life is too good to be true, but my innermost compass assures me that all is well; that to doubt the reality of absolute good is the only folly of man.

In all its syrupy sentiment, I must admit that seemingly I have met the man with whom I can finally relate. Randy has connected with me in a way beyond any I've ever experienced with another human being. I've been beside myself in a mix of wonder and almost disbelief. There are no words to describe this experience. To call it "contact" is an understatement. It's as if the most beautiful painting were livened to form multiple dimensions. It's as if my soul has quickened and arisen to a more vibrant radiation. I think I'm in love!

I've got it so bad that I feel like writing poetry. I understand how those fools can write ridiculous love songs. I understand what it's like to not be able to wipe a grin off my face. I'm experiencing the reality of ideals like "true love" and "soul mates" and "destiny." I feel absolutely overjoyed. I'm a fool in love and it's okay.

On the other hand, I see how much I have tried to control my relationships. No wonder I've never gotten the love I want. I've always been in relationships where I dictated the course. I manipulated the first "I love you." I scheduled the first kiss; the first sexual contact. No wonder!

Randy has been blowing my mind because he expresses sentiments that still terrify me to admit. I'm not in control of this and it is sweeping me away, but it's wonderful to feel small and powerless; to melt in the thought of his passionate embrace. God is blessing me now with riches beyond my wildest dreams. To be released from the bondage of my cynicism and experience an overwhelming burst of hope and enthusiasm about love is true cause for Thanksgiving.

No matter what the outcome, joyous or absolutely sorrowful, I savor this moment where hope springs eternal. Nothing is impossible in God's world! My dream of love *is* possible because, for today, I am living it.

Thank You, God. I love You.

I want to know if you can be with joy, mine or your own,
if you can dance with wildness and let the ecstasy fill you
to the tips of your fingers and toes without cautioning us to be careful,
to be realistic, to remember the limitations of being human.[238]
Oriah Mountain Dreamer

December 19, 1994

I have been experiencing the quintessential definition of love in this relationship with Randy. Our love seems to grow broader, deeper, and stronger with each passing day. I don't even really know how to describe it. For me, the circle is finally complete. Love has flowed into reception of itself.

I have spread my dreams under your feet;
tread softly because you tread on my dreams.[239]
William Butler Yeats

January 2, 1995

I feel like someone informed me that Santa Clause is real after all. I have been waiting (no *searching* until recently) for my true love; the one who would share my body, mind, and soul. I prayed for him. I dreamed of him. I yearned for his touch for as long as I can remember. As miraculous, and even corny, as it may sound, I honestly believe that Randy DeHart is this person. Each day, I become more convinced.

Randy is the most multi-dimensional person that I have ever known. We're exactly alike! I'm so grateful to have him; especially at a time when I had given up and began to believe that I had evolved to a level where I was alone. I am not alone! To be able to share my heart, mind, and soul with a person who actually relates to me and understands where I am coming from is a spiritual experience beyond description.

Jesus said, "*You shall love the Lord your God with all your heart, with all your soul, and with all your mind and you shall love your neighbor as yourself.*" (*Matthew 22:37–38*) True love is the realization that God, yourself, and your neighbor are one. This is what I have learned with Randy. In each other, we see ourselves and God. Through each other, we heal and find the truth. With each other, we will do all of the things that God has planned for us. Together, we will assume our designated roles for the ushering in of the new order where Christ reigns and God establishes His Kingdom on earth.

Dear sweet Father in Heaven, I love You and I thank You for giving me a partner and a friend—for giving me one true love.

Two lives made whole and complete,
as yearning souls meet
to form a circle of love.
Together at last, my darling.
Joined at the heart
in timelessness.
As Prince Charming's gentle kiss to Sleeping Beauty,
so does your sweet embrace
awaken me from long, yet restless slumber.
The healing balm of your selfless love
mends my broken heart...
and dreams.
The warming glow of your joyous zeal
melts protective armor
that shields my tenderness.
Free at last from self-imposed incarceration!
Free at last to love... and to be loved.
I thank our gracious Father
for all that He has given:
for Life
for Love
for Hope!
For a glimpse of Heaven
in the arms of an angel.
And gentle as a morning breeze
yet mighty as a beating drum,
my love soars to you
on eagle's wings,
to whisper softly,
"You are beautiful, my beloved, you are beautiful."

January 12, 1995

I've been in the final stages of letting go of Troy. We had an encounter the other day where he finally made that run for me; trying to get me back. I said "no!" My allegiance to Randy is greater than ever. I told Troy that I'm not walking away from something real to chase after a dream.

My relationship with Randy is a beautiful reality. The amount of growth that we share, with consequential increase in closeness, is overwhelming. I literally feel as though we have been and will be together forever. I just can't do it justice with words.

The most fantastic aspect of this relationship is that we both share the same hunger and thirst for God. To awaken and share my morning ritual with another person is beyond my wildest dreams. The joy of my relationship with God was always wonderful, but to have another at my side is Heaven! I'm just at the most peaceful and harmonious place ever and, as always, I truly believe that the best is yet to come.

Dear Holy Father,

I love You so much and I thank You for this peace and joy that You have given. I give myself humbly to Your service in any way I can. You're a wonderful God.

I in them, and You in Me; that they may be made perfect in one.
John 17:23

January 19, 1995

Randy and I went to the jail last night to take an A.A. meeting. It made the ministry vision come to life. I know he is my partner in life and ministry. He reminds me so much of Jesus.

Randy keeps mentioning the idea of us being married. It blows my mind. I like that idea so much, but because of my steadfast confidence in the process, I don't have to obsess on it. I trust that if indeed I am to be his wife, I will be. I feel more married to him than I ever did to Troy anyway.

Dear Holy Father,

I thank You for this beautiful dawn, which represents the new hope rising in my soul. I give myself to You as your obedient servant. It is my honor to serve You. I thank You for the magnificent transformative process that is my sobriety. What a gift to awaken from hell to find Heaven. I also thank You for abundant good, which is my inheritance, and for the gift of love that motivates me to keep putting one foot in front of the other. I love You with all of my heart, mind, and soul.

Whoever willingly thanks God becomes rich himself.[240]
Albert Schweitzer

January 20, 1995

Today I got upset over an argument I had with Troy. I had plans to see Randy afterwards and felt scared for him to see me upset. I hate feeling vulnerable and "showing my cards" as Randy puts it. To my surprise, rather than rejecting or trying to fix me, he prayed with/for me and it improved my condition dramatically. The experience was literally awesome.

I've experienced so much healing from this relationship. To have this absolutely radiant person, flowing with love, sit in front of me and tell me that he loves me more than anything is a fairy tale come true. He keeps telling me that I don't understand how much he loves me. Of course I understand because I feel the same way about him! What neither of us seem to understand is that we are *lovable.* Neither of us can seem to fathom that the other loves us. I guess that's sort of sad, but on the other hand, love heals all wounds. This is love.

He's in Tyler tonight playing the drums with his band. As much as I cherish my time with him, I like these times alone so I can reflect and soak-in my experience with him. He has touched my heart, my mind, and my soul. To find companionship after becoming accustomed to solitude is a real gift; a blessing. What a richly blessed woman I am.

Let there be spaces in your togetherness.[241]
Kahlil Gibran

Randy was a heroin addict in his early twenties, but he quit on his own power. He later became addicted to cocaine, but was freed from it by being born-again in 1986. He then spent numerous years in ministry training with the Episcopal Church, but became disillusioned when the Bishop decided not to ordain him. Simultaneously, he began to drink more and more until he sought help in Alcoholics Anonymous; where we met when he had almost three years of sobriety.

January 27, 1995

I really love Randy. I'm getting comfortable with him. We had a few altercations this week, though. He's under so much pressure because his sister, her husband, and his band mates have been giving him a hard time about the fact that I go to Unity Church—and that he's been going with me. He caved for a brief time and decided that not only was he not going back to Unity, but that I would have to give it up, too. It was a terrifying experience because I was afraid that we had come to a "parting of the ways." I'm not giving up Unity.

There are some other kinks to work out, but I trust the process. Randy's a bit moody and temperamental at times (like I'm not!), but he's growing so much that I know that he'll evolve out of it. He's so precious; even when he's throwing a fit.

I was just sitting here reflecting on the realization that just three and a half months ago I was still at Troy's. Right now, I'm alone at Randy's. How did I get from there to here so fast? To say *I'm at Randy's* means so much. His arms feel like the rest I have so longed for. When I'm with Randy I feel like I've come home. I'm so grateful to have finally found him. All I want is to keep being willing to accept the good that God has offered in my life and then sit back and watch our love bloom to the heavens. I have such a beautiful life; on the inside and out! I am truly blessed and for this, sweet Heavenly Father, I thank You!

Life is the flower for which love is the honey.[242]
Victor Hugo

February 3, 1995

What a week! Randy got in a tizz and went ballistic over all of the pressures. I kept trying to fix him and he ended up lashing out at me; admitting that he wanted me to lose my weight. It really hurt my feelings because I let it. I'd like to say that's the way I saw it from the very beginning, but it's not. I became mortally wounded and got a life-size picture of exactly how fast I'll bolt and run when I get hurt. I also got to see how I basically believe that once I'm hurt—forget it, it's ruined. No wonder my relationships have never been successful!

On top of that, I also got to see that I will sabotage good things in my life just because I don't want anyone telling me what to do; even if it's something that I *want* to do. My mind is just blown; especially since all of this stemmed from a situation which I once would have simply considered being an example of my being an "innocent victim." When something is going on around me, it really is an indicator that something is going on inside of me.

Things are progressing with Randy. The honeymoon phase is ending and we are moving into the real meat of true love; the work. It's like we were blessed with two and a half months of pure Heaven and now God says, *There's a taste, get to work, and come home.*

Randy is a very challenging person. We see right through each other; which is great, but also sometimes a real bummer because we call each other on our stuff. We have the nerve to question the other's ideas, actions, and beliefs. We help each other to change and grow.

Oh, that's another thing I'm seeing. I've always bragged about how easily I accept change. I now see that I accept it just fine as long as I'm the one who instigates it and as long as I control it. There's that stupid word again—"control." This relationship is causing some changes that I'm not instigating. The biggest change is to all-of-a-sudden see all of this junk that I could never see before! Life's a trip.

Dealing with a multi-dimensional alcoholic like Randy has given me a lot of empathy for what Troy must have gone through with me. I'm about a million times more qualified to deal with Randy than Troy was to deal with me. Randy and I need to be with someone like ourselves because we are both intense and difficult people. Anyway, all is well and the journey definitely continues. Thank You, God.

Patience with others is Love,
Patience with self is Hope,
Patience with God is Faith.[243]
Adel Bestavros

February 9, 1995

Last night, Randy quoted something he heard in a meeting a few years ago that really touched him. He quoted *me*. It has finally dawned on me that my ministry is not waiting to begin. It's been going all along. The bottom line is that it's not about recognition or thanks. I may never get to know if or what kind of effect I make in this world while I'm still in it. It's just none of my business.

All I know is that every choice and experience in my life has led to this now moment where I am at in my so-far peak in life with this crazy, beautiful, loving, spiritual, angel-man named Randy. God, I love him so much. The honeymoon's not over. We're just experiencing life with its continuous ebb and flow. We share so much and each day brings us closer to each other and to God.

Thank You, dear Father, for my custom-made mate who shares my heart and my soul. You've already taken me far beyond my wildest dreams and I know without a shadow of a doubt that the best is yet to come. You are my true Beloved. Without You, there is nothing else.

The essence of trust is to be convinced of the reliability of God.[244]
Brennan Manning

February 18, 1995

Randy's moods definitely keep me on my recovery toes. One day he draws me close to him, the next he pushes me away. I've really had to take a hard look at my reactions to all of this. I basically realize that I have been hanging on too tight to the idea of him being "the one." Maybe he is, but maybe he isn't. When I focus too much on that idea, I find myself, once again, trying to control outcomes. When am I finally going to get it through my thick head that I don't know what the future holds? One more time, I am faced with the vital necessity of taking life one day at a time. Otherwise, I'm playing God—*again!*

Anyway, I have realized that it is not my job to hold Randy's hand and coax him as he moves from religion to spirituality. He's got to make that transition for himself and if his time away from me results with the voices in his head making the decision that he's better off without me, then that's the way the cookie crumbles. I'm powerless over Randy's process.

The whole thing scares me because I realize that it's not good for either of us to depend on each other for the things which we must provide for ourselves (with God's help). Of course, my deep-seeded old tapes tell me that if I'm not needed, then I am worthless. Thank God that today I can see that I'm just here to be Paige—period. My only real concern is to allow God to mold me into the best Paige possible.

When Randy veers off center, I find myself wanting to run away from him. I see my intense fear of rejection in action. Thank God that I can *finally* see that. God only knows how many beautiful experiences I have deprived myself of because I couldn't face the fear of rejection and allow myself to be willing to accept the good that God has to offer in my life.

Randy is a good thing. We have both admitted that the newness has passed, but there is truly something between us worth working for. I guess we had both hoped for a freebie—something for nothing—a lasting, beautiful relationship with no work. We thought we had found an easier, softer way. Thank God again that we had the pink cloud as incentive to keep putting one foot in front of the other. We are both extremely emotionally immature so consequently, we know nothing about true commitment or even the nature of true love. We're learning together, though, and it is a beautiful thing.

Life with Randy is definitely not boring. I think I've met my match. In some ways it makes me totally grateful for who I am because he's got so many of the same beautiful qualities that I possess. On the other hand, in some ways it makes me want to surrender and work Steps Six and Seven even more because we share the same character defects.

I pray for both of us. With God's help, we'll learn how to trust and to be trustworthy. Help us, Father, to put away childish things. Help us to mature into adults who are capable of lasting and abiding love. Help us to be the people that You would have us to be. We love You. I love You, forever.

The meeting of two personalities is like the contact of two chemical substances: if there is any reaction, both are transformed.[245]

Carl Jung

February 21, 1995

I'm in turmoil this morning because Randy and I had another disagreement last night. Randy jamming up in a funk is nothing new. However, he's just about exhausted my patience for inappropriate and unacceptable behavior so I ended up being pretty shut down with him and hanging up on him.

I just realized that I'm in fear because of the fact that I expressed anger towards Randy.

Guess what, Paige? If you can't honestly express your feelings to him then you don't need to be with him.

I've been walking on eggshells because Randy tries to control people with his anger (just like I used to). However, if anyone dares to express anger towards him, he gets even angrier. I've been feeling like I should apologize for getting angry, but on the other hand, I am responsible for setting the boundary for how I will and will not be treated. The bottom line is that I am tired of this man lashing out at me at the drop of a hat.

I don't know if we're nearing the end of our relationship or if God's just teaching me a lesson in setting boundaries and Randy a lesson in discipline. I would be willing to bet that, as a child, Randy was allowed to run wild because he was too difficult to discipline (like me) and that he was never told "no" (like me). That's sad because it creates extremely self-willed adults.

I feel pretty bummed because the euphoric stage of our relationship has passed. God was that ever a wonderful experience! I really do love Randy and I am willing to walk with him, but he is difficult. He makes Troy seem like a lamb. I know that it's unrealistic to wish for continuous euphoria, but I still hate to see it go. The reality of life is that relationships are work. I ran away from Troy because he didn't seem willing to work. Now, I'm with someone who's willing to work, but the work is even more difficult. Calgon, take me away!

Not to worry, Paige. Everything is as it should be.

Thanks, Father. I love You. Please help Randy and me. Thy will, not ours, be done!

That is what unity really means:
helping one another to reach the full status of being persons,
responsible and autonomous beings who do not run away from life.[246]
Paul Tournier

February 25, 1995

Things smoothed out with Randy. He finally admitted that he was upset because a person he knew died from Hepatitis C (Randy has Hepatitis C also). I can understand his fear. There's a little fear in me about his illness also. However, I firmly believe that putting God first is the panacea for all things; including Hepatitis C. I am willing to allow myself to love Randy no matter what happens. I trust God.

I've been a little depressed lately. I have a gnawing feeling that I am supposed to do "greater" things than work in restaurants. I know that I need to work on that book. I believe that it is my destiny. I just can't let go of the idea that doing something big and meaningful for the world is still ahead of me. I certainly hope so. The idea drives me from the inside out.

Also, Laurel has been getting on my nerves and that causes me to feel guilty. I wish I weren't so selfish with her. Sometimes, spending time with her is a chore. God, please help me be the mother you would have me be.

I wish that Randy and I could live together. I love being with him, but I feel lousy about it because it's sometimes more important to me than my time with Laurel. I wish we could all be together. That's the one thing I really miss about my life with Troy—the sense of family. I want a family with Randy.

We've really had a great time. I'm so grateful for this relationship. It has stretched me and helped me to grow. We have a wonderful, conscious relationship. It hits the skids sometimes, but so far, we work through it and come together. He's a very loving man.

Well, Father, please fill my heart with the love and gratitude that brings me such joy. I love You.

To love deeply in one direction makes us more loving in all others.[247]

Anne-Sophie Swetchine

March 9, 1995

I guess I need to look at my ego in relation to my physical appearance. Lately, I've finally started losing my weight again—for which I am grateful because it is one of my biggest obstacles. However, I'm less than halfway toward my goal and I already see myself becoming more self-centered because of the attention from others.

Dear God, I earnestly pray that You give me the humility I need in order to be successful in the accomplishment of my goals without losing myself and my commitment to You and to love.

Let's talk about these goals because, frankly, I'm ready to begin. First, I want to continue to lose weight. I want to be beautiful on the inside and on the outside.

Paige, you are beautiful on the inside and on the outside. Just don't forget that the objective of life is to love Me with all of your heart, mind, and soul ... and to love your neighbor as yourself.

I also want to write that book. This is the one that's driving me crazy. I have procrastinated and procrastinated. It has been in the making since 1978 and it is definitely emerging its way into manifestation.

What are you afraid of, Paige?

I guess I really am afraid of success, but I am willing to change. There's just no denying that life calls out to me in a big way. I know that this book is important and is a part of my destiny, but I feel paralyzed about really beginning.

I'm tired of being afraid to succeed. I must do what I am here to do or I will be miserable and frustrated.

Help me, Father. Help me to begin. Take me to my true place.

With God's help I am certain that I can blossom without becoming a monster. I guess I'm really afraid of myself. It just occurred to me that I am always talking about my vulnerability (basically my inner child) being incarcerated by the protective armor I have constructed with certain behaviors and characteristics. Now, I see that a part of me has believed that I've been keeping the "boogey man" chained under the stairs so it can't destroy me.

Paige, the only thing that's trapped inside of you is Me. There's nothing to be afraid of. All that is real is Me, baby. I love you. You don't have to be afraid of Me.

Sometimes this journal blows my mind to pieces.

Thy will be done, Father.

Start by doing what's necessary; then do what's possible;
and suddenly you are doing the impossible. [248]
Saint Francis of Assisi

March 17, 1995

This week I finally came to terms with the fact that I have been neglecting Laurel. My time with Randy has been like inner child play time and I have been neglecting some of my adult responsibilities. I realized that he is not my other half who I can wrap myself up in and depend on. He's just another imperfect human being. I need to depend on God and myself. I feel kind of sad because, one more time, I get to see why they call it the "solitary journey."

Randy's band is becoming more successful. I'm happy for him, but it puts such a strain on us because his ego gains strength and because he's so much busier with the gigs. I just have to take it all one day at a time. This whole ordeal has definitely changed my perspective about show business. I understand "keep it simple" better.

I see Randy as chasing after worldly success (which is another way of running from God's will). It's hard to watch him do this because I believe that if he doesn't slow down willingly, God will slow him down. I'm probably in his life to walk with him when he stops running and starts walking. It's so appropriate that he's a "runner" **(during this period, Randy was a marathon runner)**. Maybe I'm wrong, though.

All I know is that I love Randy unconditionally and am willing to stick with him for as long as he wants me to. We're good for each other, but it's not easy. Who said life was supposed to be easy, anyway? Thank You, God.

If a relationship is to evolve, it must go through a series of endings.[249]
Lisa Moriyama

.14.

the work of love

March 19, 1995 – December 23, 1995

Love suffers long and is kind; love does not envy; love does not parade itself,
is not puffed up; does not behave rudely, does not seek its own, is not provoked,
thinks no evil; does not rejoice in iniquity, but rejoices in the truth;
bears all things, believes all things, hopes all things, endures all things.
Love never fails.
1 Corinthians 13:4–8

March 19, 1995

I just went to a meeting and it was like a breath of fresh air. I need meetings! I see that I have gotten too self-centered lately. I don't need meetings just as insurance against drinking. I need them to help me stay centered—and dead to self. I need A.A. It doesn't need me.

I also somehow got wrapped up in fear of losing Randy, which is self-centered fear. I see that Randy's emotional dependence on me has been a source of security for me. To really love him is to support him (and myself) in his quest for independence. Real love is a choice, not a necessity. I just have to trust God and be willing to stand beside Randy; not arm in arm with him.

Stand together yet not too near together: For the pillars of the temple stand apart, and the oak tree and the cypress grow not in each other's shadow.[250]
Kahlil Gibran

March 24, 1995

My fear of losing Randy has passed. I guess that my habit was to believe that the only way that I could feel comfortable and secure was to have our needy dependence on each other in play. However, the true answer was hidden in the act of detachment.

I must admit that I mourn the false sense of security that *I can't live without you* brings, but I inherently know that what we are doing now is more in tune with the truth and reality. God, this balance thing is tricky. Somewhere between *I can't live without you* and *get away from me* is the truth. I guess Randy and I are finding that middle ground.

The bottom line is that anyone can live without anyone else. In reality, no one really needs anyone. They just want to believe that they do in order to avoid the responsibility of taking care of themselves and owning their own defects of character and power. It is a lot easier to try to beat the splinter out of your brother's eye with the beam from your own.

I miss that overwhelming sense of being one with Randy, but I now see that we were just going through a process. God only knows we needed that period in order to fill our cups in the love department. We were both so starving for attention that we feasted on each other. Those were definitely the most exhilarating days of my life. I'll never forget the joy of our love when it was born.

It's maturing now and we're at more difficult stages which involve boundaries, detachment, and maintaining our individual identities in correlation with our identity as a couple. It's a very interesting process. I've never consciously witnessed it before.

I see that one of my biggest challenges will be not to withdraw and part emotionally when I feel rejected. In order to not feel rejected, I have to see that if someone is pushing me away, it's not about me. It's about their fear of intimacy and vulnerability. Now, if I start pushing Randy away—that's about me.

The hardest thing for me to see sometimes is that my feelings are about what is going on with me; not some intuitive flash inside my brother. In other words, my feelings are *my* feelings. How simple to be so hard to understand.

I'm in a pretty serene place. I'm in a place where I can let Randy do what he has to do—whatever that may be—and I can take care of myself. I trust the process and I trust God. It's a wonderful life and God is molding me into a wonderful person. Without Him, I'm nothing and, for today, I totally understand that. Thank you, God. I love You.

Learning to accept yourself is the beginning of change.
Learning to accept others is the beginning of wholeness. Love expands.
It not only sees more and enfolds more, it causes its object to bloom.[251]
Hugh Prather

March 26, 1995

Last night, the walls came tumbling down and I felt the sweet closeness with Randy that has been absent. Some of those walls were mine. I guess I am learning that boundaries are malleable; not hard as rock. It's a new experience to flow from the detachment that separates me in order to be who I am and the sense of oneness which fills my heart with love and joy.

Right now this minute, I feel an absolute surge of love for this person named Randy DeHart. This relationship is such an intense learning experience with a lot of exhausting work, but moments like this are the pay-off. It's such a tender feeling to love this man. He's so worthy and so beautiful and so sweet … and sometimes so lost and confused.

I know that sometimes he feels that he can't possibly do life alone. I feel the same way. It's funny how we all support each other so much. Alone, we stumble and fall and feel as though we can't get up again. Together, we help each other up and hold hands through the rocky and steep passages.

Life is so beautiful and God is so wonderful. I live for the moments where the poignant fragility of life trickles in my soul. Life is like butterfly wings; capable of flight, yet also capable of annihilation by even a north wind. Thank God for the shelter that is God's love. I am such a truly blessed person. I am not who I was before and I am ever-changing into the likeness of He who created me. I willingly surrender to this process, dear Father. Thank You, God!

The bond that links your true family is not one of blood,
but of respect and joy in each other's life.
Rarely do members of the same family grow up under the same roof.[252]
Richard Bach

April 3, 1995

I had an eye-opening week. I realized just how cunning, baffling, and powerful my disease is; how it can subtly set me up for a great fall. It occurred to me that every time I take even the smallest step in the wrong direction, it's like I'm adding a brick to the wall between me and God. Ways of adding bricks are things like not going to church or meetings, smoking cigarettes, taking sleeping pills, and entertaining ideas of partying with people at work.

I see that this city on a hill thing is my challenge. In the past, this is the stretch of journey where I fell off the mountain. God keeps bringing me back here. It's time for safe passage. One day at a time and with God's help, I can do it.

I had a little visit with the enemy the other night and it was frightening. Call it my ego or call it Satan, all I know is that it is a taunting, childish brat who tries to intimidate me with fear. It was weird because, once I prayed, I heard God come through loud and strong; like a firm parent. It really helped me to see who is in charge and that was comforting because it's not me.

Randy is coming out of the dark night of his soul. It's nice to see him doing well. I love him so much. Sometimes, I don't know what to think about this relationship. We're at a point where we don't necessarily want to do everything together. A part of me wants to whine that it's becoming just the Troy situation—separate lives—but I know it's actually healthy to not *need* to be together all the time.

Immature love says: "I love you because I need you."
Mature love says: "I need you because I love you."[253]
Erich Fromm

April 4, 1995

I'm in turmoil. I have a real issue with Randy concerning the fact that there is no room in our relationship for my imperfections. I don't want to be in another relationship that is all about me loving the man and end up where my needs are discounted and invalidated. I am especially upset because I work so hard at patience, tolerance, and understanding with Randy. He does not reciprocate. He seems to either be sitting on top of the mountain—looking down at all the losers—or else he's the scum at the bottom of the pond. I know that I have the same tendency, but now I can honestly see it; which allows God to change it.

We've been trying to stop smoking and I fell and smoked **(I started smoking again when I started dating Randy).** This is the first time that "we've" tried and I've been the one to fall first. He had no compassion or understanding. As a matter-of-fact, he beat me up emotionally and told me that I needed to be harder on myself. Bull!

I understand that I cannot control and manipulate to get my needs met, but I also understand that I owe it to myself to set boundaries and protect myself from people, places, and things that violate my dignity. I *don't* need someone drilling me like a sergeant.

I truly do want to quit smoking and I'm not defending my right to smoke, but I am defending my right not to get kicked around emotionally because I fell short of my expectations for myself; or of Randy's expectations of me.

I'm good enough, dammit! I love myself and accept myself *just the way I am*, but I am willing to change and God is changing me now. I didn't fail. I just haven't reached the goal yet. Setbacks are not failures—they're stepping stones.

I don't know what to think. I love Randy, but I am not interested in walking on eggshells in fear of displeasing him. He needs to grow up and join humanity. I know I'm talking about myself too. I know that he's my mirror, and frankly, sometimes I don't like what I see.

I know this much; I deserve to be treated with love and compassion because I have learned to treat others, especially Randy, with love and compassion. I'm not saying that he "owes" it to me, but I have a right to express myself when I consider the way I am being treated to be unacceptable.

I give this to You, Father. Thy will be done.

Be kind, for everyone you meet is fighting a hard battle.[254]
Plato

April 8, 1995

This was a very transformative week. I haven't smoked again since that last entry (neither has Randy). We worked through that boundary issue and have gone through a jillion other conflicts since then. Conflict resolution seems to be one of the themes of our relationship (as well as a study in the nature of true love).

I'm so proud of Randy. He hasn't smoked for a week and he did his Fifth, Sixth, and Seventh Steps with his sponsor. Smoking, the Steps, and Sponsorship have all been big dragons for Randy for a long time. Now that he has found the courage to face those dragons, he's really opening up and becoming happier. He's becoming "Randier." May "Turtle" **(his band nickname)** rest in peace.

I love Randy with all my heart. It's a lot of work standing up to him, but it's worth it. Yesterday, he got all mad because guys flirt with me at work. He said he's tired of feeling insecure. I told him that, where there is no commitment, there is no entitlement to security. Commitment breeds trust. I don't think he liked hearing that because he's one of those "have your cake and eat it too" people (like every alcoholic I know).

The bottom line is that it's probably time for us to decide if this relationship is something worth working for and then commit to it and act accordingly. As time goes by, I find myself naturally committing to Randy. If I don't, I don't even know which direction I'm going. I'm like a sailboat without a rudder (like I really know what a rudder is).

Anyway, it's a beautiful day today and I feel gloriously happy and grateful. It's a wonderful life!

Thank You, Father. I love You!

This is the miracle that happens every time to those who really love; the more they give, the more they possess.[255]

Rainer Maria Rilke

April 10, 1995

I'm in a lot of turmoil over the realization of just how exhausting the work of this relationship is. When I tap into that rejected inner child who feels so unloved, it is not fun. It's even less fun to crusade on her behalf for the love, protection, and respect that she deserves. It's a tough job, but someone has to do it. I have to do it because I love her. I love myself.

Well, I give this to You, Father, and ask for knowledge of Your will and the power to carry it out. Thank You for my many victories. Grant me victory over myself. I love You.

Trust must be purified in the crucible of trial.[256]

Brennan Manning

April 14, 1995

I've learned so many things from Randy. Mainly, I truly see that no one's living the dream life. You get out *what you put in.* There is no easier, softer way than plain and simply taking right action. The word "action" insinuates work. The grass is not greener on the other side; it's greener where you water it. For today, I continue to cultivate my little green pasture with Randy, but I also see that the most important relationship in my life is with God. We may all be one, which I believe that we are, but while we're manifesting on earth we might as well accept the fact that the true nesting fortress for each and every one of us is God within us. I can't depend on any person, place, or thing outside of myself for security. That's one of the loneliest ideas for me to accept. However, we do have each other to hold hands along the way. As Desiderata says, "*With all its shams, drudgery, and broken dreams, it's still a beautiful world.*"

No journey carries one far unless, as it extends into the world around us, it goes an equal distance into the world within.[257]

Lillian Smith

May 1, 1995

Randy and I are changing and I feel a lot of fear and anxiety. I really have no idea of what I even think is supposed to happen so the blatant uncertainty is very uncomfortable. I realize that we're never really certain about anything, but I sure like to believe I am.

I don't know what to think. I've revolved my life around Randy to the point where I don't have my own life anymore. I haven't insisted that we forge a common ground. I've just surrendered to his will. It's getting to the point where I resent it. It's my own fault. In the beginning we were just so enmeshed that all I wanted to do was to be with him.

I see that my lesson is to learn to express my wants and needs in a constructive manner. Randy is just like Troy in that he stubbornly refuses to acknowledge any sort of complaint or feedback about less-than-perfect aspects of the relationship without considering it to be "nagging and whining." Troy called it "b—ing and complaining." How do I express myself without being considered a nag? Am I not supposed to say something when I find a situation unacceptable? I really don't know. This is definitely a recurring theme.

I must remember that I went into this thing with the attitude that the joy was so awesome, it was worth the pain of being temporary. I hope I wasn't kidding myself.

Thy will be done, Father. I love You.

May 8, 1995

Randy took his first Hepatitis C Interferon injection on Saturday night and braced himself to be sick as a dog yesterday. He felt fine. I'm so glad that I didn't waste a lot of energy worrying about that. I think facing the Hep C boogie-monster has helped Randy to finally cross the line where faith grows into a knowing rather than a belief.

All genuine knowledge originates in direct experience.[258]

Mao Zedong

June 24, 1995

I've been a little irritable and self-centered lately. I truly pray for the humility

I need in order to be serene while I continue this transformative process with my appearance. I am so thrilled with the changes, but I am definitely aware of my tendencies to become a stuck-up snob. There really are some pitfalls to physical beauty. The number one pitfall is that it makes it about a million times easier to manipulate people and I'm a born manipulator. I just want to be a loving and lovable person *and* I want to be thin and healthy. With God's help, I pray I succeed.

We have become so self-centered that we go to God
only for something from Him, and not for God Himself.[259]
Oswald Chambers

July 4, 1995

What a weekend! God is working in my life in indescribable ways. I truly am becoming a believer in fairy tales and dreams come true. It really looks like Randy is "the one." We have such a fabulous relationship. I feel so safe, whole, and complete that there's no way to describe it. I just truly love him and I'm beginning to believe that he truly loves me also.

Tonight, he left to go to a gig and I felt all sorts of sad feelings; reminding me of the days when we had to go back to Dad's after visiting with Mom. It was intense. I realized that these feelings were so overwhelming to me as a child that I chose to reject the loving safety of "Mommy" rather than to endure the pain of separation from her. Thank God, as an adult, I can choose differently. Today, I choose to love rather than to avoid it because of fear of pain. What a trip.

Life with Randy is like psychotherapy, a roller coaster, the magical mystery tour, and Heaven—all rolled into one. The little girl in me says *I can't do this! Wonder if something goes wrong! I could never endure it!* Christ within me says *Don't worry, be happy. Live for the joy of the moment. Tomorrow will take care of itself.*

Life is a trip! I love my beautiful and peaceful life, I love myself, I love my friends and family ... and I totally adore Randy DeHart. He's the most beautiful person I've ever known. Thank You, God. Most of all, I love *You*!!!

I want to know if you will risk looking like a fool for love,
for your dream, for the adventure of being alive.[260]
Oriah Mountain Dreamer

July 12, 1995

I've been locked in a vacuum of loving Randy. Ever since the weekend of the fourth, he has been absolutely devoted and committed to our relationship. He says that he wants me to "be his bride." We're looking for a place that we can both call home. My home is at his side. We truly love one another.

Real love is a permanently self-enlarging experience.[261]
M. Scott Peck

During this time, Laurel and I moved into an apartment with Randy.

August 1, 1995

Life truly is the double-edged sword. With each new beginning is the grief and mourning of an ending of some sort. I go through phases where the pain of failing with Troy (and the realization of many buried hurts associated with that relationship) plagues me. I guess I just get into a lot of fear about history repeating itself. The fear of failing with Randy is overwhelming. I can't imagine the stinging disappointment if this ends in yet another broken dream. Fear and doubt block my good. However, denial of the fear blocks it even more. I must have the courage to move forward in spite of my fear. Grant me the courage, sweet Heavenly Father.

Tonight, I got in touch with how painful it is for me to feel slighted and left out where Laurel is concerned. I realize that I sometimes feel jealous of her. That is so immature, but I must be gentle with myself. My needs were so unmet as a child. They're getting met in this relationship with Randy, but it's so scary when we do things with our kids (he has two sons) because I have to play the role of "parent" when in so many ways, I am such a child myself. Sometimes, when I'm "Mommy," I'm acting.

My inadequacies in this area cause me to fear that Randy will reject me. I hate the fear of losing what I have. I still haven't learned to succeed gracefully. Help me, Father. Fear of success breeds sabotage and I know it. Hold my hand, sweet Lord. Please, calm my storm and assure me that all is well. I need You so much as I unravel even more confusion within myself. Bring me home to You within myself. I'm afraid, Father. I'm so happy with the gifts that You have given me that I'm terrified of losing them. Grant me peace. Help me to loosen the garment of this life. Lord, hear my cry. I love You with *all* my heart.

I want to know if you have touched the center of your own sorrow,
if you have been opened up by life's betrayals
or have become shriveled and closed from fear of further pain.[262]
Oriah Mountain Dreamer

August 16, 1995

The journey continues. The ins and outs of everyday living are tedious these days. I certainly see what I was running from. The illusion that I can maintain perfect balance without ever having to confront Randy with any issues is being smashed. We both have to realize that uncomfortable feelings won't break us. They indicate that something needs to be looked at. God, I've run from and numbed uncomfortable feelings all of my life rather than acknowledge that they were trying to tell me something. That blows my mind!

Sometimes I fear that Randy and I will lose our euphoric sense of love for each other. However, who's to say that losing that is a bad thing? How do I know that mature love isn't even better? I don't. God, one more time I get to see how I try to control and prevent things from changing when I have no experience with what is to come.

Let go, Paige!

I see that, as long as we remain calm, Randy and I have the makings of a beautiful friendship. We talk about things that I never even really thought about before. We're both growing. I guess we're growing up.

Lately, I've been getting in touch with some issues concerning my defensiveness. I perceive any criticism or suggestion as an insinuation that I'm not good enough. That's ancient programming. Like I told Randy about all this "original pain" stuff, *It would sure be nice to make a bowl of cereal without being interrupted by childhood issues.*

Life's a trip. It really is just a journey home—to love. God gently illuminates every dark corner that shades the reality that *God is Everything.* I guess it's time to stop believing in monsters—that I'm a monster.

Thank You, Father.

The root of evil is within you. As you begin to understand this,
you stop making demands on yourself, you stop having expectations of yourself,
you stop pushing yourself and you understand.[263]
Anthony DeMello

August 20, 1995

Randy seems to have had some sort of awakening. Tonight, he spoke with authority and conviction. He sounded just like me! It made me realize that I am not special. I'm God's kid. If someone sits before me in audience to my Father through me, I am witness to another kid being blessed by his Father. I need to learn to let God love me too.

I see that my stupid spiritual pride has been in play—once again putting me in the position of superior guru. How does this keep happening? As the layers peel, the same old defects become more subtle, but they're still there. Help me, Father! Of myself, I cannot change. Of myself, I'm nothing.

Anyway, I'm willing to be vulnerable and I'm willing to meet the challenges of adulthood.

September 2, 1995

This week has been a rude awakening for me. I get to see how I thrive on crisis: how I love to coax unreasonable men into reasonableness; how I find self worth in "fixing" other people; how I play God. This whole week had been uncomfortable because Randy has been embracing life rather than resisting it. Immediately I began resisting Randy, trying to keep the turmoil in action … trying to find some sort of balance.

All of this makes me frantic because I'm seeing that I'm not well; that I still have issues … that I suffer from a disease that tells me I don't have one. My first reaction is to beat up on myself for not being perfect or shame myself because I'm not, which means, I guess, that I was beginning to think I was.

Ego! Spiritual Pride! Cocky Self-Assurance! Get behind me, Satan! I guess the bottom line is that God has a gentle way of reminding me that He's God—not me. It seems that the deeper I go I find new levels where I have not yet come to believe that I am lovable and worthy. I'm willing, though.

> **Guess what, Paige? You're not super-human. You can't do it alone. You need Me and you need other people in your life to love you. You need Randy just as much as he has needed you. It's okay to need people.**

I feel like such a fool. I can be so grandiose and self-centered.

> **Precious child, it just doesn't get any bigger on planet earth than being**

a child of God. I love you, Paige. Everything is as it should be. Relax. Surrender. Let go.

I found my security in believing that Randy needs me to help him and to fix him and to save him. I guess I just realized that he *does* need me still, but not because of what I can *do* for him, but for what I *am* to him. Not doing—being. How many times have I learned that? Our worth comes not from our actions, but from our inherent being. If true to ourselves, then good works just naturally flow. New ideas become old ideas which, when released, give birth to newer ideas ad infinitum. Life's a trip.

Your freedom when it loses its fetters becomes itself the fetter of a greater freedom.[264]

Kahlil Gibran

September 22, 1995

Am I ever worlds away from thinking I'm perfect! I have realized that I'm such a crisis junkie because it distracts me from the subtle storms raging deep within me.

Randy got real upset when his divorce was final. We ended up having a long talk and the subject of inner child work came up. I ended up pulling out John Bradshaw's *Homecoming* and reading it (for Randy of course). Well, it was God's way of tricking me into finally looking at this work myself.

I've read the book before, but this time is different. This time it's put me on the emotional roller coaster from hell. I've been experiencing feelings that have always scared me. They still scare me, but at least today I know that they won't kill me and that they will pass.

I've found a part of myself that has been lost. I'm not sure who she is, how old she is, or what she's been through, but she's there and she still thinks and behaves in all of the old ways. I haven't even gotten her to trust me yet; much less trust life or the process of recovery.

Uncovering all of this pain and turmoil has shown me a lot about my crisis creating and about my rescuing. This onion peeling thing is no lie. It's like you finally calm the storm and keep moving forward—only to find a deeper storm. I know this much: I am willing to do this and feel this because I'm tired of ancient emotions coloring today. I'll be damned if this disease is going to take me down. I will not be a fatality to alcoholism or to dysfunctional family systems.

The realizations concerning my childhood emotional life are very painful. No wonder I've always felt hollow and cold. No wonder I shut down. It's time to thaw. Last night, Randy spoke of *building a life together.* He used terms like "loyalty," "security," and "family." I know nothing of these things. I feel so sad for the kid I once was. Being separated from Mom left such a big hole.

There's something inside of me that tells me it's not okay to feel sad for myself, but what about my yesterday self? I can't help but feel sad for her; to feel her sadness.

Yet the journey continues ... the ride's a bit bumpy these days. Thank You, God, for the unfoldment of my life according to Your purpose. Thy will, not mine, be done. I love You.

I saw the angel in the marble and carved until I set him free. [265]
Michelangelo

October 4, 1995

What a two weeks! During that last entry, I was having a terrible time emotionally. It was the craziest place I've been in for a long time. I had forgotten how insipid insanity can be. I needed to remember. So much has been going on. I've really had to look at my tendencies to run away—to favor comfort over commitment. I've also gotten to look at the fact that sometimes I have to take a step back in order to move forward.

This relationship with Randy has turned out to be just about as life-altering as the program. If I had known what the implications of meeting my true mate were to be, I probably would have passed on the opportunity because I would have considered myself incapable. I'm learning that there is no such thing as incapable; only *unwilling.*

From the time when Randy and I first got together until the time we moved in together, I felt like "Daddy's Little Princess." I loved it. It's not like that so much anymore and at first I thought it was a "bad" thing that it had passed, but tonight I could see that what we have now is deeper and more mature. I've never been here before.

Randy is not my daddy and I am not a little girl. He is not my hero and I am not his guru. He's not a prince and I'm not a princess. Randy is my partner and friend and, together, we're learning about things that neither of us have a clue about. He's not here to indulge me, but to love me. One more time it is hitting home with me that *I don't have a clue about anything that I have not personally experienced and I have never experienced enduring love so where do I get off thinking that I know what it's supposed to be like?*

Something happened to me in the meeting tonight. I sat there and, for once, felt grateful that I don't know all the answers because that gives me hope that the lesson's not over.

Paige, the lesson's not over.

I sat there feeling grateful for the very things that seemed a burden to me before my setback. Sometimes I lose perspective on exactly where I came from. I came from hell.

Anyway, I can accept Randy's imperfections and hopefully, he can accept mine. In the good times and the bad, he's still the best friend I've ever had. I truly love him.

Thank You so much, Father, for this life and these wonderful lessons. You never cease to amaze me. I love You so much and I surrender to You.

God bless us all.

When I have once again been made aware of my fallibility,
I become predisposed to learn.[266]
Hugh Prather

November 9, 1995

Where have I been? I've been living and loving with Randy DeHart. Our love became new again so we rode the tide of our joy. I basically figured out (one more time) that I just have to let Randy be the boss. It's not a Daddy/Princess thing so much as it is a Husband/Wife thing. The feminist in me fights the idea, but hey, someone's got to wear the pants and when I wear them I end up having no respect for my partner. There's got to be some middle ground between resentment of their strength and disrespect for their lack of strength. Oh, well, we're learning. Even though the loving feelings are great again, we still have conflicts, but we're learning about loving each other through them, but not running away—literally or figuratively.

Randy left yesterday to go to Europe with his band. I feel like a real fool because my fear of abandonment caused me to emotionally regress to the state of an eight-year-old little girl. Needless to say, my perspective was skewed. It's a long, drawn out process for me to learn to trust. I felt so abandoned and rejected because he was going away, but those are old feelings.

Even though I pretty much guessed that having time to myself would be an enjoyable experience, I'm still pretty amazed to see the boogey-monster of loneliness is nothing but a very peaceful state of aloneness. I guess there's a big difference between lonely and alone.

I'm okay alone. Thank God! However, even though when I'm alone I can keep the house cleaner, listen to whatever music I want, read and pray at my own pace, and eat cake for dinner, I still like it better with Randy DeHart sitting in my face. That man is truly a gift from God to me. We go through all kinds of junk and still come out on the other side holding hands. I've never been here before. He's my best friend. I guess he really is "the one."

If a man could mount to Heaven and survey the universe, his admiration of its beauties would be much diminished unless he had someone to share in his pleasure.[267]

Ralph Waldo Emerson

December 2, 1995

Randy's trip was a huge success. The band came back in a blaze of glory and then the leader decided to quit. Randy was upset. I was relieved. When he got back, he was so focused on the band again that I was in real fear about his sobriety. I know that he loves music, but that demon ego of his sometimes soars when he gets too wrapped up in it. It just makes it easier for him to rationalize unacceptable behavior. Whatever happens, though, I know that I have to try to accept life on life's terms and not fight what's going on with the band—just like he needs to try to not fight what goes on with me spiritually.

We had another big debate over Unity vs. The Episcopal Church. We go round and round over whether or not I believe that Jesus is the "one and only" Son of God. The bottom line is that I need to let Randy be a musician and Randy needs to let me be a metaphysician. God will take care of the rest.

I see that I used to create crises because I was afraid that balance and serenity would be boring. I've realized that balance and serenity are hard work because of the ever-changing nature of life. Every time the dust settles, God challenges us to new growth.

Each day has enough trouble of its own. (NIV)

Matthew 6:34

December 23, 1995

The day before yesterday, Randy came home with a beautiful engagement ring. The energy between us was leading up to marriage so I wasn't surprised, but I was still enthralled by the moment because I actually hadn't played it in my head a million times. It didn't happen "just the way I dreamed" because I didn't sit around dreaming about it too much. I've just always tried to let go and to trust that everything will be as it supposed to be with Randy. I keep pinching myself because, since November of '94, my life became a beautiful dream.

The only fear I have is facing the day when it all ends; when Randy or myself dies. I guess for a life of beauty, I can deal with that when it happens. We're so close that I doubt that even death could separate us. We *are* joined at the heart in timelessness. He is my soul mate and, believe me, true love is not under-rated.

Thank You, God!!!

At last I know what love is really like.[268]
Virgil

.15. home at last

January 1, 1996 – January 30, 1997

The course of true love never did run smooth.[269]
William Shakespeare

January 1, 1996

Another year gone by—eighteen now with the journal. It's hard to believe how quickly time passes. I still feel like the same girl I was when the journal began. I'm thirty-four now. I guess I'm not a "girl."

Well, so much for a calm and serene life. On December 24, we found out that I am pregnant. We've both been going out of our minds. It's a very confusing circumstance because on one hand, it's wonderful, but on the other, it's scary. Of course, all of the negative thoughts concerning it are driven by self-centered fear on both of our parts. I guess it's time for us to work on our self-centered fear.

As beautiful and joyous and full as the spiritual path is, there's just no getting around the fact that the farther you go, the more narrow the path becomes. It's definitely a survival of the fittest thing because there's just one seemingly huge obstacle after another that could easily be one's undoing. I know that *all* that matters is guarding my sobriety with vigilance because as long as I take right action, I will be in the flow of God and all will be well. I just can't get over what a trip life is.

Sure, dreams come true—and I believe in fairy tales and dreams come true. However, in fairy tales and dreams you don't see the part about the huge amount of work and character building required to maintain them. As time goes on, the words of the preamble for A.A. and the words of Jesus, Emerson, and other great thinkers ring so true to me. There is no easier, softer way. Life is not supposed to be easy; just lived to the fullest.

I just can't believe that I'm going to have another child. I've always had a hunch that Randy and I would have a little girl named "Hope."

My only real concern is what this will do to my physical appearance. I guess it will help me because I've obviously over-identified with the beauty queen image. I can get ego and self-esteem so easily confused.

Of course, Randy's fears are basically financial. Also, he has fears about the responsibility and selflessness involved in parenting. It's not like we're not already parents. It's also not like we don't need another opportunity to do things differently—to amend our past and the way we passed the responsibility of parenting to other people. We both did that and we both have guilt and shame about it. God is giving us the opportunity to change that.

God ... what a wonderful, most gracious Father. Even though it's hard, I love my life. I truly love the person that I am becoming. I told Randy, *Just like all of the other things that we don't understand, God will help us to understand what all of the emphasis on marriage and family is about.* It's not that marriage and family are not all that they're cracked up to be; it's that we haven't comprehended their greatness yet.

1995 was the best year of my life, but I know in my heart of hearts that the best is yet to come. Here's to a blooming 1996 when Hope (or Jesse) will come into the world.

I want to know if you will stand in the center of the fire with me and not shrink back.[270]

Oriah Mountain Dreamer

January 2, 1996

We've had a very difficult few weeks. Of course, we've made it difficult on ourselves by resisting our lives rather than embracing them. I see that we tend to label life situations as "good" or "bad" when there's really just "comfortable" or "uncomfortable." In meetings this year I heard that we should choose character over comfort and that acceptance doesn't mean approval. Being comfortable is just another name for resting and I know good and well that you need rest on the path, but not so much that you get complacent and start moving backwards. Like I once heard, *"The universe is either constructing or destructing at all times."* No lie.

It seems that we meet challenges, practice principles until we achieve some sort of mastery of the lesson, rest for a minute, and then move on. I guess that's life and if I can accept that, I just don't have too much to argue about. I realize that most of my problems have been a result of the belief in concepts that simply weren't true. If I can accept the fact that life is difficult and its objective is *not* about getting my way, I can get free of a lot of the reactions that make me miserable.

Randy and I have really had to do some soul searching lately. We've both had to look our selfishness and our immaturity square in the face. I know that we can't change ourselves into responsible adults, but if we are *willing* to change and to *act as if* we are responsible adults, God will do for us what we cannot do for ourselves—change our character.

I guess the whole deal with life is about learning because, even when I fall and wallow in self-pity, I still learn something from it. I guess nothing really happens in God's world by mistake. I'm so grateful to be sober. I literally walked around blind until then.

Randy and I are getting married on February 10. I told him that as long as we are *willing* to stay together, no matter what, we'll make it. If he and I can't make it in this relationship with each other, we might as well give up on relationships because we are truly a match made in Heaven.

Thank you, God.

Love is blind—marriage is the eye-opener.[271]
Pauline Thomason

February 19, 1996

Well, the wedding came and went. It was beautiful and all, but it was really no big deal. The big deal was meeting Randy. We went to Vegas and hated it. We noted that before, a lot of our experience was wrapped up in events and in our surroundings. Today, our experience is about *being who we are.* We don't even have to leave the house to do that. Life really is so much simpler than I ever imagined.

Sometimes, it's even sad to realize that all the hype and glamour and drama that I thought was so appealing was really nothing but illusion; absolutely meaningless in the reality of eternity. If you can't take it with you, it's not really worth striving for. I guess it's the love and joy that you take with you.

I think I'm finally realizing that I'm not destined for "greatness"—at least nothing beyond being a worthwhile child of God. Sometimes, it's hard for me to believe that my most important role is not *savior of mankind* or *prophet of God*, but *wife* and *mother* and *sister* and *friend*. What a trip. I just got off the phone with the Girl Scout leader and thought to myself, *I'm the mother of a Girl Scout, I drive my child to school every day, I pack sack lunches, and I mop floors and do laundry.* I'm just a normal person and that's okay. I never knew how to do that before. I was always too good; or too afraid of failure.

Anyway, I'm learning. The farther I go, the less grandiose I become. The simpler I become, the more okay it is to just be. One more time, all I can say is that I have everything I need *and more!*

Thank you, God!

The invariable mark of wisdom is to see the miraculous in the ordinary.[272]
Ralph Waldo Emerson

March 13, 1996

I've been doing prayer time with Randy that excludes writing; it excludes a lot of things I enjoy. I always wanted someone to "share my life" with because I was so hungry for companionship, but on the other hand, I can't share my relationship with God. It's a one-on-one so, basically, there's a crowd when Randy's included.

I learn so much from my life with Randy. One thing I'm learning for sure is that I love him, but I don't *need* him to be whole and complete. Everything I need is inside of me.

I've been having a pretty rough time with this pregnancy. I'm starting to show and, frankly, I see nothing attractive about it. I feel like a fat cow. I know that I need to quit thinking like that, but it's just an automatic reaction when I look in the mirror.

Hey! Stop looking in the mirror!

I know that this thing is a lesson in finding my inner beauty, but it's still a pain to watch my body balloon. My body tends to expand easily anyway. It *really* responds to being pregnant. However, this is temporary and after it's over, it will be worth it.

I've really been in touch lately with my deep love for Laurel. The idea that there's going to be another child of mine here amazes me. One more time, life will expand.

Randy and I have been having a hard time dealing with the step-parent/

step-sibling issues. I know that a lot of it has to do with me. I have a real hard time loving Randy's kids. It's like I'm blocked or something. There's something inside of me that doesn't want to love them and include them in my family. I guess it's just plain old selfishness.

Help me, Father, to be the step-mother that you would have me be. Please give me the willingness to act as if I truly love them until sincerity follows.

In situations like this, I disappoint myself with my pettiness and selfishness.

This is a difficult time in my life, but it's not characterized with wallowing self-pity and defeat as in the past. I always like to compare life to mountain climbing. I've just come to a steep and rocky passage. However, carefully placing one foot in front of the other will lead me to greater clarity and even a higher horizon than before. Experience tells me this and I believe it.

Each day that passes amazes me more and more with my absolute intense gratitude for being sober and for the program of Alcoholics Anonymous. It truly is a school for living. Randy and I have been doing a little ministry training for Christian Counseling, but I already know the stuff we are learning. I've already learned to be a God/love-based counselor in A.A. We really are *all saying the same thing in different words.*[273]

A priest at the church where Randy and I were both raised told Randy that Unity is not "Christian." Who cares *what* you call yourself? A rose called by any other name *would* smell as sweet and a person with a heart full of God is just as loving whether called "Christian," "Buddhist," or "Alcoholic."

Sometimes I get very resentful towards the doctrines of traditional Christianity because they are so rigid. I understand that it is very meaningful to Randy and I truly respect that, but I have great fears about his immersion in the Episcopal Church because, in the past, he has become so rigid in his beliefs that he has deemed me and my experience as invalid. He claims that he has realized that I am really God-centered and that it doesn't matter how I've gotten here. I hope so.

I just have to give all of this to You, Father.

The bottom line is that I don't believe that "Christianity" is about Jesus. It's about Christ and Jesus was Christ, but Christ was before Jesus and continues to live on in all of us. That's all I know. I don't believe that 2000 years ago, miracles were more miraculous than they are now. I don't believe that miracles can defy law, but I believe that they *can* defy appearance. Jesus was a Master of Illusions because He could see beyond appearances. If I'm wrong, I put myself at Your mercy, Lord Christ, and beg that You show me the truth. I am open and receptive to You, Holy Spirit. Show me the way.

If you believe what you like in the gospels, and reject what you don't like,
it is not the gospel you believe in, but yourself.[274]
Saint Augustine

April 21, 1996

I woke up this morning almost in tears because I'm so grateful to share my life with this wonderful man who is my best friend, my soul mate, and my husband. Watching him change and grow this last year and a half has been a beautiful experience. He really is surrendering his ego and also finding the joy and beauty of just being rather than constantly doing and pushing for a tomorrow that never comes. Tomorrow really does take care of itself if today is well lived.

Not much happens these days except *life!* There's no big deals; just comfortable and uncomfortable experiences that *teach me what I need to know that I may be made more whole* (lines from an old poem).

I'm starting to get excited about the baby. The sonogram was about 90 percent conclusive that it's a girl. I'm not surprised because I've had a sense for over a year now that Randy and I would have a little girl named "Hope." Well, Hope is on her way. Seeing her little feet on the sonogram and being able to feel her moving and kicking has helped me to gain more acceptance about the changes in my body. I can't say that I'm in the *best* mood about it, but I'm better. I can't wait to see her tiny face and to rock her in my arms. I can sense that I already have a relationship with her. I couldn't do that with Laurel because I was too sick.

Everything is quite peaceful and beautiful these days (if I will let them be). I can absolutely see that I have everything I need. Having my needs met seems new to me, but it makes all the difference in the world. However, it somewhat removes the desperation that breeds drama.

Sometimes I miss high drama so I create it. I'm sure that this too shall pass. I guess I'm just growing up—and I like it.

I have become someone that I once would have hated. No, I *was* someone that I *did* hate and now I've become someone that I can love. I have become someone who is capable of loving. Love really is the bottom line and, for today, my life is full of it—*love* that is.

Thank You, sweet Heavenly Father. Most of all, I love You!

I want to know if you can be alone with yourself
and if you truly like the company you keep in the empty moments.[275]
Oriah Mountain Dreamer

May 31, 1996

The beat goes on. We've been going through the wringer over our inabilities to grow up and to face responsibility. I've never thought about things like job security and insurance benefits for my family. I've been such a child for such a long time.

It's three months until the baby comes. I can't imagine getting any bigger than I already am. This pregnancy *shows!* Anyway, for today, I accept it. Hope's a kicking little jumping bean. I'm looking really forward to meeting her (and to being able to resume my fitness regime). This pregnancy has been stressful, but it has helped both Randy and me to grow up in a lot of ways. We have moments where we absolutely do not get along, but we get through it. Life is the good and the bad; the joy and the pain.

We recently found out that Kelly is pregnant also (due 12/30). It's really special to me that God is giving us the gift of doing this together. I really love her and we've learned to work through our conflicts.

That's been a major theme this year—conflict resolution. I grew up in a system where, if someone got angry, they were "disowned for life." It's taken me a long time to learn that this manner of dealing with conflict is neither mature nor healthy. I'm learning how to disagree and conflict with others without it being the "end of the world." I've had big arguments with Kelly and we're still friends. That's definitely progress.

I really like the way life is unfolding. Everyone's life is getting fuller, richer, and more mature. Even though some of this stuff is hard, I trust God and the process. Everything is exactly as it should be.

Thank You, God.

Friendship is seeing differences, accepting differences,
yet continuing to love and be happy.[276]
Hugh Prather

July 22, 1996

Life is very good. I never fail to be amazed at what a wonderful friendship Randy and I have. We have both changed so much since the beginning of the relationship. Together, we're learning about loyalty, commitment, and integrity.

He has been so good to me lately. He consistently tells me how beautiful I am (I'm as big as the house!). He's really been wonderful. The thing I've noticed is that, for once, I can let him be peaceful without creating a crisis.

It's real nice.

God is removing our defects and building our assets one day at a time. I have utter faith in the process. I have found my way home.

August 23, 1996

Hope Kelly DeHart was born yesterday at 3:16 P.M. She is an angel and my life is a blessing.

Thank You, God!

Your children are the sons and daughters of Life's longing for itself.[277]
Kahlil Gibran

October 3, 1996

I feel like I've lost a part of myself in the process of being "Mother" and "Wife." I've been having a lot of melancholy feelings lately. I really think that I just need a little time to myself. Sometimes I feel as though I'm pushed to give when I feel that I have nothing left to give.

Lately, I tend to romanticize last fall, but I realize that I could not go back to that lifestyle even if it were possible. I know that having Randy play in the band while I wait tables and spend most of my time being obsessed with my appearance would seem insipid to me now. The only problem with right now is that I'm still not comfortable with who I am. Sometimes I tend to lament over who I'm *not* rather than embrace who I am.

The old grandiose thoughts that I'm someone important in the "Big Picture" are slipping away. I sometimes hang on to the idea by telling myself *Maybe by letting go of the idea, it will happen,* but I really doubt it. I think my lesson is that I'm *not* important—just valuable and worthwhile. I'm just no big deal except to the people who love me. The people who love me: I still have such a difficult time being loved. It's so uncomfortable and I feel so powerless over it.

I really did feel so much more comfortable coaxing Randy and loving him through his turmoil than I do having him reach out to me when I'm camping out behind my wall of silence. I know that everything is as it should be. I just have so much to learn.

The key to motivation is to look at how far I have come
rather than how far I have to go.[278]
Hugh Prather

October 5, 1996

I think I'm addicted to being a martyr. Why else would I respond more lovingly to Randy when he's moody and discontented than when he's balanced and loving? That's a perplexing question to me. I need clarity here, Father. I need You to help me be okay when things are *wonderful.*

I have everything I've ever dreamed of: a wonderful, handsome, loving, successful husband; a beautiful home; the opportunity to be a stay-at-home mom to my precious newborn; two beautiful, healthy daughters; sane relationships with the members of my family; and a strong A.A. program that has helped me to not take a drink for over five years. I have it all. What the hell's the matter with me that I want to nit pick for flaws rather than sing alleluia? Is it because of the responsibility? Is it because it is difficult? It's because I'm immature! Help me grow up, Father! I don't want to sour this beautiful man who tries so hard to love me. Help me, Father! Help me to count my blessings!

I guess the bottom line is that I haven't been putting God first, which is the only way that I am capable of remembering who I am. I am a child of God who is here to serve and to love and to be loved. Once again, I give myself to You, dear Father, and ask that You mold me and help my capacity to love expand with all of the changes in my life.

October 26, 1996

A lot of things have been going on with me. In answer to the *Why do I nitpick for flaws?* question, I would have to say that I do it so that I don't have to look at some things about myself that are a bit disconcerting.

Randy has really grown lately. The problem for me is when he took a huge leap forward, it showed me as big as day the size of the gap between where I am now and solid maturity. It "appears" to be one of those "journey of a thousand miles" things. Thank God I know that appearances aren't reality and all I *really* need to change is my mind.

Anyway, my parenting issues have really been under scrutiny and I get to see how really *not* loving and caring I am at times. Randy has pointed out to me that I disregard requests as "unimportant" that are very important to children. I automatically think that things don't matter because I never experienced them. If these things are so important to children and I didn't experience them, what does that say about *my* childhood?

I know that I am so negative about little league and school carnivals because

I have been too immature and self-centered to see these things as enhancement for the lives of our children (and consequently for us I suppose). The ten-year-old in me feels jealous of Laurel and Mike (Randy's youngest son). My immature thoughts clamor, *I didn't experience this so why should you?* Then I feel mad at Randy for wanting to participate in these things with them. These are a child's feelings and thoughts—and these are angry thoughts. I guess I know that underneath there's sadness.

I really have minimized the neglect I experienced as a child. Anyway, now I see that I have this huge challenge of rising above these childish feelings and letting the adult take charge. I guess I need to take my inner child to the carnival.

Shannon was recently talking about the responsibilities and commitments of parenthood. It made me realize that this huge job of carrying on the human race and attempting to improve its future condition by producing superb human beings has become so mundane that people have lost sight of its importance. I certainly never looked at it that way. All of my pregnancies were products of sex with no birth control. Besides Randy, the motive for the sex wasn't even love. It was about confusing love with sex and just trying for one minute to *be* loved. Man, have I ever been lost in space.

Anyway, I guess it's time for me to quit thinking about myself and take responsibility for the fact that I have been blessed with the task of guiding two beautiful little girls into humanity. I especially need to pay attention to undoing any harm I may have done to the first one.

It breaks my heart to realize how incapable I was of truly loving Laurel the way that she needed to be loved. Thank God for Ruthie and Mom. My love affair with Hope is showing me so much about my insufficiencies with Laurel. I know that God will show me the way to make it up to her.

Even though I feel like a fool for having been so clueless, I am grateful for the new awareness I have lately. It's the beginning of setting a new course. Who knows, there may be a day when headbands, keds, mini-vans, and the PTA feel normal. Who am I anyway?

The soul is healed by being with children. [279]
Fyodor Dostoevsky

November 21, 1996

No matter what hat I wear or role I play or appearance I project, I am still a spiritual child of God. The challenge is to stay in touch with that. I realize that lately I may have been fooling myself into thinking that my service work begins at home. Somehow, it just doesn't seem to work that way. I've realized that I want or need for nothing and I can still find discontent within myself. Rather than letting my cup run over, I try to keep from spilling it. My priorities can sure get whacked.

External success can sabotage my spiritual growth. The trick is not to lose myself in prosperity. The bottom line is that it is time to give back what has been so freely given to me; to love my neighbor as I love myself; as God has loved me. It's time to dive back into my involvement with Alcoholics Anonymous.

I truly believe that I must step up to the plate with my program *and* live life. There's just one deepest heart's desire that hasn't been fulfilled yet in my life—to earn an income doing what I love to do; allow God to express Himself through me. I truly believe that if I will extend myself in A.A., that dream will materialize, but that is not my motive. I have realized that if I don't extend myself in A.A., I will not be happy because my happiness is not contingent on fulfilling my heart's desire, but upon extending myself to others. However, I could never really do that with no ulterior motive until my own needs were met. What a catch-22.

Anyway, here you go, God. My desire is to earn an income by doing what I love to do. In the meantime, I'll do it for free. No, I'll do it for freedom … from the bondage of self.

What at trip You are, dear Father. I love You with all my heart. Please untangle the knots in this heart of mine as You prepare me for my destiny. Make me a channel of Your peace.

We are not channels, we are instruments.
Channels give nothing of their own, they just let water run through them.
In our action, we are instruments in God's hand and He writes beautifully.[280]

Mother Teresa

November 30, 1996 – 35th birthday!

Ten years today … on this roller coaster ride to freedom with my God. I can't believe the changes. No, I *can* believe them. I *do* believe them. What a wonder is this God of mine—this power of Life and Love that is the Truth.

I've realized that the only thing that really matters in my life is seeking contact with God. Without that, all of the riches and pleasures of this world would mean nothing. With it, all of the riches of Heaven are mine in the blinking of an eye.

What a thrill to finally realize that *all* I really need is right here; available at all times—contingent on nothing but my willingness to seek knowledge of God's will and the power to carry it out. The rest is just frosting, but I don't have to have it. There's a big difference between wanting something and believing that you need it. I *have* everything I need—always and forever. There's a lot of freedom in that realization. There's just a lot of freedom in true living.

Now the Lord is the Spirit; and where the Spirit of the Lord is, there is liberty.
2 Corinthians 3:17

December 4, 1996

I've been in a great place lately; which fires me up. That surge of enthusiasm about the journal being significant is back. Reading Deepak Chopra validates that it's okay to believe that I have a purpose and that I am capable of making a substantial contribution to my fellows by doing what I do best—writing and public speaking (and chewing gum too!).

The most secret wish that lies at the bottom of your heart is the very thing that God is wishing you to do or to be for Him. And the birth of that wish in your soul was the voice of God Himself telling you to arise and come up higher because He had need of you.[281]
Emmet Fox

January 23, 1997

I've finally decided that I *don't care* if the journal is significant or not. If the work is meant to get organized, it will, but I'm tired of concerning myself with it. Sure, I'm willing to share my experience, strength, and hope, but on the other hand, I'm busy *living it.* I had a nagging feeling about not having enough time to write. I told myself, *I just have to do something worthwhile.* Then the little voice said,

"Living your life is worthwhile."

The little voice is right.

I don't need the world's approval for my life to be worthwhile. I just don't need to be a big deal anymore because being an ordinary human being is enough. My deepest heart's desire *has* come true because I've found the love, acceptance, and belonging that I believed would come from being "important." Who would have thought that being a housewife and mother would hold the secrets and treasures of existence? I wouldn't have and that point exemplifies exactly just how much I *don't* know. I just give up.

I realized the other day that one of the acronyms for GOD is "Good Orderly Direction." I see that I confused "direction" with "details." All I can do each day is face in God's direction and let go. It's like being a sailboat and God is the wind. I don't know which way the wind is going to blow. I just have to concern myself with getting the sails up; not with painting angels on the side of the boat for all to see. All I have to do is *live;* one day at a time.

The other day I was sitting in my rocker, nursing Hope, and listening to Laurel and Mike bicker over homework. I had dinner in the oven and about a million loads of laundry to fold. All I could think was, *This is fun.* Last night, I woke up and realized that what I had been experiencing were the sounds and feelings of a "family"—*my* family. I guess that's all I ever really needed—to be a part of a family. It's just not over-rated. I'm just so grateful to be experiencing these simple things. I'm so grateful to *live!* I love my simple, beautiful life.

"What do I want to do in life?"
Here I assume a reason for living that is separate from life.[282]
Hugh Prather

January 2, 1997

I keep having drinking dreams. They're just awful. I'm so grateful to be sober. We watched *The Days of Wine and Roses* the other night. It sent shivers up my spine; especially when they read the preamble from A.A. I felt so grateful and full of awe over the power that A.A. has had in my life; the power that God has had in my life. I've come a long way from living in a two-room duplex with trash piled in the corner, the ironing board sitting in the middle of the living room, the cat drinking from the cat box, and the fridge having nothing in it but vodka, wine, and beer. I can't even believe that person was me, but I remember it. I hope I never forget.

All I've ever wanted was to be was happy. I have all I ever wanted and so much more. My life is overflowing with an abundance of love and joy and laughter and friendship. I am whole and complete.

Thank You, God!!!

The Lord is my shepherd;
I shall not want.
He makes me to lie down in green pastures;
He leads me beside the still waters.

He restores my soul.
Psalm 23:1–3

January 30, 1997

Sometimes I have such bittersweet feelings because I know that this precious time when Hope is my little baby is so fleeting. However, how do I know that there aren't more precious times ahead with Hope and Laurel and Mike? Sometimes I wonder where I've been all of my life. I guess looking forward to the best that was yet to come. I realize that better things may very well be coming, but that the best, so far, is right here and right now. Who cares if this great and poignant beauty of life is not forever? It's here and I see it. I am experiencing it.

Sometimes I just hate the way that joy and sorrow are so similar. I guess the seeming polarity is what keeps it all in balance; in perspective—what keeps it all from becoming mundane and keeps me from becoming complacent.

I am enjoying motherhood so immensely. It's still so hard not to suffer over what I missed with Laurel, but that's just another way of depriving myself of enjoying my time with her right now while she's my sweet nine-year-old. She's such a beauty; so smart and inherently generous, sensitive, and sweet. I am so blessed to have such precious children; and to have such a gentle and loving husband. We have come such a long way together. I don't even recognize us anymore yet the peace between us is so anciently familiar. We are truly learning to live and let live. I have a wonderful life. I just need to quit being so dramatic and not let the fact that it's transitory get me down.

That's just life, Paige, eternal yet so fleeting.

Like Chopra says, it's just a *parenthesis in eternity* and if we can manage to *"touch each other and love each other—it is worthwhile."*[283] My life is worthwhile. I have no cares for tomorrow for my present moment is well lived.

Thank You, God.

The issue of guilt over Laurel's early childhood continued to plague me for many weeks. The intense joy I experienced as Hope's mother grieved me because I knew that it was the first time that I was capable of truly being present for the experience of motherhood. Many times I tearfully cried to God to help me forgive myself. He gently reminded me that I had been mentally ill when Laurel was a baby and that I had done the best that I could. Nonetheless, I still could not release the horrible sense of self-condemnation concerning the issue.

As mentioned in the opening chapter, I was separated from my own mother at nine because she had to go to a mental institution for a year. Afterwards, we lived with Dad so I missed the experience of growing up in a home with a mother. For most of my life, I greatly resented Mom over this and considered her to be "weak." I believed that if she had really loved me, she would have fought to keep me.

During this ordeal with myself over Laurel and the Lord's continuous reminders that I had done my best, He finally made it clear to me that I would find compassion for myself when I found compassion for my mother. I immediately understood that Mom had done her best as well and I was able to forgive her—and myself. I also realized that I was not a person whose Mommy didn't love her—I had only believed that I was. Ultimately, I came to understand that my mother's loss was even greater than mine.

Being given the truth in exchange for terrible lies is the essence of forgiveness.

It's never too late to have a happy childhood[284]
Tom Robbins

.16. becoming human

March 1, 1997 – April 1, 1998

"Know Thyself" was written over the portal of the antique world.
Over the portal of the new world, "Be Thyself" shall be written.
That is the secret of Christ.[285]
Oscar Wilde

March 1, 1997

I have been having a recurring dream that I live in a house and realize that there is a whole wing of the house that is uninhabited. At one point in the dream, it occurs to me that I should start using the extra rooms. I finally figured out what the dream meant and then I quit having it.

Anyway, to me the dream is saying that I am my house and the uninhabited wings are the parts of me that are yet to be discovered. They are the possibilities for me if I dare to cross my comfortable thresholds and explore beyond the present boundaries of where I live and move and have my being. Like Jesus said, *"In My Father's house are many mansions." (John 14:2)*

I came to this momentous realization because of coaching Laurel's YMCA basketball team. God, I was terrified and now it's just another part of me. I stepped forward and did something new (and frightening) and added a new dimension to my experience (my consciousness).

The farther I progress into my transformative process, I understand the jargon of the program better—like doing the same thing over and over again; expecting different results. My experience was very limited (partying and making up my own rules as I went along) and I was absolutely unwilling to do anything that I couldn't be a know-it-all at. That didn't leave much room for growth.

When I came to the program, my only goal was to clean up the mess that was my life. As I worked the Steps, the debris was cleared and power became available to actually build something. Anyway, life has been interesting lately.

I've found myself feeling negatively towards Randy because I've been self-centered and thinking that his actions are about me. I know I just have to let Randy do things the way he does things (rather I approve or not) and if I don't like it, keep it to myself (unless it is legitimately my business; which it usually is not).

If he wants to be messy, I have to let him. If I want the house to be neat, I have to clean up after him. I can request, but I cannot demand. I get hung up on thinking that my way is the best way to do things. Even if I do know a better way, so what? Please help me to leave Randy alone, Father! I really do love him and I don't want to destroy this relationship with my attitude of superiority. Help me to live and let live and *not* to criticize, shame, and judge.

When I complain about me or about you,
I am complaining about God's handiwork.[286]
Alcoholics Anonymous

March 24, 1997

The prayer about leaving Randy alone worked wonders. I can't even remember what that was about. The bottom line is that everything ebbs and flows; including Randy and me. Things have been beautifully peaceful lately. Life really is so simple. Love God. Love yourself. Love others. The way to love is to serve with joy. The willingness to serve with joy comes from forgiveness that extends from the willingness to live and let live. Above all else, don't sweat it. Willingness really is the key.

I made a joke the other day about finding my identity in the midst of Tupperware. Then it dawned on me that I have found my identity in the midst of being a part of something greater than myself; in the midst of A.A., in the midst of Unity, in the midst of my family. In my willingness to serve, I found salvation—true freedom.

Life is good. God is great!

It is more blessed to give than to receive.
Acts 20:35

April 28, 1997

I've been in turmoil lately because of my selfishness and self-centeredness. I realized that my "lovingness" is usually only there when there's a pay-off for my ego. How sickening to realize the depth of my self-centeredness. It even disguises itself as love. Anyway, needless to say, I have a tendency to feel hopeless, but I know better. I truly believe that God has a plan for me.

There are two types of selfishness.
The first type is the one where I give myself the pleasure of pleasing myself.
That's what we generally call self-centeredness.
The second is when I give myself the pleasure of pleasing others.
That would be a more refined kind of selfishness.[287]
Anthony DeMello

May 7, 1997

For the first time in years, I have felt really confused about what's going on inside of me. I have been seeing some stuff about myself that is very disappointing. Even worse, I realize that I am powerless. I guess that's not "even worse" since "powerless" is a good place to be in a Twelve Step program. I'm at Step One with some character defects that are becoming quite debilitating.

I have a tendency to be hurtful to the people I care about the most. My hurtfulness basically stems from nitpicking (perfectionism), down talking (superiority/pride), and complaining (self-centeredness). Basically, I'm bottoming out with self-centered, perfectionist, control issues. Ouch!

I'm tired of being a hurtful grouch. I'm either high on the mountaintop —superior to everyone—or a total jerk. I complain that I don't want to be like everyone else, but that's just my ego telling me that I'm unique or different. I *am* like everyone else. I am a child of God.

One of the things I really respect about Randy is that he has limits concerning the amount of unacceptable behavior that he is willing to tolerate from me. That scares me sometimes because I fear that I can't change, but it also stops the tornado and helps me gain clarity. I know that I can't change myself, but I truly believe that God can and *is* changing me according to my willingness to surrender.

That's what blows my mind: I can be an alcoholic tornado whirling destruction through the lives of those I love and not even recognize it. Talk about denial! The good news is that rather than wallow in self-pity because, once again, I've realized that I'm not as nice as I fancied myself to be, I can be grateful that I'm at a turning point for new horizons.

My journey has taken me so far that sometimes I tend to think that I have "arrived," but I remember now that it *never* ends. There is no permanent plateau. That's exciting and even a bit unbelievable. I'm already at places I never dreamed of. However, when Randy talks about "building a life" and I feel confused because I don't know what he's talking about, I see that I have a long way to go. I remember when the word "loyalty" baffled me. I remember when I didn't understand the concept of the word "consequences." I remember when the word "God" made me angry. I have a long way to go, but I have also come a long way. At least now I understand that if I don't understand what someone is talking about, *I'm* the one who's in the dark. It doesn't mean that *they* don't understand what they are talking about.

More good news is that these issues are messing with me like never before because, for the first time, I'm attempting to form a true partnership with another human being—however feeble the attempt. I just need to get with the program and forget about what it is I think I want and need. Sometimes I totally forget that I blew my chance at running my own life and that I have no right to complain about nor dictate the circumstances in my life. Left to my own devices, I would be dead.

Dead, Paige, dead!

God saved me. I am here to represent Him.

I'm realizing how selfless a person needs to be to have a *real* life. I see that one of the reasons that I never tried to step up to the plate was that I didn't know how. Another was that I was just too self-centered to bother. I find myself thinking, *If I keep spending my whole life just doing for others, what will be left of me?*

Just the REAL you—silly fool!

So the difference between "the boys and the men"
is the difference between striving for a self-determined objective
and for the perfect objective which is of God.[288]
Twelve Steps and Twelve Traditions

June 3, 1997

Sometimes, I think of myself as "nicer" than I really am because I judge myself by my thoughts and feelings rather than by my actions. If I'm having "happy" thoughts, I believe myself to be nice. I guess I'm sometimes oblivious to my actions and the effect that they have on others. This helps me to understand principles like "act your way into right thinking," "examine your motives," and "don't judge your insides by other people's outsides" better. However, true authenticity is to have my actions and thoughts aligned. I've got a long way to go.

Better to return and make a net, than to go down
the stream and merely wish for fish.[289]
Chinese Proverb

July 4, 1997

Life is so good. The best thing about it is that I truly believe that no matter what happens, "good" or "bad," I can endure because *nothing* has the power to remove God's love and grace from my life; not even death. What a trip! Anyway, the pieces are falling into place and my work is beginning. God only knows that I am willing to go as far as He'll take me. *In Christ I live and move and have my being. (Acts 17:28)*

For I am persuaded that neither death nor life,
nor angels nor principalities nor powers,
nor things present nor things to come, nor height
nor depth, nor any other created thing,
shall be able to separate us from the love of God
which is in Christ Jesus our Lord.
Romans 8:38–39

July 28, 1997

I've realized that I am finally free to trust ... not that people won't let me down or that there will not be times that I don't feel pain or that life will never be messy, but that *always* there is more to learn.

July 31, 1997

There's a big difference between giving advice and sharing my experience.

Only he who is able to articulate his own experience
can offer himself to others as a source of clarification.[290]
Henri Nouwen

August 21, 1997

Well, the circle continues to flow round and round. I went through a big process of extending love whether I felt like it or not. Lately, the flow stopped and I'm beginning to understand why. *A Course in Miracles* says that everything is either an *act of love or a cry for help*. I have been practicing the recognition of those cries for help in others so that I may meet them with expressions of love. There's just one person whose cries for help I fail to recognize—my own.

I guess I'm at a place where I get to practice letting others extend themselves to me. I am a part of this circle also. I am not above or below the humanity and imperfection that seemingly separates us by our broken dreams or the true spirituality that binds us. Once again, I see the need to come down off my pedestal and to let others love me. This thing cycles for me. I realized in '94 that the Saint Francis Prayer doesn't *just* address giving, but once again, I've tried to sacrifice my vulnerability in the name of heroism. I sometimes become a self-appointed "untouchable." That's just pride, ego, and self-centered fear. Anyway, here I am again—a part of the circle of life—learning to love and to *be* loved.

Help me, Father, to reach out to those in need and to allow others to reach me when I'm in need. My need is Your opportunity to fulfill it and my neighbor's opportunity to let You be Yourself in him or her.

Remember that, Paige; it's important. Every time you hide, you deprive someone that you love the opportunity to practice being loving and helpful. Others need to be there for you as much as you need to be there for them. Let others help too, sweetheart. Everyone must give AND receive. This is the lesson.

Someday, after we have mastered the winds, the waves, the tides and gravity,
we shall harness the energies of Love.
Then, for the second time in history, man will have discovered fire![291]
Teilhard de Chardin

November 11, 1997

I recently got involved in an intense study of the A.A. book that intuitively feels important. Randy is interested in it also. Of course, this study guide is the *only* spiritual book I've ever been interested in that I *didn't* try to persuade Randy to read. One more time—powerless—that truly is my dilemma.

I've been experiencing a great surge of motivation lately to work on the journal project. I really believe in that idea, but on the other hand, I don't want to delude myself. I guess it really doesn't matter because I have truly found what I was looking for and no one can ever take it from me—except my self-will.

For today, my will is to do the will of God. I have been having some awesome experiences lately. God has blessed me with the ability to be helpful; to truly be of service. It is so ironic that the greatest lessons come with simply being willing to do what is mine to do.

We alcoholics crack me up. We go from being totally self-destructive maniacs to wanting to be the next Mother Teresa. Today, I see that in the first things first department, we have to stop the madness. Next, we have to learn to live a healthy, normal, balanced life. For most of us, that's a lifetime achievement. Then and only then are we able to progress on to "greatness." Without the program, my tendency is to do *last* things *first.* Who would have dreamed that being a good mother is more important than being an inspiring speaker?

Well done is better than well said.[292]
Benjamin Franklin

November 21, 1997

I've been editing the journal and, as if for the first time, I can clearly see the course of my life. I cried with gratitude and joy last night when I came across a list of all the things I wanted from God **(May 5, 1988 entry)**. It was a real wish list. Today, it is a check list for my reality. It is uncanny to truly realize the power that is God.

There just aren't words to express my gratitude for this marvelous adventure with God. His light literally blazes in my life and it is awesome. Finally, my desire is to give rather than to receive.

I'd be lying if I said that I don't want to be "recognized" for who I am, but I can live without it. For all I know, recognition could be a big pain in the butt—so that one's up to God. All I know is that I have a tremendous desire to share this experience and this presence that explodes continuously in my life. I am blessed with the faith that literally moves mountains. I truly believe that I can do *anything* through Christ who strengthens me—even make a dramatic impact on the world.

We can do no great things—only small things with great love.[293]
Mother Teresa

November 22, 1997

I started my new Fourth Step. I really didn't see the point in doing it until I read the journal from '88. For the first time I could see why everyone was so mad at me. I was a selfish fool. I just thought everyone was picking on me. When I saw the truth, I knew I had to get to the roots.

This is the very perfection of man, to find out his own imperfections.[294]
Saint Augustine

January 5, 1998

I have felt disconnected. It's becoming obvious to me that being a perfectionist and over-achiever is *not* an asset—it's a cover-up. Trying to hide my weakness with cocky bravado is a form of denial. I need to kiss my demons, not bury them. This is what *"do not resist an evil person" (Matthew 5:39)* means to me.

February 7, 1998

I've been doing the *Big Book Awakening Fourth Step,*[295] which has put me on an emotional roller-coaster; torn between sadness, anger, and fear. Thank God that my mentality is focused so that I can process this experience with discernment rather than just freak out with utter fear that I am going insane.

I can see that I have been deeply programmed to believe that negative emotional excess is crazy ... that I better stuff it and not let anyone know how unmanageable my feelings really are. Thank God for books and people who have gone through this process. They validate for me that weepiness, anxiety, and rage are all a part of the unmasking.

I am not crazy and God will pull me through this. Although I am terribly uncomfortable, this too shall pass. Even though I am tempted to judge this as a "bad" experience, I know that it will lead to more freedom and authenticity. I'm ready, willing, and able to rise above all limitations within me ... with God's help.

This inventory process is showing me how emotionally unavailable I have really been. It's hard for me to believe that "Miss A.A./Miss One-With-God" has been yet another disguise for my ego; another mask for my deep-seeded fears and insecurities.

To get into the core of God at his greatest,
one must first get into the core of himself
at his least,
for no one can know God who has not first known himself.[296]
Meister Eckhart

February 9, 1998

This inventory is showing me that my idea of serenity has been to stand vigilantly at the door of a basement that is full of hungry dogs. I can't believe how much I've lived in my head in order to deny my true emotions. I realize that I am terrified of being vulnerable, of being imperfect, of not being in control, of needing other people, and of making mistakes. In other words, I'm terrified of being human. I can now see that if I deny being driven by fear, I might as well accept that I am being driven by delusion. In denying my vulnerability, I have almost denied the part of me that loves.

Prior to metaphysics and God, I *was* my emotions and that wasn't okay either. Then I became my thoughts, but that was still quite a delusion because I was so out-of-touch with my own weakness and limitation. Hopefully, I'm on my way to integration.

Yesterday, it occurred to me that to invite Jesus to be my personal Savior is not the same thing as saying that I believe that He's the *only* way to God. Even if it is, who cares? I *can't* work out my own salvation with diligence because I keep getting in my own way. It amazes me how I can continually forget that *I* am the problem.

Jesus Christ did not come only to teach.
He came to make me what He teaches I should be.[297]
Oswald Chambers

February 14, 1998

I had a realization in an Al-Anon meeting: I've never really looked at the fact that the objective in communication is to make a connection with the person you're communicating with. My agenda has always been to get my point across. I debate and lecture. My conversations are monologues. No wonder my only tool for living was a hammer. I realized this as a result of reading *Giving The Love That Heals.* Hendrix and Hunt talk about conscious dialogue … the components being mirroring, validation, and empathy. I see in my recent inventory that I have a tremendous need to be validated. That is why I am sometimes overbearing in my opinions. My opinions are not necessarily the truth. Wow!

The A.A. literature says that there is a difference between a request and a demand. That's news to me. In my family of origin, there was but one ultimate authority and it was *not* a loving God, but Dad. There were no "requests" … only orders. The result was either resentful compliance or pure rebellion. This really helps me to understand why a request can be perceived as a demand and why compliance with the requests of other people can feel so much like engulfment.

This new inventory in conjunction with the willingness to see the truth is a real eye-opener. I am grateful to once again be able to see that I am a work in progress. I need to get it through my thick head that the feeling of having arrived equals a resting period.

I must do these things in order to communicate:
Become aware of you (discover you).
Make you aware of me (uncover myself).
Be ready to change during our conversation.
And be willing to reveal my changes to you.[298]
Hugh Prather

February 21, 1998

This extensive method of doing the Fourth Step is showing me the truth behind my ideas of myself. I guess it's showing me the beliefs of my heart … and some of them are very different from what my head says. I guess the journey from the head to the heart is the longest journey, but once again, I cannot *"put new wine in old wine skins." (Matthew 9:17)* I must deny the lies before I can really believe the truth, but before I can deny them, I must identify them.

For example, because of an ingrained belief that I will *never beat Dad,* my heart whispers *Don't win*. However, my head clamors *I am a winner.* No wonder I swing from one extreme to the other. No wonder I'm an egomaniac with low self-esteem. I'm beginning to see that the ideas imprinted in my heart were done so by a small child with a very limited perspective. No wonder growing up was so difficult. What I'm beginning to see is that what I want to be when I grow up is *grown up.*

Even though some of these realizations are painful because I am experiencing some ancient frozen emotions, I am pleased with the course that my life and recovery are taking. The hot-shot hero is fading away and a real person is coming into focus. All is well. What a gracious Father.

Therefore you shall be perfect, just as your Father in heaven is perfect.
Matthew 5:48

In Greek, perfect means "complete or of full age."

March 3, 1998

I have really been tapping into the core of my being and it is not the exhilarating experience that I had imagined. I am in touch with the fact that at a very deep level I believe that I am inherently flawed and defective. I am absolutely driven by a thousand forms of fear and delusion. I had no idea that I was so afraid. It's actually a bit disconcerting. It seems as though, in many ways, my ego has been masquerading as God.

At least as a result of this, I can see on a whole new level that, of myself, I am nothing. I realize that all of this does not necessarily change anything as far as my goals and aspirations go, but it is changing everything concerning my *motives.* My tremendous need for recognition has come from deep, unmet needs for validation. External recognition is probably the last thing I really need right now because my ego gobbles it up before it ever makes it to my center.

"Project Charlie," a volunteer program that I am teaching at Laurel's school, is helping me to see that I am someone special … not because I am "chosen" or because I am super-evolved above others, but because there is no one else in the world exactly like me. My value already exists. I don't have to achieve anything to bring it about. That concept is very hard for me to comprehend. I am already there if being valuable is the objective. Now, *realizing it* is a whole different story.

I put *Toy Story* on for Hope yesterday. The scene that stuck out to me was when Buzz Lightyear realized that he was "just a toy" and not really a "space ranger." He was bummed. I could relate. Woody told him that there was no such thing as "just a toy." He was *someone's* toy and the little boy who he belonged to thought that he was a really cool toy.

I know that I have circled through this same thing over and over again, but I guess it's just a deeper level or something. It feels like the first time. Once again, I'm realizing that I am "just a human being." However, yesterday I got to see that I am someone's mother and someone's wife and someone's friend and that they love me. Even more I could see how blessed I am to have these "someones" in my life.

In a sense, we really are nothing without relation to those around us. Einstein's theory of relativity goes a lot further than time or space. I guess the bottom line is that I am seeing that I am not separate from those around me. We are a part of each other ... a part of this cosmic weave called "life." I *am* someone special, but so is everyone. Once again, on a deeper level, I see that there is no such thing as an ordinary person in an extraordinary world.

> *Service, gladly rendered, obligations squarely met, troubles well accepted or solved with God's help, the knowledge that at home or in the world outside we are partners in a common effort, the well-understood fact that in God's sight all human beings are important, the proof that love freely given surely brings a full return, the certainty that we are no longer isolated and alone in self-constructed prisons, the surety that we need no longer be square pegs in round holes, but can fit and belong in God's scheme of things—these are the permanent and legitimate satisfactions of right living for which no amount of pomp and circumstance, no heap of material possessions, could possibly be substitutes.*[299]
>
> **Twelve Steps and Twelve Traditions**

March 16, 1998

The sermon at church was about Jesus' seamless life; absolutely no delineation between His intentions and His actions. How could I have been so deluded as to think that I have achieved such a thing? I'm pretty disgusted with this ego of mine. My head is full of knowledge, but knowledge without love is worthless. I know a lot of things—so much that people might really think I know what I'm talking about. I can't even open my eyes without the power of God's love.

I am confused because I am not sure if I am beating up on myself for being imperfect or if I am becoming aware of how truly self-centered and mean-spirited I can be; probably a little of both, but I suspect more of the latter.

One of my daily readers made reference today that our singleness of purpose is to work on improving the quality of human relationships as opposed to striving for material success. How can I be so backwards? I stink in relationships. I want more than anything to be a truly loving and supportive wife and mother rather than treating everyone as if they're extensions of me and then withholding approval or attention if they don't comply with my every demand, but I am powerless to do those things. *Help!!!*

I believe in my heart of hearts that God is taking care of this because it is coming into my awareness so fiercely. Still, seeing what a jerk I can be is very painful.

Your conscience is the measure of the honesty of your selfishness.[300]
Richard Bach

April 1, 1998

As I uncover my delusional process, I see how truly "insane" I can be. It's more than taking the first drink, it's more than the crazy things I did while drinking, and it's more than doing the same thing over and over again—expecting different results. Insanity is believing two things that oppose one another.

I can see that the recovery process is a continual process that is like gardening. I recently reread *The Parable of the Weeds (Matthew13:24–30)* that shed some light on what is going on with me. Jesus said not to pull the weeds while the good seed is still a seedling—to let them grow side by side until the good seed is a strong vine—to pull the weeds at the time of the harvest. The lies inside of me are the weeds.

When you drop your errors you will know the truth.[301]
Anthony DeMello

.17.

from belief to trust

April 27, 1998 – October 14, 1998

We have grasped the mystery of the atom and rejected the Sermon on the Mount.[302]
Omar N. Bradley

Until now, I have minimized explanation of my belief system that was developed through metaphysical books and Unity Church. Metaphysics is basically a philosophy of being and knowing that brings one to the conclusion that God is at the core of every human being and that by using various psychological and spiritual methods, one can access the divinity within. This understanding can be validated through the sacred Scriptures of many religions such as Hinduism, Taoism, and even Christianity. Consequently, the meaning of the Bible is interpreted beyond literal understanding. With this perspective, one can see that the Bible is really the story the inner world of each human being. There is validity in this understanding, but without literal consideration of the Bible as well, the key significance of Jesus' life is overlooked.

Unity[303] is an organization that believes that the nature of each human being is divine, but also teaches the practical application of truth that was taught and exemplified by Jesus. However, they believe that He was simply the "Way-Shower;" a Teacher who demonstrated the importance of thoughts, words, and deeds in shaping the life and world of the individual—a special person in history who expressed perfection and thereby became the Christ.

Unity also teaches that God is Divine Mind and the Source and Creator of all. The nature of God is absolute good so there is therefore no other endur-

ing power. What is called "evil" is a limited or incomplete expression of God. Consequently, any theological paradigm that includes the capture of humanity by a sinister enemy with the consequential need for a Savior to rescue and redeem it from the power of darkness is unnecessary.

I spent ten years at Unity Church where I experienced a loving and tolerant environment that enabled me to grow spiritually and to learn many practices that effectively worked in my life. However, my experience has taught me that, without full acceptance of the Gospel of Jesus Christ, access to the Christ within is thwarted in a dangerously deceptive way. As you will see throughout the next several chapters, my attempts to accept the Gospel and the implications of what that would mean to my life and ministry were blocked by "something other" than myself.

For we do not wrestle against flesh and blood, but against principalities,
against powers, against the rulers of the darkness of this age,
against spiritual hosts of wickedness in the heavenly places.
Ephesians 6:12

On Good Friday of 1998, I felt led to attend the services at the Episcopal Church where both Randy and I were raised. At that service, the inner voice of God spoke loudly and clearly. He said,

"Paige, it's me—Jesus. I'm the One you've been having a relationship with."

April 27, 1998

I don't know where to start. I guess the bottom line is that all of my prayers and pleas and searching have led me to Jesus. Now I see why I've been conflicted. There's Him and there's me. I am aware of His presence in me a *lot,* but the reason there's still this "other" part is because my self is not yet crucified. Jesus is *in* me, but we are not one and the same. There is a difference. Of myself I do not have the power to do the right thing. Of myself, I am nothing.

Anyway, I guess the bottom line is that I am truly realizing that this supernatural spiritual journey I have been having for all these years is tied to Jesus and that the work I feel called to do is *His* work that He began and continues to do through me and the other vessels.

I have been so competitive and unfair towards Jesus. My pride wanted to tell me that I am equal to Him on my own merit. My recent experience with the Fourth Step showed me that on my own merit, I should be dead. I need to accept that this love and loftiness that is *in* me is *not me* and that I cannot claim it for my own glory. It is mine in order to do what is the will of God. I have been wrong.

I'm just blown away by this majestic power that is yanking the shingles from my eyes. I truly feel like Saul/Paul. I made and continue to make many mistakes, but have been blinded by the light of Jesus after many years of persecuting Him in the name of God. My eyes are seeing clearly now and all I can say is Jesus Christ is Lord and Savior of my life.

Christianity is not a message which has to be believed,
but an experience of faith that becomes a message.[304]
Edward Schillebeeckx

April 28, 1998

I spent a lot of time this week trying to sort through all of the information I've been getting about Christianity. I was under the impression that Christians believe that Jesus was the "originator" of the Holy Spirit, but I was mistaken. Jesus is the *author* of *salvation.* This makes sense to me. It's like He's the director of the Holy Spirit or something. I read in *Christian Believing* that Jesus has a future as well as a past. In other words, the work is not over.

I feel as though I have been having some sort of long distance love affair for the past twelve years and now I have finally met my Beloved face to face. Some sort of veil has been lifted. Something is going on between us that is beyond anything I can describe. I guess that's why they call Him "Wonderful."

And his name shall be called Wonderful,
Counselor, The mighty God, The everlasting Father, The Prince of Peace.
Isaiah 9:6

Shortly after this experience, I was led to attend a three day spiritual retreat that was hosted by the Episcopal Church—Cursillo. During the weekend, the presence of the Lord was overwhelming. He gave me many visions of the future and showed me how several of the doctrines of the Church were misused and harmful to the people. He also told me that Randy and I were to be priests in His Kingdom and He commissioned me for my future ministry.

However, at the closing ceremony, I was overtaken by another dominating spirit that caused chaos, confusion, and humiliation. The experience dam-

aged the seed that had begun to grow in my acceptance of Jesus Christ as Lord.

The thief cometh not, but for to steal, and to kill, and to destroy: I am come that they might have life, and that they might have it more abundantly.
John 10:10

May 29, 1998

The purpose of life is to know God and to do His will. When I was at Cursillo, I was filled with the presence of God and He told me to get Him off that cross—that He needed to be out in the world. I am so irritated about what's going on with dogmatic Christianity. To motivate people with fear and cause them to believe that Heaven is about hell prevention as opposed to abundant life is abusive.

I really resent the Church for treating the "sheep" like they're idiots. The visible church is a playhouse compared to the vastness of the invisible church. The whole Cursillo deal was an unpleasant experience **(Randy was frightened by the experience and took me to a psychiatrist who diagnosed me as psychotic, but I was regrouped and normal within three days after the retreat).**

Anyway, Jesus' life, death, and resurrection; the whole act of creation is an act of love from God to us and from us to God when we become aware of it. As much as we need God's power to have manageability in our lives, God needs our cooperation to have power in His world. This is a two-way street. The knowledge of good and evil is meant to be *understood* and is what gives life texture and context.

One thing that I see very clearly reminds me of Richard Bach's reluctant messiah in *Illusions*—people don't really want to know the truth—they just want to find ways to justify themselves without being too uncomfortable. Anyway, I need to quit doing the visible Church's inventory. I am just amazed by how ignorant people choose to remain.

There are many people who have sought light and truth, but they look for it outside themselves, where it is not.[305]
Saint Augustine

June 14, 1998

Everything is totally crazy today. It seems that God is telling Randy that he is supposed to be an Episcopalian priest, but Randy is sure that he will never be ordained as long as I'm his wife (which is probably true). Anyway, for the first time, the possibility of my marriage with Randy coming to an end is entering my mind. I feel awful.

I am so sad and depressed, but I just can't argue over either of us having to do what we have to do. I have always seen a distinct possibility that one of the last hurdles for each of us could be to face the challenge of being alone. I've never been alone for long and Randy's *never* been alone. I'm talking about physical aloneness. Psychologically, we were both alone our entire lives until we met each other. I just can't believe that this is happening.

He said the meanest things to me. He said that he has to lie to people about me because the truth about me is embarrassing. Lately, because of things I see in him that I never wanted to believe, I don't know if he means these things or not. I'm not sure which of these personas is really Randy. He says that who he is now is who he *really* is and that the person who married me was just a confused, spinning man. He says that he has finally gotten well.

I know that Randy is fighting like hell to hang on to his old ideas and that I represent a new thought process that is so threatening that he tries to tear me down in order to feel secure about his worn-out beliefs. I also know that he really loves me. The thing that breaks my heart is that I'm not so certain that he will surrender; especially when he thinks that he already has.

I just have to hang on tight to God. I would be willing to sacrifice *anything* for my relationship with Randy—except my relationship with God. I cannot lie and pretend in order to keep up an appropriate appearance for him to play priest. If I could, I would, but I can't.

Anyway, I pray for Your highest will, Father, and I do not presume to know what that is.

The only way someone can be of help to you is in challenging your ideas.[306]
Anthony DeMello

July 17, 1998

Things are amazingly better between Randy and me. My fear of allowing Randy to have his own experience was a big part of the problem. Miraculously, those particular character defects of mine seem to be slipping away. Consequently, we're better even though he's still studying to be an Anglican Priest and I'm still motivated to reform Christianity and bridge it with Metaphysics and the principles of the Twelve Steps of Alcoholics Anonymous. We make an interesting pair.

I am having a real experience with Steps Six and Seven. For example, I can really see how my persuasive arguing harms Randy. It invalidates him.

My motive behind it is absolute fear of vulnerability. The recent inventory revealed in Technicolor that I have been literally driven by the fear of rejection, confrontation, abandonment, being alone, vulnerability, and not being able to take care of myself. This has led to approval seeking, people pleasing, and extreme attempts to be the center of attention. The bottom line is that somehow I have deeply believed that I am some sort of monster and without the validation from another human being, I'm dead—or even just plain atrocious. That's sad.

However, I am really starting to see that those beliefs are lies. Unfortunately, the only way to confirm this is to risk rejection, abandonment, vulnerability, and confrontation and to take care of myself by setting boundaries and telling the truth and by letting Randy have his experience that I am not directing. That means risking being in his life without trying to make myself indispensable; just being in the relationship *to be.*

If you have become a necessity to someone else's life, you are out of God's will.[307]
Oswald Chambers

July 22, 1998

True service is inspired by the love and compassion that stem from the *experience* of living according to spiritual principles. After God assists us in our salvation, He asks for assistance in the salvation of His world. God's will is to carry the message (hope for the hopeless) to the suffering human being. God helps us, but He needs our help in order to fulfill His plan. To humbly seek God is to fulfill our destiny—Mission Possible.

We have the choice to deny the mission because of free will, but we'll end up with a perversion of what is intended. We can only create in truth with the assistance of the Holy Spirit. Of ourselves, we miscreate because of misperceptions (lies and false beliefs). God's help is a gift to the unconscious, but it is a *contract* with the consciously aware. Mainstream Christianity has a very limited perspective of the "truth."

If you embrace what you resist, it will dissolve what is not real and emphasize what is. There is one thing for sure that will not go away if you embrace Him and that is Jesus Christ. *Blessed are those who believe without seeing* (John 20:29) is the same as *Blessed are those who can learn from the experience of others.* Some of us just have to have our own experience; to put our hands in His side.

Most people use Jesus as hell prevention or as a mere comfort in life. There comes a time when we have to follow him at *any* cost.

If any man will come after me, let him deny himself, and take up his cross, and follow me.
Matthew 16:24

August 8, 1998

I am having a spiritual experience as a result of The Steps. I have woken up to a new experience—larger than ever. About two weeks ago I was feeling the nudge to volunteer to do The Steps from the podium. Within two days, I got a call and I did the first of five weeks last Monday at an A.A. group. For preparation, I've been doing my own intense study of the A.A. literature and my life will never be the same.

My strange capacity for information retention is working just as well with the A.A. literature as in other situations. I am literally armed and dangerous. Seriously, I feel as though I have finally donned my last piece of armor and am now marching my way to the front line where my command post is waiting. For today, it is clear that my ministry is in Alcoholics Anonymous. I do not have to go to seminary. I have been in seminary for twelve years. Suddenly, it all just came together and my effectiveness in the program has advanced beyond anything I had previously imagined.

Now that I have direct experience and better understanding of the Twelve Steps, I am equipped with the capability not only to share the experience, but to literally direct the way for others to follow and to have their own experience. *That's* what it's all about, Alfie.

To watch people recover, to see them help others, to watch loneliness vanish, to see a fellowship grow up about you, to have a host of friends—this is an experience you must not miss.[308]
Alcoholics Anonymous

August 23, 1998

My life is moving in a direction of greater accountability and responsibility, but I cannot be hyper-responsible for everything. Lately, I've been acting with great responsibility, but becoming painfully aware that I am absolutely powerless over outcomes.

I've been having surges of feeling very depressed and anxious, but I think I'm just scared because my dream is coming true and I'm starting to get a glimpse of the pressure that is involved with this sort of thing. When you have a public life, people don't love you—they assassinate you. I'm afraid of failing.

I guess the good news is that it doesn't really matter what happens because it's God's deal. The world doesn't really need my contribution—I just need to make it as an act of my own creativity. I guess that's what Richard Bach meant in *Illusions* when he said that we can write a beautiful story or tear the pages. I don't *have* to do anything. I guess I sometimes take all of this and myself too seriously.

Gee, Paige, you think?

Anyway, I'm getting in touch with my nature to sabotage my successes. I'm still a lot more fearful than I realized. I guess this is a good way for me to see just exactly how much I need God.

I need You, God.

Paige, if a shadow looms before you, you have turned your back to the light.

Pray as though everything depended on God.
Work as though everything depended on you.[309]
Saint Augustine

September 11, 1998

I have really been feeling myself growing and changing lately. The nice thing is that my concern with myself and "who I am" has been fading away. I'm finally losing interest in how other people perceive me and am being able to just concentrate on "being" me; which is really about learning, growing, and attempting to be of maximum service.

I finally see that we have to come to love ourselves enough to stop caring about ourselves so much. We can only take the focus off ourselves after some healing has occurred. When I say I "love myself," I'm not even sure if it's me I'm talking about. The bottom line is that this person that is living my life is *not* me. It's not who I was—ever—as Paige. Sometimes my experience is as if I am more of an observer *watching* how God operates and thinks.

The other night I was reading a science book. Afterwards, the information was processing and I had almost total recall of everything I had read. It just blew my mind because *that* kind of learning capacity is just foreign to me. Sometimes I feel as though I'm waking up to the awareness that I'm from another planet or something.

No, Paige, you're from another PLANE.

I'm truly beginning to understand that God's "chosen" leaders don't have to worry about competition or someone trying to take them from their rightful position. I see that everything's coming to a head or a close or whatever and that the only ones who will be able to get us out of the mess we're in will be the one's who know God enough to be able to understand what's going on in the first place. Everyone else will *have* to get out of the way because they won't know what to do.

> *God desires urgently that you, the creature, get out of his way—*
> *as if his own blessedness depended on it.*
> *Ah, beloved people, why don't you let God be God in you?*"[310]
> **Meister Eckhart**

October 7, 1998

The past two weeks have been sheer hell. I have really gotten in touch with the fact that I have a deep sense of not mattering; which explains my drive to *do* something very important; to make my mark. All of this grand realization has come about as a result of Randy's impending ordination. If he doesn't need me to save him, what am I for? That's really a dumb question, but it's there.

Worse, I get to see how truly self-centered I am. I tell God I'm willing to "go to any length" to do "the right thing," but once again I get to see how I can color my self-determined objectives up and call them "the right thing." I've said that I'm willing to die for the cause of being the person that God would have me be, but am I willing to step down from the throne and be "the wife" to another leader? Am I willing to be supportive of a cause that doesn't place me front and center? Am I willing to let go of every preconceived notion I've ever had—including any and all notions of who I am? Am I willing to forget about myself and truly seek to be loving, understanding, and consoling more than I am to be loved, understood, and consoled?

These are hard questions to answer. These are also my current instructions and, believe me, my ego has been kicking and screaming all the way to the crucifixion. Truly, more than any "grand" idea of who I could be, the current situation offers more opportunity for character building than I could ever have imagined. Maybe this will be a stepping stone to "great" demonstrations, but that's none of my business. Besides, what does it matter if I reach the ultimate goal in consciousness, yet be unable to support my husband in the achievement of his greatest desire? It wouldn't mean anything. I'm willing, God. I surrender.

Though I speak with the tongues of men and of angels, but have not love, I have become sounding brass or a clanging cymbal. And though I have the gift of prophecy, and understand all mysteries and all knowledge, and though I have all faith, so that I could remove mountains, but have not love, I am nothing. And though I bestow all my goods to feed the poor, and though I give my body to be burned, but have not love, it profits me nothing.

1 Corinthians 13:1–3

October 14, 1998

Besides the "not mattering" and the "need to be center stage" stuff, I'm also getting to see a lot of intolerance and unwillingness to change. I see that I have a lot of resistance towards the idea of becoming a "priest's wife." I'm beginning to see that I defend my "right to be me"—to defend my right to be irreverent and opinionated and bawdy and sometimes inappropriate; to defend my right to be *wrong*. This is a call for a measure of meekness that I don't have. I guess more than a realistic perspective of where I am with a true vision of where I need to be, humility is also the recognition that I don't have the power to get from point A to B—at least of myself I don't have the power.

This whole deal has been very difficult and I have really wanted to run away, but when the objective is be and do what God wants, balking at difficulty defeats the purpose. In the process of progress, there is much imperfection. To tolerate and endure the imperfection and discomfort builds character. The lesson truly is: *do not give up.*

I would never have guessed that seeing my limitations more clearly would make me more tolerant.[311]

Hugh Prather

.18. preparing a servant

October 18, 1998 – January 2, 2000

Your self-sufficiency, your selfishness, and your intellectual pride
will inhibit His coming to live in your heart
because even God cannot fill what is already full. [312]
Mother Teresa

October 18, 1998

In just one week I've learned a tremendous lesson and had a great realization. I see that, because of a deep sense of not mattering, etc., I have either depended on other people way too much or else let them depend on me—so that I can be indispensable to them—so that they will need me—so they won't leave me (fear of abandonment). Anyway, that scenario has always left me superior, inferior, or just on the outside looking in. People who either did not need my help or me theirs were simply not a part of my life. I have been unable to truly be interested in other people simply for who they are because I was driven by this fear. No wonder I've thought I'm not enough; because no one else has ever been enough to fill the deep void within me. Anyway, all of this seems to be changing.

As I've faced this fear of losing Randy and my position as "top spiritual dog" around the house, something interesting has been happening. I'm beginning to see Randy in a new light. Watching him reach out to life in his own way (without me holding his hand or pushing him into it) is giving me great joy. I am so proud of him and I am able to truly see how worthy and beautiful he is. He doesn't need me; he just needs God.

All along, what I've thought I needed was attention, validation, and recognition. What I've really needed also was the ability to pay attention to, validate, and recognize the beauty in the people around me—not as a reflection of myself, but as a true perception of how much we're all the same. Beyond the opportunity to recognize our own value, life offers us the true kinship and joy of loving our neighbors as ourselves. I feel truly humbled; and awed. God and this tremendous transformative process never cease to amaze me.

As previous certainties desert us, we become vulnerable and open.[313]
Brennan Manning

October 31, 1998

Dear Heavenly Father,

I finally see that it is right that I be afraid of my "self." For only You can lead me in the right path. Please relieve me of the excruciation of the bondage of my selfish ego desires and guide me in Your ways in thought, word, and deed.

Bless all of Your wondrous creation, Father, and bring forth those of us who are chosen to carry this Light into darkness as never before. May all of creation unfold in cooperation with You.

Thank You, Father, for this opportunity to grow in power and beauty as You slowly chip away my sharp edges and fill me with the gentleness of Your love. You are wonderful. You are the only Power. Guide me, Oh God, and help me to think of You until You become my only thought; until I become merged with You—for the world.

Though I fail miserably, I trust that You are correcting my error. Lead me to mastery. Save us from ourselves. Protect and strengthen all who work together for good.

Salvation consists wholly in being saved from ourselves
or that which we are by nature.[314]
Andrew Murray

November 1, 1998

My God,

On this special day for my precious husband, one of the *many* treasured gifts to this silly life of mine, I sit in quiet meditation as I reflect on all You've done for me. You raised me up from spiritual death in an immoral life, set my feet upon the Path, called me to order, and then bestowed upon me a worthy partner—who today becomes a Deacon. How do I thank You for my good and faithful companion? He is a gift to me; to temper me and discipline me; to protect me from my foolishness and impatience. May Your light illuminate his way.

November 7, 1998

I feel a little uncomfortable today because sometimes I don't know where "being supportive" of Randy turns into enabling and not taking care of myself. I've had a hard time this week watching Randy wear his collar and talk about how the ordination has "changed him." I've just been jealous.

I keep judging him and comparing myself to him and then feel like he doesn't "deserve" it because I'm "more evolved" than him. I need help, Father. Please help me to be supportive and loving and encouraging to him, but also, Father, please give me the courage to follow my own calling.

I know that the real thing that is stirred up is the fact that Randy is *doing* what I've always *wanted* to do. I had given up on the idea of ordination just as he had. Now, I see the desire is consuming me again. However, it's a little scary because we all know that the type of "priest" that I could be would probably not be stereotypical.

Whoever is afraid of what others will say will not even try to advance.[315]

St. Augustine

November 21, 1998

Well, I've evened out over Randy's ordination. For one, I have really prayed and sought clarity and I see that I do not feel led to seek ordination at this time. I am supposed to continue to put my energy into my studies and spiritual growth and to write/edit the book.

I guess I just got jealous, but now I can truly see that I can't do everything at once and getting Hope past toddler hood is the priority. I can accept that. What a conflict to believe in your heart of hearts that you're destined to be a global spiritual leader while being a suburban housewife and the mother of a toddler. Either I'm a nut or God has a hilarious sense of humor (or both).

I really came to terms with a new truth this morning. I see that all of that "do the opposite of your own best thinking" stuff in A.A. is another myth. Doing things differently is not necessarily doing things oppositely. What's really necessary is to look at the opposites, compare the two extremes, and then find the middle—the truth.

We've spent 3000 years waxing philosophically and debating the *definition* of reality rather than *experiencing* reality in a way that leads to what God wills. I guess the purpose of time in the first place is to waste it (or use it for this process). The point I'm trying to make here is that it seems like it's definitely time to start putting our beliefs into action so that us humans can get on the beam and discern what we need to be doing in order to save the planet and to perpetuate the race.

Christ has made Himself dependent on the faithfulness of His people for the extension of His kingdom.[316]

Andrew Murray

December 7, 1998

Randy and I have been struggling. This "struggle" is tiring, but I'm starting to see some new things (or at least they're "new" today because I probably have seen them before but forgot).

Anyway, as I was saying, I'm starting to see that my relationships don't work not because I'm in relationships with the wrong people, but because I don't know how to respect and value and accept people for who they are. I'm too busy focusing on how they're *not* how I need them to be in order for my life to be the way I *want*—talk about the "director." I'm dying to say "we" in all of this and drag Randy's process into it, but that's another "new" awareness; Randy is none of my business.

I have a greater understanding of "security." I can see that in the past, my security in relationships was based on dependency and need and then it shifted to being based on loyalty, trust, honor, and commitment. However, I'm beginning to see that the notion of "security" is an illusion when referring to anything that is visible. I need to give up all notions of my security having anything to do with Randy at all; no matter what it's based on. The only thing I need to be secure in is the understanding that God is working out my process for my highest good. God only knows what that means.

I don't know what to think. I can see how going separate ways from Randy would be a valuable learning experience for each of us, but I can also see how learning to truly love, respect, and honor each other would be equally valuable. I guess it doesn't matter. The decision's not really mine. It will all work out the way it's supposed to.

We trust infinite God rather than our finite selves.
We are in the world to play the role He assigns.
Just to the extent that we do as we think He would have us,
and humbly rely on Him,
does He enable us to match calamity with serenity.[317]
Alcoholics Anonymous

December 20, 1998

I just realized that "sharing" your life with another doesn't mean living the same life—never being apart. To truly "share" is to have two separate lives that meet; and that meeting place is the nest of the heart; the place that is always with you—even in your lover's absence. When I go into my separate life, yet still have full awareness of Randy's reality, I have a window into a whole other world through him.

Neat things are happening. The storm seems to be calming for today with a new sense of peace and connection between Randy and me—even though he's a Deacon in the Anglican Church and I'm back at Unity. Forget trying to do it together. I think that believing we're supposed to has been the problem.

I was recently instructed by God to focus on the solar plexus—the love chakra—chakra four. Anyway, ever since, my world has been changing. I can finally see the blossom in my brother's heart. Does this mean that I am just now blossoming myself? I don't know. I don't even care. All I know is that I feel more a "part of" than ever before. I want to say that I "finally" feel a "part of," but I think I've realized that statements like that are absurd. There's no *finally* on an infinite journey. So, I probably haven't experienced the peak of a "part of," but it's new, improved, and richer than before. This journey really expands my mind.

These days my whole life is just about patiently observing the unfolding of the events that I have spent twelve years anticipating. I know who I am and my time is coming.

Love one another, but make not a bond of love:
Let it rather be a moving sea between the shores of your souls.[318]
Kahlil Gibran

January 3, 1999

1999! This should be an interesting year. The collective consciousness of the human race is going nuts. I'm curious to see whose beliefs will build the critical mass. There are the ones who believe that the world is coming to an end by supernatural powers, there are the ones who believe that entropy is winding us down to hell in a hand basket, and there are the ones who believe that the New Kingdom is being established and that the ushers are being put in place (this is what I believe). I'm convinced that there are many of us being placed in position for the mass awakening that is coming. The ushering process is more like being an usher at an arena—leading everyone in towards the center.

I have a dream that some day every valley shall be exalted,
every hill and mountain shall be made low,
the rough places will be made plains,
and the crooked places will be made straight,
and the glory of the Lord shall be revealed,
and all flesh shall see it together.[319]
Martin Luther King, Jr.

February 1, 1999

One of the girls I sponsor fired me because I directed her to read stuff from Saint Augustine's prayer book; non A.A. approved literature. Some other people in the program persuaded her that going outside of the box is dangerous. There are people in A.A. who think I'm a nut because I believe that I can hear God's voice.

Situations like this can be painful and frustrating. However, this is probably an eye-opener for me to realize that I need to focus on my studies and the book so that I can reach a like-minded audience. Many of the people in A.A. are like Pharisees who want to believe that only "pure" A.A. recovery is valid; that religion and psychology are invalid. Just as the eastern teachings of Buddha can be discerned in the teachings of Jesus, the higher truths can be discerned in the Twelve Step literature. However, I guess if you don't have direct experience with these things, you just can't see that they're there.

Sometimes being able to see clearly is a royal pain. It's definitely a great lesson in patience and tolerance. Of course, he who has the greatest level of understanding has the responsibility to demonstrate it. Therefore, they get to think that I'm a nut and I get to love them, tolerate them, and pray for them until nothing but warm regard floods my heart.

Now, Paige, what is so bad about that?

I guess I get the point. Silly me.

When love and hatred cannot affect you,
Profit and loss cannot touch you,
Praise and blame cannot ruffle you,
You are honored by all the world.[320]
Lao-Tzu

April 15, 1999

I'm on a big ship sitting in front of the Cayman Islands (Randy's Dad died and we inherited a small fortune). This "vacation" has really made me appreciate my life. I guess a person is pretty blessed when being in gorgeous surroundings, being waited on hand and foot, and having no responsibilities is a sacrifice because it means being away from a rich, beautiful, and fulfilling life; not to mention being away from my precious, adorable children and from my friends.

This trip has made me realize that a lot of the joy of life comes from the relationships and the connectedness with others. I guess I came here to relax and to realize these things. There truly is no place like home and home is where you are planted so that the beauty of your heart springs up around you.

The best and most beautiful things in the world cannot be seen or even touched.
They must be felt with the heart.
Helen Keller

June 29, 1999

The theme of the month has been the process from "belief" to "faith." I can see how even the tiniest amount of willingness to believe with reciprocal action can lead to a small faith that in turn will lead to a willingness to believe in something a little more profound until belief + action = a willingness to believe that, with God, *all things are possible* ... even for us *all* to live happily ever after.

August 17, 1999

It's occurred to me that I need to consider the possibility that *everything* I've ever believed is *not* true; not pick and choose what to let go of, but to just let go of it *all* ... and see what remains.

Wonder if I'm *not* who I think I am? Wonder if I'm just Paige, the housewife? Wonder if the most important thing I'll ever do is love the people around me? Wonder if I *am* Paige the Prophet for the twenty-first century? Wonder if, even then, the most important thing I'll ever do is love the people around me? Something has changed, but I'm not sure what. What once seemed alluring to me about myself is becoming rough and jagged.

I have already received the highest level of recognition that I can ever receive—*I know who I am*. But I am truly realizing that a greater recognition is who I am *not*. I am *not* God. The Spirit moves through me at times, but that has *nothing* to do with me. I am nothing of myself. I must be an empty vessel—suspend all judgment against others … and against myself. By thought, word, or deed, harm no one … not even me … be an empty space … take the "I" out of me and create a space in Paige … a blank page to write the names of everyone I meet in love … and don't forget my name also.

I tend to switch back and forth between judging others and beating myself up for judging others. Peace … be still … and know that I AM is God … something is changing … the wind is changing. I release myself into Your hands, Abba … my Father … my Mother … my All … my God.

Man is not blessed because God is in him and so near that he has God—but in that he is aware of how near God is, and knowing God, he loves him.[321]

Meister Eckhart

October 7, 1999

I've been having an experience with humility. Like I said before, something is shifting. All of the things that once seemed important just don't matter anymore. Just trying to be a nice person is what matters … and believe me, that 'aint easy. I feel myself becoming quieter. I know this is about Steps Six and Seven and relying even more on God.

It is so true that there are no big deals. The inheritance, having a flock of sponcees, everything going "my way" … all to find out that these things don't matter. The *only* thing that matters is love … and sometimes I don't know how to love. I guess life really is all about learning just how much I need God.

If God is for us, who can be against us?

Romans 8:31

November 17, 1999

It's 5:00 in the morning and I woke up to a startling revelation. At least I thought it was until I read the last two entries and saw that this is a process that has been happening to me for the past several months.

I've been having a life-sized version of the experience with the lesson of *just because you can do something doesn't necessarily mean that it's the right thing to do.* Yea, yea, yea; what the mind of man can conceive and believe, it can achieve ... but what is the motive behind the desire for the achievement?

There's a huge difference between activity and achievement. I'm beginning to see that the only achievement that matters is love. The only activity that is worthy is that which consists of actions that are motivated by love. That's it! Examine your motives! If love is not the motive, then move on to what you are to do that *is* motivated by love. Needless to say, I'm definitely becoming aware of the fact that a lot of my goals and aspirations have not been motivated by love, but by the tremendous need for recognition, approval, and attention. That need was a character defect. My instinct for prestige was out of whack. *That* is what has been changing ... it is going away.

Life is not about sitting around dreaming up things to accomplish or master. It is about relationships ... with God, myself, and others. It is about love and love is *work* made visible. That's another way of saying that love is service to others and that service to others is the highest form of loving oneself.

I've been learning a lot about limitations and their transcendence. I once told Randy that we have to become aware of our limitations in order to transcend them. That is true, I suppose, but we must examine our motives for wanting to transcend them. Sometimes a fence is at the side of the road as a way of saying, *do not enter.* Why would I think that in the invisible realm, a barrier (or limitation) means *get a bulldozer and tear it down?* Talk about self-determined objectives! I'm starting to see that maybe I should stay within the limits in order to find out where the fence ends. I trust it ends at a love that knows no bounds. I see that I have been like a kid on the cars at Six Flags who had the idea that the point was to jump the tracks and to drive the car to whatever place I could dream of. When I look at it that way, I can see how full of self-will those ideas are. I think I better just scoot over and enjoy the ride; just get on the unicorn and quit telling it where we're going!

I see why they say to put yourself at the top of the Eighth Step list. We don't work these Steps; we just step into a process that works us. My experience is putting my name at the top of the amends list because what is happening to me is the removal of defects that have driven me and caused me to miss out on so much joy and love. I've been so busy trying to be spiritual that I couldn't be still.

I heard someone say in a meeting last night that if she is in a room by herself, she can't practice her defects. That's just not my experience. If life is about relationships, the most important relationship is the one between God and me (which also includes the one between me and myself). The defects that affect *that* relationship are the most devastating and I can practice those anywhere and in any situation. I do not need other people around to separate myself from God.

All the harm I have caused other people stems from the harm that I experience when my character defects block me from God. Though the idea is to *do unto others as you would have them do unto you*, the reality is that we *do unto others as we do unto ourselves.* Think about that for awhile. "Easy does it" is taking on new meaning.

Back to the limitations: I'm beginning to believe that true transcendence of limitation is to let go of the idea that you have to push beyond the limit in the first place. One more time, peace of mind is the name of the game … that's the gauge. If the red light flashes … indicating a lack of peace … that's a warning sign. One of my biggest limitations was the belief that I have to be important and special in the eyes of others in order to be important and special to God—another lie shattered by the power of God's amazing love.

Life's a trip—enjoy the ride.

Who shall separate us from the love of Christ?
Shall tribulation, or distress, or persecution, or famine,
or nakedness, or peril, or sword?
In all these things we are more than conquerors through Him who loved us.
Romans 8:35–36

January 2, 2000

2000! Brother, I expected to be queen (no princess) of the universe by now. No kidding—what we think is going on is not what is going on. I really can see that maybe we do know where we're going, but *objects in our mind may be farther away than they seem.*

More important than my goal of establishing a church that unifies tradition and universal principles (my ultimate, long-term goal; which includes ordination, etc.), I now need to learn to love and respect my husband. I'm beginning to truly see that the latter is a step to the former. I know that I've observed this before, but one more time I'm seeing that God provides what I need; which aligns my *wants* with His will. I *want* what I want *now!* I *need* to learn to be patient.

Rome was not built in a day.
Rome was not built in a week.
Rome was not built in a decade.

It's taking a lifetime to build Rome.

It's okay, though, because the experience of building Rome is what it's all about. That's the point of all creation … for God to experience Himself … for us to experience ourselves.

I guess I've always needed to believe I was accomplishing a lot in order to feel good about myself. Now, I'm beginning to see that I don't need to feel good about myself anymore. I can just feel good about being a part of this marvelous dance of life.

The journey really is a celebration of sobriety; which is really just another word for "conscious awareness." I used to dream of walking the "Master Path." Recovery *is* the Master Path because if you continue to take personal inventory and to make amends (which means *to change*) you get to shoot beyond the stars.

Twenty-first century, here I come!

Whatever you can do or dream you can, begin it.
Boldness has genius, power, and magic in it.[322]
Johann Wolfgang Von Goethe

.19.

beginning ministry

February 10, 2000 – September 24, 2001

The first and most basic task of the Christian leader in the future will be to lead his people out of the land of confusion into the land of hope. Therefore, he must first have the courage to be an explorer of the internal world and to articulate his discoveries as a service to the inward generation.[323]
Henri Nouwen

February 10, 2000

Anniversary #4!

Randy left the church where he was ordained and our ministry together is beginning! We got accepted by the Free Catholic Church and gathered people for feedback; which ended up beginning our church, *One Hope.* Every detail is coming to me in perfect synchronicity. It's true! This is real! I've always known it was real, but to see it finally beginning to manifest is an experience I just can't describe. It's a mixture of relief, excitement, and fear—all at once.

I've prayed and prayed for God to show me the truth if I'm just a deranged, deluded lunatic with grandiose dreams, but all I get back is

> **"Why don't you just trust what you have been told for thirteen years and stop being afraid?"**

I'm afraid to stop being afraid. I know this is all silly because this not my deal, but the energy has definitely shifted. The church beginning to manifest is grounding *and exciting* me.

Conduct your triumph as a funeral.[324]
Lao-tzu

March 3, 2000

Randy had a series of experiences right after our anniversary that catapulted him into a new experience with God. He's more open now to a bigger truth. God is an awesome God!

We're moving into the Lenten season, which is the perfect time to correlate the sacraments of Baptism, Confession, and Reconciliation with the process of Steps Three through Nine. I had a realization that the Trinity is like a handshake. The Holy Spirit is activated when we reach our hand in response to God and say, *Yes, I will cooperate ... I am willing to take you as my partner* (Third Step—Baptism). This is the birthing of Christ. The maturation of Christ occurs through the process of facing and being rid of the causes and conditions that block us. Until Christ is expressing Himself through us, we are still immature. Spiritual Man will not be complete until Christ is expressing Himself through loving service to the entire Body. I really believe that what is going on here is a way to bring true Christianity, the Steps, and the Sacraments into a living, breathing reality for people.

I feel so alive and in my element now that the prep is finally over and the true service has begun. Not that I don't need further preparation. It's just great to finally have the church I've always known was coming. And You, my precious Lord, sit on the throne—leading the way. You did not make me for myself. I live for You and I accept my cross and my mission. Give me the strength and courage to carry through.

I will prepare and some day my chance will come. [325]
Abraham Lincoln

April 1, 2000

Randy has been having a huge struggle. My sponsor helped me see that I have to look for loving, thoughtful ways to respond to him. I basically see that between "*ask and it will be given to you*" (*Matthew 7:7*) is the journey of self-examination concerning what really motivates us, accountability to another human being, a willingness to be different, and responding in different ways.

This is the difference between being able to wear life like a loose garment as opposed to allowing life to choke you to death.

I just had an epiphany. I see Randy resisting life when he says, *I'm so tired of… whatever.* I've been saying *I'm so tired of always trying to point out truth to Randy. I'm not his sponsor, his therapist, nor his conscience.* However, maybe I better face the fact that I *am* those things to him because any behavior that is less than loving is a cry for help. Whenever anyone, anywhere, reaches out for help, I want the hand of God to be there. For this I am responsible. What is the hand of God, but the voice of truth?

Do you want to do something beautiful for God?
There is a person who needs you. This is your chance.[326]
Mother Teresa

May 4, 2000

The church is moving right along, but not as successfully as we had hoped. It's just not as simple as saying, *Come, I'll make you fishers of men.* The energy of attraction takes time to build momentum. A lot of people run their heads about wanting to be ministers, etc … and then can't keep moving forward when push comes to shove, but who am I to judge? Staying committed to things is one of the hardest things for me also. A.A. is the first thing I never quit; which has helped to teach me not to quit my marriage, my job, my ministry … and which has helped me not to give up on my dream … which is definitely coming true by the way.

I'm excited, but I have a very busy, tight schedule which will wear me out if I don't stay poised mentally. I'm getting a crash course in how to stay focused on one thing at a time (the thing in front of me). This enables me to be capable of myriad tasks. I'm able to work, workout, study, clean house, be a mom and wife, sponsor two people, have a church and do all of it's administrative stuff, do the book work on the business, plan sermons and readings, and be a Step speaker all at the same time … and … keep a reasonable meeting schedule. That made me tired writing it. However, like I said, as long as I plan and prepare well and then only focus on one thing at a time, it's no big deal. It's actually quite amazing. It really is all about letting God express Himself through me to greater heights.

I spoke at my home group on May 7. It was like the pinnacle of A.A. speaking engagements and it went very well. They turned right around and asked me to do the Steps there. I start tonight. It is almost unreal to me that I am going to do the Steps at that group. I want to say that I can't believe it, but of course I believe it … I've even always known that this would happen. It's just like everything though; when it's actually happening, it's not anything like you would imagine it to be. Rather than feeling all excited and grandiose, it's actually kind of humbling. I have a very strong sense of stillness about it all. I feel quite certain that the only way to walk through this is slowly … holding God's hand all of the way. This whole thing is really no big deal anymore, but it's one heck of an experience!

If you ever let yourself feel good when people tell you you're okay, you are preparing yourself to feel bad when they tell you you're not good.[327]
Anthony DeMello

June 6, 2000

The Step speaking was a great success and the church is picking up. Randy and I are doing the back-to-back sermon thing that I always envisioned. It's great, but it's very draining. The prep for the sermon (research, etc.) and the energy created for its delivery just zaps me. The Steps zap me each time also. I can definitely see why Jesus went to the top of the mountain to pray alone. Being a conduit for the Holy Spirit is exhausting.

Of course, all of this is the "down" side of the dream—the hidden part—the part that builds the character. I sometimes regret that I am getting such a late start at all of this, but I also know in my heart of hearts that being an alcoholic and an actively involved member of A.A. is meant to be a part of it.

Everything's very interesting. We're having horrible financial problems, but I figure we'll go broke if we're supposed to go broke. No kidding … freedom's just another word for nothing left to lose. No, it's another word for nothing left to *fear* losing. There's nothing I am afraid to lose as far as material possessions go so I don't really care what financial level ends up being the one we can maintain on.

Well, even though the road seems to have ended at the cliff of the mountain, my instructions are to keep moving forward so, once again … I jump.

Alone and without his nest … the eagle shall fly across the sun.[328]
Kahlil Gibran

August 8, 2000

The church is going well. Preaching has made me totally uninterested in sharing in A.A. A.A. itself is becoming a drain because so much of its focus is on *not drinking*. The level of spirituality is so base in there compared to what happens when you hitch your wagon to Jesus and the other sacred traditions. Even though the A.A. literature says that libraries and places of worship are full of great books about prayer and meditation, most people just read the *Daily Reflections,* go to a meeting, and live by the motto that we "never rise above human." All that bores me, but this is probably just a stage. I know I'm judging so I just have to practice compassion.

One can never consent to creep when one feels an impulse to soar.[329]
Helen Keller

October 18, 2000

The church has been dwindling, as well as my enthusiasm for it. I'm really starting to realize that most people really don't want to grow any more than they have to. This has made me much more easy-going on the structure of the church so we're going to switch to a more conservative Bishop. I don't care either way. It's kind of a relief to realize that I don't have to figure out a way to get people to dive in spiritually. I just have to do it myself—which is my pleasure.

Most people tell you they want to get out of kindergarten, but don't believe them.[330]
Anthony DeMello

December 26, 2000

I am wiped out! My biggest dream has been to be a minister, but I never bargained for what a hard job it is. Things are definitely going according to plan, but the new has worn off. God always told me that I would have what I want when I could care less about it. I see what He meant. What He didn't tell me was that my dream would become a pain.

I'm just tired. The Christmas season was intense and, like a fool, I agreed to do the Steps at an A.A. group also. That always stresses me out. However, watching all of this unfold is nothing short of amazing. Since my ego has already grown tired of the gig, I get a life-size picture of how it is *not me* writing those sermons and delivering those talks. They literally come through me and they are fantastic!

I've decided I don't care if I ever learn to fly. I'm tired of trying so hard to get something I already have. I know the sages of old say that no one can ever know God without years of active pursuit, but that just hasn't been my experience. Maybe I don't know God at all, but I trust the process. I cannot put my family on hold while I sit all day in meditation saying, *Go away kid, I'm getting spiritual.*

With all that's been going on, I can now see that I am a disciple of Christ, but I am not Christ. The line of delineation is too clear. Of myself, I am selfish and hateful. All I have is a daily reprieve contingent on the maintenance of my spiritual condition. Some days I maintain better than others.

The years are flying by and I am becoming aware that I am middle aged. I guess I'm just growing up.

Today I don't want to live for,
I want to live.[331]
Hugh Prather

January 26, 2001

Wow! It's the crack of dawn and I'm locked in the bathroom so I can have a place to write without waking everyone up. I just had an experience with Jesus. He told me that we literally send our substance to one another with our thoughts. A soul built on prayer is a blessing to all because it radiates at a higher level and automatically has concern for the world. No act of kindness is ever wasted. Even the smallest thoughts of concern send love to that person. On the other hand, negative thoughts send that energy also and harm those who have not consciously claimed protection for themselves. So the more we allow our soul to be cultivated by God, we help Him to take the maturity of the whole race to a different level.

My beloved Lord Christ, thank You for this opportunity to be a part of this great work. I give myself completely and I take this opportunity to declare that I send my love into this world to break the bonds of darkness and superstition. I release all error everywhere and substitute it with the great reality of Your Way, Your Truth, and Your Life. Thy will be done. Power to the mission! Look out world—His kingdom comes!

For God so loved the world that He gave His only begotten Son,
that whoever believes in Him should not perish but have everlasting life.
John 3:16

And this is eternal life, that they may know You, the only true God.
John 17:3

March 9, 2001

I did some energy psychology with a therapist yesterday. It irritates me that those people charge so much money for services that should be just that—service. Anyway, I addressed the energy block I sometimes experience in my lower chakras. It's all about my vulnerability. It's time for me to literally extend my body affectionately; to stop holding back my embrace. Before being a mother, the only way I could express myself physically was sexually. The Lord told me that vanity was vulnerability playing dress-up. It's all been a façade to cover the child in me that wants to throw her arms around the world and say, *I love you!*

Life is either a daring adventure or nothing.
Helen Keller

April 26, 2001

I have been having a weird experience this week. I was finally ordained as a deacon last Saturday and it had a strange effect on me. I am beginning to see that this is not a joke and that I had better start taking my calling more seriously. This is real and it's not about being larger than life, but about living the life of Christ. On some level, I have been in denial about all of this. All my ego could see was fame and attention, but now I see that I am here to glorify God; not myself.

For the first time, I am not cock-sure, but very apprehensive and reluctant. I am willing to do and be whatever my Lord would have me be, but I see clearly that I am absolutely incapable of doing or being those things through my power.

The one thing that I am responsible for throughout my life I cannot generate.
The only thing I need to do I cannot do.
But such is the meaning of radical dependence.[332]
Brennan Manning

May 2, 2001

I think it's a big cosmic conspiracy that Mother God has been taken out of the picture. Randy and I were talking and he said that the balance of female/male energy is what we need. Ironically, he needs to blend more male with the female and I need to blend more female with the male.

I've been too guided by intelligence, order, and organization and it sometimes overrides the little child within me. In the branch of Jesse (Isaiah 11), it says, "*a little child will lead them.*" Love is a feminine energy and it should be the lead and guiding principle. However, it needs the male energy to protect it, but not immobilize it. That's my challenge personally; not to let the pragmatism of my male energy block me from the beauty and reality of pure innocence and love.

For the human race to have a chance to survive, this cosmic sacred marriage between the feminine and masculine forces within the One has to be mirrored and enacted in our being at every level. At every level there has to be a fusion between our masculine and feminine energies, a fusion between those polarities we have been taught to keep apart—between our vision of "heaven" and our vision of earth," between what we have called "sacred" and what we have called "profane," between our innermost mystical awareness and our political, technological, and economic choices.[333]

Andrew Harvey

May 5, 2001

Putting others first can turn something that you don't even want to do into a spiritual experience. We took the kids to a corny show last night; one that we would never go to alone unless we were just bored. Anyway, enjoying it with the kids brought back magical feelings I had when I did things like that with Dad. I just realized that for years after I was grown, I wanted to get dressed up and go out to fancy restaurants in order to recreate scenes like I had with Dad. I always had to use alcohol to get the feeling just right. It just occurred to me that the magic was spending time with Dad and feeling as if I were loved; "making memories" as Shannon calls it. Anyway, it was a blessing to make some memories with and for my own kids. We went to the show and then took them dancing. It was a joyous blast!

Thank you, precious Lord, for the gift of these children and for making me the parent you would have me be.

For in the dew of little things the heart finds its morning and is refreshed.[334]

Kahlil Gibran

May 8, 2001

The new agers say that we have to "stake our claim," which I know has validity, but the Bible says to *ask* and you receive. There seems to be a fine line here. It seems like some think that we are supposed to *take* what He wants to *give* us.

July 12, 2001

I co-facilitated a *Big Book Awakening* retreat in Nashville and the Lord led me to baptize people, wash their feet, and give them communion at the end. It was awesome. Words can't adequately describe what happened.

I've had a huge breakthrough this week. I realized that on some level I have believed all anger was "wrong." Last night I prayed and asked what to do with my anger and I was told

> **"to use it to move me toward right action."**

The other day I had a very long and deep meditation in which I hit into a deep pocket of very old pain. I asked what it was and I was told that it was

> **"my fear of being open and vulnerable."**

I thought that meant I had a fear of being open and vulnerable in a sweet sort of way; like I do with Randy sometimes. I now realize that it's also a fear of speaking up and standing up for the truth. I understand in the program that when we are "defending our rights" we are usually in self-pity, but I think that this is different; it's older. It's more like standing up and defending what is right—period.

My fear of people manifests itself in different ways; depending on whether the person I'm afraid of is male or female. The typical way in which I have viewed my fear of vulnerability has been in regard to males. I'm afraid that if I open up to a man I will be overwhelmed and consumed, but I see that I fear that if I "stand up" to a woman I will be abandoned.

This is all so obvious if you look at my situations with Mom and Dad, but it's taken my whole life to come to light. My abandonment issues are with my Mom. I have issues with women that make me a horrible people-pleaser and very scared that I will be hurt through abandonment. These realizations will help me to break the cycle and respond differently.

Thank you, precious Lord, for the clarity to see the truth.

It often requires more courage to dare to do right than to fear to do wrong.[335]

Abraham Lincoln

August 13, 2001

I realized that our only job in this world is to get out of God's way (like that's a big realization).

My step-son, Michael, has come to live with us. This is a huge struggle because I know it is what is best for him, but it is very disruptive to my comfort level because I feel invaded. I just pray that the discomfort passes. I have periods where I feel very resentful about it, but Randy has always been welcoming of Laurel and he is so happy to have Mike here. My immaturity and self-centeredness are getting a run for their money.

When Michael came to live with us, I felt very threatened by him. I wanted to love him as my own child, but I was too selfish and immature. I had a big breakthrough with this issue when I finally threw myself on the bathroom floor one morning and confessed to God the level of petty hatred within me. Over time He exchanged my *ashes for a crown of beauty* (Isaiah 61:3) and I grew to genuinely love Michael as my own son.

I tell you one thing—
If you want peace of mind,
Do not find fault with others.
Rather learn to see your own faults.
Learn to make the whole world your own.
No one is a stranger, my child;
This whole world is your own.[336]
Sri Sada Devi

August 28, 2001

I am seeing why I am sometimes too soft—not able to make a stand. I bend over backwards at times to be nice in order to fend off my old deep-seeded fear that I am bad. Every time I lose my temper or have angry thoughts, the old tape says, *See, you're really just a jerk!* My loving Father says it isn't so, but I'm having a real experience with it because I keep beating myself up and telling myself that I'm an imposter.

I am really starting to see how vitally important conscious contact is because nice, set rules don't always apply. To promptly admit when I'm wrong or to settle matters quickly with my adversary don't always apply. Actually, they do apply, but I have to go deeper to get to the truth. I have to promptly admit to myself my own wrong doings, but I have to let God time-out the amends.

I see that I do a lot of appeasing just so I can be okay because I don't want people to dislike me. I make amends as a way of people pleasing.

This is all a bit confusing, but I guess I'm getting to take my life to a new level of sincerity because I'm getting to see that the real adversary with whom I need to settle matters quickly is *me*—that I may see clearly to take the speck out of my brother's eye. In my case, the beam in my own eye is the tendency at times to beat up on myself for certain situations, which probably need further investigation, and then to try to patch things up without getting the wound totally cleaned up.

I was crying to God that I was powerless, and He told me that I have all the power I need; I've just been using it to try to control others—ouch!—but true. If recovery is about owning the lies we tell ourselves—wouldn't the ultimate thing be to own the truth?

The hero of my story is The Truth.[337]
Leo Tolstoy

September 24, 2001

I have been in a bad place. The disaster at the World Trade Center has had a devastating effect on me. I've really had to search my soul to figure out what the point of all this is. The point is to grow along spiritual lines—period.

I've gotten to see lately that my motives for the ministry have not necessarily been to serve, but to succeed. It is not meeting my expectations so at least now I can surrender those expectations and just suit up, show up, and do my job. The outcome is really none of my business, but I have a hard time remembering that.

I know in my heart of hearts that all that really matters is to learn to love (and that's a full-time job). This WTC thing has been good for all of us. It's showing us what really matters. My problem is that I'm not turbo-charged with enthusiasm over what really matters.

Getting to the core (allowing myself to be vulnerable enough to really love) is very painful to me. No wonder I've been super-woman. Getting the wind taken out of my sails has shown me how much pain I have inside of me.

On a deep, deep, level, I still have the idea that I'm just not enough. I have faith, though, that this is being worked out. I regret that I have been less than compassionate with depressed people at the group because I had forgotten what it was like to be paralyzed. It's not so easy to put one foot in front of the other when all you want to do is lay down.

I know that this too shall pass. The sun is still shining behind the clouds.

Sometimes it is just hard for me to accept that life is difficult. When innocent people die in a senseless and loveless way, you just can't get around that.

Any Christian writer who ignores the grim realities of raw, undifferentiated heartache, cosmic disorder, and the terror of history or dismisses them as inconsequential is either naïve, dishonest, or disconnected from the trust busting anguish of many struggling seekers and believers.[338]

Brennan Manning

.20. seasoning salt

October 11, 2001 – August 25, 2002

You are the salt of the earth;
but if the salt loses its flavor, how shall it be seasoned?
Matthew 5:13

October 11, 2001

I am no longer depressed and paralyzed over the idea that my priorities were messed up. I accept it and am now enthusiastic about what really matters, but not driven. I see that there is a difference. To be enthused about something is to do it *with Spirit.*

I have decided that I do not want to preach every Sunday anymore. Since the WTC disaster, the church seems insignificant to me, yet the *people* at the church don't. I realize that that they don't need me up there preaching as much as they need me to just be there for them and to love them.

Anyway, I am willing to accept the fact that the church is just a small little group of people who pray and love together. I am not the hub of the wheel. They don't come to hear me. If they come, they just come to be a part of.

I am here to serve—not to succeed—that my ministry may be a joy rather than a job.

That's a good one. I still feel very motivated to write that stupid book, but I also feel apprehensive about it. I'm not sure if I need to write it because it will help someone or if I just need to get it over with so I can forget about it. All I can do is share my experience, warts and all.

What is most personal and unique in each one of us is probably the very element which would, if it were shared or expressed, speak most deeply to others.[339]
Carl Rogers

October 16, 2001

I am uncomfortable with all of the High-Church protocol at *One Hope.* Mainstream Christianity gives me heartburn because it just doesn't gel with my experience. I have felt very hostile towards Randy because I feel as though he is standing in the way of allowing the church to move in its own direction and to take on its own identity.

Randy and I are in definite disagreement about a few things. He says the job of the deacon is to preach and to serve at the altar. Forget being a deacon, then. Besides, I thought the job of the deacon was to be the liaison between the priest and the people.

Randy keeps saying that the people aren't informed or committed enough to have an opinion. I think that's nonsense. How can we serve them without having a finger on the pulse of their needs and wants? Randy keeps telling me not to talk to the people about stuff. I suppose that's protocol at a lot of churches, but I think that's nonsense too! What I yearn for is real community where people feel that they are heard (including me) and where we can agree to disagree.

I've been reading *A Different Drum* about community building in which Scott Peck talks about "pseudo community;" a gathering where everyone sits politely, smiles, and pretends to be like-minded. In my opinion, that's where Randy is trying to lead us. I think it's more important to celebrate our differences and allow the community to express itself in order to become something bigger than any of the individuals.

I feel like I need to go solo if Randy and I can't come to a compromise. This situation is really bothering me, though, because I have a deep fear of being wrong. There's an ancient belief that tells me it's not okay to have my own opinion. There's a part of me that needs Randy to agree with me in order to feel valid myself.

Maybe I'm really just a quitter and a poor leader. I guess there is a difference in realizing that something is not for me and "quitting." No, I am afraid of looking foolish! This is about the fear of how I look to others! By God, I just need to stick to it so nobody can say I'm a "quitter." Heck, I only went through the ordination process so that no one could say that I was illegitimate. But I'm beginning to see that to take action in my life in order to try to control what others think about me is pride and manipulation. However, soliciting honest feedback from other people I trust is humbling.

I want to believe that to try and fail is hopeful, but there is something deep within me that still believes that to fail is to be a loser. Quitter—loser—bad girl. My deepest fear is that this is the truth of me. What is this thing within me that will not let me rest in peace?

Pride has its root and strength in a terrible spiritual power, outside of us as well as within us. As necessary as it is that we confess and deplore pride as our very own, of equal importance is the recognition of its satanic origin. If this leads to the utter despair of ever conquering or casting it out, it will lead us all the sooner to that supernatural power in which alone our deliverance is to be found.[340]

Andrew Murray

December 6, 2001

My 40/15th birthday came and went. On one hand, I can't believe that I have been on the path for fifteen years, but on the other, I can't believe that all of this has happened in *just* fifteen years.

Mom gave me a "surprise" party and I acted like an ingrate. It was very painful to be such an ass. A deep inventory showed me that "Baby Paige—Mad Baby Paige" is in there begging for love and then toughly saying *I don't need anybody—and no matter how hard you try Mom, you'll never be able to be the Mom I need. You'll never be able to make it up to me!* Not pretty, huh?

One element of maturity
is the realization that we don't get away with anything.
Progress is dirty business.
We are taught the smell of the ego's reward
as well as the fragrance of the heart.[341]

Hugh Prather

December 31, 2001

This year flew by and I basically only learned one thing—above all things, love is the greatest. Both the ordination and September 11 point to this one thing only. Nothing really matters except our ability to love—and my ability basically stinks sometimes.

I mentioned the two events that caused this revelation, but I forgot to cite the two blessings where this love was fulfilled: Dad and Michael. This was the year that I fell in love with both of them.

And now abide faith, hope, love, these three; but the greatest of these is love.
1 Corinthians 13:13

January 12, 2002

I started a group to discuss Gwen Shamblin's *The Weigh Down*. It is causing me to have a tremendous experience with the Bible. Anyway, I am getting into a new level of obedience and it is truly changing me.

I'm starting to get some insight about my viewpoints on education and intelligence. In *A Different Drum* (excellent by the way), Peck gave one of the most intriguing and intuitively satisfying definitions of evil—*militant ignorance.*

When I think of ignorance, I basically think of uneducated people and when I think of militant ignorance, I think of extreme Islam or Christianity. However, I'm reading Huston Smith's *Why Religion Matters* and it is shedding a whole new light on things for me.

I'm beginning to see that ignorance and stupidity are not necessarily the same thing. Ignorance is darkness whereas wisdom is light. There are many viewpoints that Jesus is God's "Sophia"—"Wisdom." Yes, grace and love are aspects of Christ's nature, but I'm beginning to see that wisdom is paramount because it is the balance between both love and intelligence.

Anyway, I'm beginning to see that extreme intellectualism is also evil. A person can be intelligent and ignorant simultaneously. I have been that way when I have gotten too out of balance with trying to intellectually figure God out. And I have been way too judgmental with people who have a more emotional, faith-based approach to their world-view.

The human race has become so intelligent that it is absolutely ignorant to the truth. That's sad and it's frightening. The Apostles were writing letters about man-made rules and losing sensitivity to God 2000 years ago. Obviously, we haven't been listening.

The Christian ideal has not been tried and found wanting.
It has been found difficult and left untried.[342]
G.K Chesterton

January 14, 2002

Whew! I am in the middle of a mind-blowing spiritual experience. Yesterday, we did Philippians 2 at church. I love that scripture, but focusing on His humility got me in touch with my own arrogance. Jesus wasn't focused on His equality with God—He was focused on obedience—unto death—on a cross!

Yesterday, I got emotional and went into the bathroom to pray, but Hope wouldn't leave me alone. When I told her to go in the other room, she got mad at me and said, *I don't care about you.* I ignored it because I was caught up in my remorse over my arrogant attitude towards Christianity. As the words were coming out of my mouth, *Lord, please forgive me if I have done or said anything to dishonor you,* Hope knocked on the door saying, *Mommy, I am sorry I said that I didn't care about you.* Perfect synchronicity. My response was, *It's okay honey, I didn't take that seriously.* Exactly! It hit me like a ton of bricks.

"It's okay, honey, repentance and forgiveness are connected."

The admission that we are wrong is enough truth to let the light dawn in the darkness. It was a powerful experience.

Coming to terms with the magnitude of Jesus is showing me that the Holy Spirit is the captive remnant in all of us. We must die to self in order to return to the source, but the deception that self can accomplish the death of self is its last vestige of maintaining its identity. We cannot take the final step alone; we have to be led—ushered in. It is our Father's good pleasure to *give us* the kingdom. We have to *receive* the kingdom; not storm it ourselves. We don't get to seat ourselves at the wedding. We can't be seated in Heavenly places without Jesus.

Working the Steps, mystical practices, etc. all tie in to the experience—which is designed in order to motivate us to carry the message—but ultimately the bottom line is that we don't go home alone. We *can't* get home alone. We must become nothing so that God can truly be everything. This oneness with God *is* home; the Kingdom.

It's funny, on inventories, everyone's worst fear is to become nonexistent—to not matter.

Exactly Paige—not matter. You are not matter; you are spirit, but the final relinquishment of self requires surrender to the Teacher/Master—ME.

Duh, we can't use self-will to die to self. I've heard it a million times, but I finally get the point. Today, I abandon myself utterly to you, Jesus Christ, my Lord and Master. Thy will, not mine, be done.

Let this mind be in you which was also in Christ Jesus, who, being in the form of God, did not consider it robbery to be equal with God, but made Himself of no reputation, taking the form of a bondservant, and coming in the likeness of men. And being found in appearance as a man, He humbled Himself and became obedient to the point of death, even the death of the cross. Therefore God also has highly exalted Him and given Him the name which is above every name, that at the name of Jesus every knee should bow, of those in heaven, and of those on earth, and of those under the earth, and that every tongue should confess that Jesus Christ is Lord, to the glory of God the Father.

Philippians 2:5–11

January 16, 2002

The mind, heart, and soul blowing continues … Bottom line, Jesus is bigger than religion. Abstract concepts of God (the Godhead, ground of being, Father/Mother, etc.) all express concepts of the fact that God is indescribable, but that's the point—it can't be defined, figured out, etc. God has to be *experienced* to really be understood. Jesus is the only One who can really get us past the veil of self.

Authentic spirituality is not so much about the *death* of self as it is about the transformation of self into the nature and likeness of Jesus. He turns water into wine. This is the final surrender, but our awareness of being separate from others remains intact because we are meant to be a family; not just become one with the "One," break the cycle of birth and death, or even just go to Heaven. The Kingdom of Heaven is within. This story will not end until the Utopian Garden of Eden is restored on earth and inhabited by the universal priesthood.

We are at a true climax for this particular piece of history (the beginning of recorded time until now) because the human race is basically on a stretcher in the emergency room—dying if something doesn't drastically change. Our current ways of coping are ineffective because the monotheists are basically on a morphine drip to ease the suffering, the intellectuals are happy just to understand *why* we're dying, the new agers pretend that the crisis is not real, and politicians are happy as long as the patient *looks* alive.

At this time, right here, right now, Jesus is present and available to tell us what to do to save the patient (and don't forget that sweet mother earth is the patient too). The King is calling us to the round table to make us privy to what we need to know. There is one hope in God's call to us. He is going to save the day. Something big is getting ready to happen that's going to get our attention, but rest assured, victory is a done deal.

God's great objective in salvation is to acquire possession of the heart. God sent Christ to accomplish a redemption by which man's heart could be won back to Him ... Christianity is nothing if it is not, from the beginning to end, through all in all, the hidden, but direct and mighty, energy of the living God continuing and working out the great redemption that He accomplished in His Son ... A revival among God's children cannot even be thought of unless the average standard of religion with which we have been content is replaced.[343]

Andrew Murray

January 19, 2002

I woke up this morning with the words *The Kingdom of Heaven is Within You* bursting inside of me and then I realized that we are to live our lives from the inside out. It is our job to bring forth everything that is within us—what we don't will destroy us. I saw in the mirror clearly in order to see that the mirror is self and beyond it is eternal God. For every turkey, there's a Thanksgiving, but after the crucifixion is true celebration. We are meant to be Higher Powered and we are meant to be one.

What hinders us from the Holy of Holies? What but the presence of a veil in our hearts. It is the veil of our fleshly, fallen nature living on, unjudged within us, uncrucified and unrepudiated. It is the close-woven veil of the self-life which we have never truly acknowledged, of which we have been secretly ashamed, and which for these reasons we have never brought to the judgment of the cross. These are the hyphenated sins of the human spirit. They are not something we do, but something we are, and therein lies both their subtlety and their power. They dwell too deep within us and are too much a part of our natures to come to our attention till the light of God is focused upon them. Self can live unrebuked at the very altar.[344]

A.W. Tozer

The spiritual experience continued for three days; during which I had many dramatic visions and revelations. The occurrence became so frightening for Randy that he called 911 and had me taken to the hospital where I was diagnosed as having had a "psychotic break." However, I left against medical advice without being admitted and leveled out within three days.

February 4, 2002

I am in a lot of turmoil. Randy and I are at a standoff and I feel that I have no alternative than to resign from the church. I just can't play "Christian" anymore. Both times that I have had a big Jesus experience **(Cursillo and the recent experience)**, something crazy happened to derail the whole thing; which leads me to the conclusion that fall-redemption theology is a lie.

I really feel that the marriage is over also, but I'm willing to sit with that longer. All I know is that Randy and I are definitely not on the same page spiritually and that we actually deter each other rather than edify each other. I don't think that we love each other anymore. I enjoy the freedom of not having to work, but having to live in this turmoil is really not worth it. I don't know if staying together for the security of the family is good for the kids or not. We are so unhappy, but most of our conflicts concern our religious beliefs. Please God, show us the way.

That whole ordeal over the past few weeks has turned everything upside-down. Believe me, this prophet deal is a pain in the rear. I must admit that sometimes these experiences teeter on the edge to the extent of being frightening, but if I begin to doubt my experiences, I might as well just hang it up. My whole life depends on my ability to hear the voice of instruction.

Show me the way, Lord. I need to hear from you *now*.

Satan does not tempt us just to make us do wrong things—
he tempts us to make us lose what God has put into us through regeneration,
namely, the possibility of being of value to God.[345]
Oswald Chambers

After that experience, I got two new sponsors and quit the church; which caused me to become increasingly estranged from Randy. Simultaneously, Randy got involved in Kairos prison ministry and became more and more of an evangelical Christian and began to accuse me of having a belief system that was influenced by the "dark side." I became so outraged by that accusation that I moved out of our home with Laurel and Hope and rented an apartment.

June 27, 2002

It is amazing to me how my mind tries to rewrite history in a positive way concerning Randy. My memories of him are just like romantic memories of drinking. I remember the pseudo warm-fuzzies and not the life draining turmoil and oppression.

As time continues to pass in my separation from him, I question whether

I ever really loved him because I question whether or not I really know what love is. I hope I get to find out. My new sponsors were right; what Randy and I were doing was *not* love. I think that the relationships I have with Hope and Laurel are the closest I've come to manifesting true love because I really do care about what's best for *them*.

Leaving Randy was one of the most loving acts I performed in the relationship as far as his best interests are concerned. It saddens me to realize how dependent on each other we were; to see that so much of our love affair was about using each other to avoid pain and responsibility. I'm not saying that we didn't have some beautiful moments, but the relationship wasn't built on the foundation of mutual respect so it couldn't sustain for the long-haul. It has been a devastating blow to face these truths because I had one hundred percent believed that we would stay together forever. Divorce was not an option—which is pretty draining in a situation where it is inevitable.

Our scientific power has outrun our spiritual power.
We have guided missiles and misguided men. [346]
Martin Luther King Jr.

July 5, 2002

I have come to see that everything I perceive as attractive or exciting is a red flag that false identities are coming into play. All that mumbo-jumbo about love is a waste of intellectual energy. It seems that the only way that I am not surrounded by red flags is if I think, say, or do nothing. How outside-in I've been. To continue to follow in the direction where these "attractions" and "excitements" lead me will keep me in the cycle of delusion. *Be not a slave to desire and fear.*

No attachments. I AM …

I don't have much to say in the journal because so much is going on in my e-mail correspondence with my sponsor. He is truly an enlightened being. His very presence dispels darkness. He is certainly helping me to see what a child I have been. I'm learning that I always hang on to the idea that the voice inside of me is Jesus because I don't want to take responsibility for who I am. The fact is that it's really just me because, at the highest level, God is not personal. I have believed a fantasy so that I don't have to face the reality of my aloneness.

> *The nature of sin is not immorality and wrongdoing, but the nature of self-realization that leads us to say, "I am my own god"… Condemnation comes*

when I realize that Jesus came to deliver me from the heredity of sin, and yet I refuse to let him do it. From that moment I begin to get the seal of damnation.[347]

Oswald Chambers

July 14, 2002

So much I've been learning pertains to the lessons that I am in delusion if I think I know what's going to happen; that it's not my job to create my reality, but to let it be created through me by the universe. However, I can't deny these visions of the future that I've had since 1986 and I can't deny that the voice within seems to be something other than me that really cares about me. I'm confused.

Paige, let everything blossom—not yank the petals yourself. Hold the visions, but don't hold on to them. It's My job to bring them into manifestation. Hold your dreams in your heart and write them in here. A part of your mission is to be living proof that it is My good pleasure to give you the Kingdom. The evidence is these journals. Yes, they'll be published in time.

The way My highest ideals are projected to earth is through My creations—you. Never minimize the power of your thoughts, but know that I reside way beyond your thoughts or constructs. I am not your mind, but use it as a medium to communicate My ideals. However, the way to manifest them is to focus on the present moment and to be absolutely honest with yourself. Just like in sports, the eye must be kept on the ball, goal, etc., but the focus is internal—within the player.

Remember the vision, but observe the present moment. Be true to yourself and all will be added. Everything is as it should be. It's not over. Don't minimize all that I have told you these past sixteen years. You are one of My messengers, but you are not here to keep harping on the same worn-out message and you are definitely not here to conform to the Christian Church in its current state. You are here to bring the Church to repentance in true humility—that it may truly worship Me instead of the hateful doctrines of some very mediocre minds.

And I will not leave you without a worthy partner. I am as near as your breath and he is in the wings, being drawn as we speak. Don't give up on the dream five minutes before the miracle! It's all true, My love. I have given you the gift of vision; not to turn you in to a work horse, but to assure you that all is well and to give you the opportunity

to chronicle everything as evidence that I AM REAL! Hold the vision. Focus on the present moment. Hide nothing. I will have My way.

If we obey what God says according to our sincere belief, God will break us from those traditional beliefs that misrepresent Him.[348]
Oswald Chambers

August 20, 2002

Randy had a huge spiritual awakening and is back in the picture. I am experiencing some neediness and attachment that scare me because I don't want to lose myself in the relationship with him again, but it's still very nice to feel warm regard for Randy and to want to be with him again. I just want to be able to love him without being attached to him. I'm really starting to remember why I love Randy and to be proud of him and grateful for him.

I'm still a little in shock about everything because I truly had accepted that we would never get back together and I had really given up on the idea that he would wake up. It has taught me a lot about letting go and letting God.

A successful marriage requires falling in love many times, always with the same person.[349]
Mignon McLaughlin

August 25, 2002

I had a whirlwind weekend with Randy. By yesterday, we were wrapped up in romance and saying things like *I never want to spend another night without you.* We bought new wedding rings and went to the church and blessed them.

This morning, the first thoughts on my mind were that I am supposed to be doing something with the church. The Lord then told me this deal with Randy is about more than romance.

Randy and I ended up having a discussion about the religion stuff and I came to see that I am judgmental about his belief system, but I don't get it. I adore Jesus, but I just don't see how Randy could buy into all that "died for our sins" stuff. I don't know if we're going to be able to pull this thing off or not. I give this to You, Lord, and ask you to show us the way.

Love, the magician, knows this little trick whereby two people walk in different directions yet always remain side by side.[350]
Hugh Prather

.21. the power of the cross

November 16, 2002 – October 19, 2004

I believe what I believe is what makes me what I am
I did not make it, no it is making me
It is the very truth of God and not the invention of any man[351]
Rich Mullins and Beaker

Shortly after Randy and I were reunited, God told me that I was to serve on the upcoming Kairos prison ministry team that was just a few weeks away. Randy made the arrangements and I was on the outside team where we prepared food and prayed for the penitentiary inmates that were being served by the men's team that was inside the prison.

One evening of the weekend, I was awakened with the words *Humble thyself in the sight of the Lord* in my head and throughout the weekend the words *The wisdom of the world is foolishness to God* kept crossing my mind. The final morning of the weekend, as I was reading Oswald Chamber's *My Utmost for His Highest,* the voice within me spoke forcefully,

"The Gospel is true, Paige! The power is in the Gospel."

A few hours later, I went for a drive in the country. Since I didn't know the radio stations in the area, I searched through Randy's glove compartment and found an unmarked copy of a Rich Mullins CD. I had no idea what it was, but put it in so I could listen to some music. Just as I drove

past a small church, the song "Creed" began to play as I read the words on the church sign, ***Has not God made foolish the wisdom of this world?*** **(1 Corinthians 1:20)**

Immediately I felt as if streams of love and light were raining on me inside the car. I pulled over to the side of the road as the words; ***I believe in one God, the Father Almighty, maker of heaven and earth, and of all things visible and invisible. And in one Lord, Jesus Christ, the only-begotten Son of God*** **[352] began to burst from within my soul. I sat at the side of the road for over an hour—crying the words,** ***I believe it . . . I believe it!*** **At last, I was free indeed.**

For the message of the cross is foolishness to those who are perishing,
but to us who are being saved it is the power of God.
1 Corinthians 1:18

November 16, 2002

Many things have transpired and all I can say is that I am convinced that the Bible is absolutely true in even a *greater way* than literal. I am convicted that I have been under a huge spell and that it is broken now. I am convinced that there is only one true God and that the only way to Him is through Jesus because Jesus is the only One capable of defeating the enemy. Lack of power is our dilemma, but to believe that there is only *one* power in this world is a lie.

Anyway, let's just say that I have had a change of mind and heart and it is clear that my mission, if I actually have one, is to proclaim the name of Jesus Christ, to preach the Gospel, *and to denounce Satan.*

I see that the some of the concepts I've believed all sound good and get you to do the right things, but without acceptance of Jesus' crucifixion they're a setup that leads to a barrier that can't be broken. To merge with the cosmic "One" is to end up alone—believing that to care about and want other people in your life is an "attachment."

The biggest trick that Satan has played on us is to convince us that he doesn't exist. Believe me, he is real—but the Lord of all life has defeated him.

Jesus is not just a Way-Shower, a prophet, or a teacher; He is *the Way.* Jesus is God. He is the meek Lamb who was slain to take away the sins of the world *and* He is the mighty Lion who fights our battles for us. He is a warrior and He has won me from the darkness. He labored for sixteen years to deliver me and I am eternally grateful and in His service. Jesus Christ is the *only* power who can relieve me of the bondage of self.

We are ensnared by the wisdom of the serpent;
we are set free by the foolishness of God.[353]
Saint Augustine

December 8, 2002

Praise to the Lord, Jesus Christ! I am having the time of my life. My anger and fear have been dispelled and I am in love with my life, my husband, my children, and my precious Lord.

It has been a very strange experience to realize that my entire belief system has been veiled to block me from the Gospel. I am so grateful that the ministry took the course it did because I might have been lost beyond recall if I had not been in the Bible so intensely to write those sermons each week.

I was thinking about everything this morning and thought *thank God for Randy.* What would have become of me if he had not come along with his deep-seeded beliefs in traditional Christianity? He was literally used to save my life and I am so grateful to him.

In the same way that it was once revealed to me that the love I feel for others is God's love for them—and for me—this morning I heard in prayer that the hatred that arises within me belongs to Satan. I must realize that the things and people that provoke bitterness and hatred are the things and people that are being especially attacked. The Lord told me to be vigilant about this and to immediately rebuke all anger and negativity while praying for the people who I experience that with.

I guess I can see why the enemy didn't want me to get back to safety; because I'm going to blow his cover—big time! I've always known that the book will be called *Unmasked*, but now I see that it's not just me who is getting unmasked. Satan and his tricks are being exposed; which will help the Lord to be revealed. No lie that we all need to get to the causes and conditions that block us from God because it's not defects of character, but *defective characters* that embody us.

I guess for the record that I have to admit that while I'm sitting here—absolutely covered with the helmet of salvation—I am still being told by the Lord that the finale is going to be more beautiful than we could have ever imagined because the Plan really is about the return of the ultimate prodigal and the reconciliation of all polarity.

The cow and the bear shall graze;
Their young ones shall lie down together;
And the lion shall eat straw like the ox.

The nursing child shall play by the cobra's hole,
And the weaned child shall put his hand in the viper's den.
They shall not hurt nor destroy in all My holy mountain,
For the earth shall be full of the knowledge of the Lord
As the waters cover the sea.
Isaiah 11:7–9

As my deliverance finalized, I was ordained to the priesthood and Randy and I started our own Christian Twelve Step group because A.A. was too limited.

January 19, 2003

I have been reading a lot of Christian stuff and the big mystery seems to be how evil could exist.

If God created everything; why does He allow it? This brings me back to what I have believed for a long time—that we had to be expelled from the Garden in order to be given the tools to get back and to be able to live there as mature children of God instead of nursing babies. Like Augustine said, *"For, were it not good that evil things should also exist, the omnipotent God would almost certainly not allow evil to be, since beyond doubt it is just as easy for Him not to allow what He does not will, as for Him to do what He will."*[354]

Sin is kind of like homeopathic medicine. It was put into our spirits so we could learn to fight it. Our identity as being created in the image and likeness of God was allowed to be corrupted in order for us to understand our absolute need for total dependence on God. God Himself came to earth, demonstrated true obedience unto death, rose from the dead, sits at the right hand of the Father, and sends His Holy Spirit to all who believe in order to *restore* our identity.

Christianity always aggravated me because it seemed that the Gospel insinuated that a loving God would smite you to hell if you didn't accept Jesus, but now I get it. The Bible says, *"For God did not send His Son into the world to condemn the world, but that the world through Him might be saved. He who believes in Him is not condemned; but he who does not believe is condemned already." (John 3:17–18)*

We're already condemned without Jesus! The "accuser" is holding us hostage—telling us that we're nothing, that we don't matter, that the world is not safe, etc. Condemnation is the captor!

A lot of people can't accept Jesus as Savior because they don't really understand that they're in bondage. That's a trip. It reminds be of the movie, *The Matrix.* We're all being held captive in a situation that is so deceptive that we're not consciously aware of it. At certain times, we get the creepy feeling that something is not quite right, but we just can't figure it out. In the movie, the ones who have broken free offer the "red pill" to the ones who want to know the real truth. The red pill is like the blood of Jesus. Hey everybody, *take the red pill* so we can get out of the matrix!

We all need to realize that Satan and his deception are real and that the blood of Jesus is the *only* way to get free of them. And we need to start believing this *ASAP* because the planet itself is losing its ability to sustain human life and Jesus is the only One who can do anything about it because He is the only One who can truly change our hearts and minds and bring us together in cooperative effort.

Our global population is now approaching 6 billion people.
Another doubling of the population—
expected to happen within the next 40 years—
will bring us beyond the estimated carrying capacity of earth.[355]
Barbara Marx Hubbard

In the 24 hours since yesterday, over 200,000 acres of rainforest have been destroyed in our world. Fully 13 million tons of toxic chemicals have been released into our environment. Over 45,000 people have died of starvation, 38,000 of them children. And more than 130 plant or animal species have been driven to extinction by the actions of humans ... Recycling won't save the world, birth control won't save the world, and saving what little is left of our rainforests won't save the world ... Even cold fusion and the elimination for the need for oil, with free electricity for everybody, will not "save the world" ... Nothing but changing our way of seeing and understanding the world can produce real, meaningful, and lasting change.[356]
Thom Hartmann

May 24, 2003

It was this time last year that Randy and I were separated. I thank God every day that my life was restored.

I have heard some great lessons on the radio. Jack Hayford said that prophecies say that God's children will help in establishing His Kingdom. He said that it is not that God "could not" do it Himself, but that He "won't" without the invocation from others; He does not go where He is not invited. That makes me think of *God could and would if He were sought.* [357]

Michael Usef said that "falling from grace" is falling into legalism—in other words, trying to do it yourself. These are great things to consider.

The pastor at the church we have been attending told us about a lady who had a vision of water pouring down from the mountain and converting even the most cynical. Hayford said that our prayers are put on our hearts as a promise. Both of those things give me great hope because the prayer of my heart is that *all* may know that Jesus is Lord and that they may receive his love and mercy.

> *"I will put My law in their minds, and write it on their hearts; and I will be their God, and they shall be My people. No more shall every man teach his neighbor, and every man his brother, saying, 'Know the Lord,' for they all shall know Me, from the least of them to the greatest of them," says the Lord. "For I will forgive their iniquity, and their sin I will remember no more."*
>
> **Jeremiah 31:33–34**

June 6, 2003

I've been reading *The Purpose Driven Church* and it has brought everything that has been going on for the past seventeen years into clear focus and perspective. I think that I can assuredly say that the ministry has begun. We are basically a church for the black sheep. We are prodigal shepherds.

I'm starting to understand the real issues and pressures of being a leader. It's definitely more than just being in charge. I think that one of the hardest aspects of leadership is making decisions for the whole that disturb the few. Let's face it; you cannot please all of the people *any*time! But that's the point; it is not about "pleasing" people, but about making sound decisions that edify the whole. Upsetting the few is not fun to walk through, though. Leaders definitely have to have a good balance between the courage of their own convictions and their willingness to listen to others. I definitely need to work on listening to others and counting to at least ten (maybe one thousand) until I respond.

The direction of the ministry is definitely moving toward exposing the twisted truths of A.A., mystical/scientific Christianity, and even the Christian Church. When I dreamed of being a leader, I used to fantasize about how "loved" I would be. Now I see that going against doctrine that has been ingrained in so many people is not going to make me very popular.

The church has sunk down to a life in which the spirit of the world and of human wisdom is far too prevalent ... It is only as the written Word ministers the life of the Eternal Word, and as the Holy Spirit, who knows the things of God, makes them life and truth to us, that our study of the Scriptures can be edifying to us ... The Christian experience of the church is not deep, intense, and living enough to meet the world's needs ... The twofold charge against the church; that of neglecting its own members and neglecting the unbelievers entrusted to it, does indeed call for the deepest contrition.[358]

Andrew Murray

October 7, 2003

Since the last entry, Randy and I served on an *Epiphany Ministries* team. When we got back, it became pretty clear that our whole ministry revolves around correlating the Steps with true Christian spirituality and then using this correlated system as a discipleship process. We registered the name of our Twelve Step group as *More Than Conquerors Through Christ Jesus.* The Sheriff's Chaplain for Tarrant County, who is one of Randy's deacons, has asked us to bring meetings into the county jail. We are going in instead of A.A. or N.A.

January 11, 2004

We started going into Tarrant County Jail and it is going well. It has forced me into that correlation deal with the Steps and Christianity. There are too many "new creations" that can't stay sober to try to lead them through recovery without using the tools that I *know* work. I have been compiling information and worksheets for the inmates that are self-contained and can be transmitted through the mail.

Well, I don't even know how to get started on this next subject. Ruthie fell and broke her hip in mid-November. We thought she was going to be okay, but to the contrary, she deteriorated and died within two weeks. It's still pretty surreal.

Kelly and I stayed with her until they took her body to the funeral home and Randy and I got to do the funeral, but there is really no describing this grief. I used to think that it wasn't a sad thing when old people died, but it has nothing to do with their age—it has to do with their significance in your life. Ruthie was a very significant person in my life; one of the top five! Fortunately, God has a way of letting things sink in slowly so that it is not overwhelming, but it is still very hard to believe that she is gone. I miss her.

I had a beautiful experience the Sunday after she died. The service was very sad and getting focused on worship wasn't easy, but as we were praising Him, He reminded me about Isaiah 61; how He turns our mourning into gladness. Right in the middle of the worship, He met me in my brokenness and turned my sadness into joy! It was a beautiful thing.

I loved (love) Ruthie so much and am so grateful for her. She was the rock of my life before I knew the true Rock. Thank you, Ruthie. I love you. Thank you, Lord, *for* Ruthie.

This week I heard a preacher say that who we are in Heaven is contingent on how well we respond to the onslaught of hell that comes against our lives. Someone else said that we bow to the enemy when we succumb to judgment, fear, doubt, etc... This was very important because the Holy Spirit then reminded me that what He is able to do *through* me is contingent with what He is able to do *in* me. I sometimes (a lot of times) get distracted with impatience in waiting for Him to move the ministry faster when, in reality, He is waiting on me to move out of the way as He perfects that which is within me. Thank you, Jesus, I'm Yours.

The Spirit of the Lord GOD is upon me; because the LORD hath anointed me to preach good tidings unto the meek; he hath sent me to bind up the brokenhearted, to proclaim liberty to the captives, and the opening of the prison to them that are bound; To proclaim the acceptable year of the LORD, and the day of vengeance of our God; to comfort all that mourn; To appoint unto them that mourn in Zion, to give unto them beauty for ashes, the oil of joy for mourning, the garment of praise for the spirit of heaviness; that they might be called trees of righteousness, the planting of the LORD, that he might be glorified.

Isaiah 61:1–3

February 13, 2004

Here's one straight from the horse's mouth that He told me to write down so I don't forget.

> **You cry to Me to see My face—to experience Me in extreme and spectacular ways. Let Me remind you that you have had many such experiences. However, you have many times used them to distinguish yourself from others and therefore to divide and separate. I now charge you with the greatest challenge, which will also be the fulfillment of your heart's cry to see Me and to know Me. I am everywhere! Expose Me. See Me. Know Me. Unmask Me in everyone you encounter.**

The previous entry was one of the few times that I heard from the Lord in the almost year and a half after my final deliverance. After that, He started talking to me again about my "destiny" and I got scared that I was being deceived by the enemy. I contacted one of the priests in our diocese and he counseled me not to rebuke my own thoughts for thirty days. A few days later, he sent me an e-mail telling me to get ready for my biggest breakthrough ever. He also sent me a Scripture that he said the Lord told him to give to me. It was John 14:23, "If a man love me, he will keep my words: and my Father will love him, and we will come unto him, and make our abode with him." Shortly thereafter, the Lord started integrating all of the things I had ever believed through the grid of the Gospel of Jesus Christ.

June 1, 2004

Paige, I am with you always; especially at the end of the age. Listen AND speak to Me in order to keep the lines exchanging. Prayer and meditation are a similar exchange to the continuous transformative process between mass and energy. It's all about dialogue.

Everything is a macrocosm of a microcosm, but the micro is greater than the macro. In reality everything is a *macro*cosm of a *micro*cosm, but I am both the Alpha and the Omega—the beginning and the end—the invisible and the visible.

I will save Sodom if just one person is righteous (and that does not mean good, but obedient). The only way to have My righteousness is to abide in Me, but everyone must realize that abiding in Me goes way beyond a morality issue. I hold the key to all things and to those who abide in Me, I will give the hidden manna.

I am the author of all life and believe Me, I'm no Shakespeare. This is not a tragedy. I speak life. I speak love. Do you love Me? Then, feed My sheep—every day—until you are all filled with hidden manna. Earth is Heaven's promised land just as Heaven is earth's.

I am everywhere, but you have to know Me personally or you won't be able to receive instructions. Then again, no one pays attention to the directions anyway and that's the problem in the first place; trying to do things that you don't know what the hell you are doing (like creating hell). Disobedience creates hell. That's food for thought; and fear if you don't know Me.

But don't worry, Paige. There is no death for those who know Me, and believe Me, My intention to know all will be fulfilled. I have over-

come death, but I need My soldiers as vehicles. It takes a village, baby, but not of idiots. Do not fear. My peace I leave with you. I am your peace. Abide in Me and don't do one thing I don't tell you to. I love you.

Ok, ok, ok, I hear you. Remind me never to say *speak Lord for your servant is listening* again.

Nobody ever wanted anything as much as God
wants to bring people to know him.[359]
Meister Eckhart

June 20, 2004

When I began to incorporate my mystic/recovery world view back into the picture through the scope of the Gospel, it was as mind-bending as the time I got delivered out of that belief system. I was scared that I was being deceived, but after reciting deliverance prayers, binding, rebuking, praising, worshipping, and taking communion, the Lord told me that I was just going to have to accept the fact that it was Him who was talking to me.

The bottom line is that everything is about Jesus. It is pretty ironic how a life can begin by trying to preserve itself and then come to a place where the goal is to die; that He may live. As Paul said, "*To live is Christ, to die is gain.*" (*Philippians 1:21*)

The anticipation of the sweep He's getting ready to make is breathtaking. He has assured me that He is going to save the day—like any perfect hero. I live for that day; when every knee will bow and every tongue will confess that Jesus is Lord. What a glorious day that will be—and I can feel it coming.

When passion takes on a purpose
And searching ones embrace the light
When skeptics find themselves down on their knees
You'll know it's here
It's the revolution, can you feel it?[360]
Jason Wade

June 26, 2004

I am the Lord your God and I say to you, "I hear your cry." Would I leave you homeless—an orphan? Do you think that you could possibly have a problem that I do not have a solution for? Of course not, My

beloved children. I love you and My greatest desire is to lovingly care for you always.

You say that you are desperate for Me. Well, I am desperate for you also. We share the same longing for each other. You cry for more of Me—more love, more power. I have given you everything already. Stir it up! Press deep down into My love for you. You cannot even begin Maslow's climb without my love for first cause is not the mind of God, but the heart of God; not thought, but love.

Before I return, you must prepare My bride. To enable this, I am tearing down Babylon; and Jerusalem will rise from the ashes. As I invade Satan's towers—science, academia, religion, the media, technology, the arts—I will recover what was stolen from Me. Nothing that is hidden is not meant to be revealed and I have saved My best wine for last. The hidden manna will be revealed and it will be glorious for knowledge of My love for you will cover the earth as the waters cover the sea.

As you press in to My love for you, I will rise up within you for this is the hope of true glory; to share it with you. You are My weapons of mass destruction, yet I destroy with fierce love for nothing can contain the Spirit. But you must contain your flesh if I am to rise up to meet Myself in My coming again. Contain your flesh in order to withstand the power that I am sending to you. The Joel outpouring is NOW. Prepare the bride! Turn off the television and turn IN to Me!

Receive My love and all else will follow. I am your God and you are My beloved. Be of good cheer for I love you ALL. Your worst fear is a nightmare for YOU ARE LOVED—beyond anything that you can imagine. But it will not be real to you until you open the door and let Me in! Receive My love for I am as near as your breath. The only thing that travels faster than the speed of light is LOVE because it stands forever. I am with you always–even until the end of the age–but that is just the beginning of what I have for you for the very best is yet to come—FOREVER!

September 18, 2004

I am finding that truly pausing is a very uncomfortable experience for me. There is still a very deep pain inside of me. I'm just so ready for Him to take it. Less of me; more of Him—none of me; all of Him. Your will be done, Lord.

The deep pain really is the fear that God will not take care of me. It is the part of me that does not truly trust Him, but I can't change that because my will power cannot conquer self will. I just have to wait—and pray (believe and be obedient).

This is hard to finally be at the place where I truly know that there is nothing for me to do—when I ask for directions and hear nothing in return. The job of doing nothing but sitting silently in solitude is the hardest one yet.

The Lord told me to be patient—that internally there is major reconstruction being done. That is exactly how it feels sometimes: like a giant wrecking ball is knocking down walls that have some really old and heinous stench behind them. There is so much rage and hostility wrapped around that inherent fear of being alone and unloved. I know that He will unravel all of this.

I'm ready, precious Lord. Show me the truth. Tear down all of the walls and create a huge empty space that You may fill.

All of my life
I've been in hiding
Wishing there was someone just like You
Now that You're here
Now that I've found You
I know that You're the One to pull me through[361]
Jon Marsh and Helena Marsh

September 24, 2004

Paige, this is all about the understanding of My resurrection power. Death is required for resurrection. The original state had to "die" in order for the false self to be born into creation in order for it to die so that resurrection power could be understood (true wisdom/intelligence). The garden can't be appreciated without the contrast of separation and you can't eat from the tree of life until you have experienced the resurrection which reveals all things.

This is why My strength is perfected in your weakness. The more dead you become, the greater the glory of My life (I Am Life!). This is why those who are forgiven little have little love; no contrast. The way I descend into hell is by being born into the least: the more heinous the sinner, the greater the descent, but the more glorious the resurrection.

The whole powerless/broken thing has not been popular in Christian circles because they think that only what feels good is My will.

Yes, My joy is your strength, but My strength is displayed in your weakness. Like Gibran said "Your joy is your sorrow unmasked."

But the only TRUE identity is Me. Without redemptive revelation of Me, there is always a veil because the final mask is self. Anyone who wears that mask can be influenced by the angel of light who masquerades as "The Christ"—trying to draw earnest seekers into union with him (merging with the One). Even the one true God isn't "one" because the Trinity is "God in community."

Merging to a conscious state of oneness with no physical body is completely antithetical to what this is about. It is all about communion; with Me and with each other. The Omega will be (is) Me having a relationship with Myself, but in a BIG way. Believe me, the kind of "Catholic" family I desire is beyond comprehension.

September 26, 2004

I need those who worship in Spirit and in truth. When you accept Me, your spirit is purified, but that still leaves your soul and body. The body is the outward manifestation of the soul's activity; which is governed by the Spirit. However, the problem here is that the Spirit is not governing in most people because they are not near as willing to surrender as they fancy themselves to be.

Self-will has many disguises and in order for you to truly be filled, you have to be EMPTY. You can't put new wine in old wineskins or fill what's already full—of expectations and old ideas. To worship in Spirit and in truth, you must be transparent and this is contingent on your capacity to be honest; with yourself, with others, and with Me.

I am the inspiration behind the recovery movement. The operation within the Twelve Step process purifies the soul and removes the interior blocks that hinder the work of the Holy Spirit. Once these blocks are removed, the deeper operations of the Spirit come into play (the Spirit of the Lord: the Spirit of wisdom and understanding, the Spirit of counsel and of power, the Spirit of knowledge and of the fear of the Lord).[362]

Your steps being "ordered" by the Lord insinuate **G**ood **O**rderly **D**irection, but detail to the inner is more important than detail to the outer. Self awareness is nothing but allowing Me entrance into the inner chamber of your soul. Exterior changes are limited. The idea of changing the outside to try to fix the inside has been proven to be ineffective on anything but a short-term basis. It's an inside job. BEWARE of being all bright and shiny on the outside when you're filthy on the inside. Clean first the inside of the cup.

I have been with all of you since BEFORE the foundation of time, but you have been oblivious to this fact because you are insensitive to My presence. The most important thing you can ever do is nothing; to sit quietly in solitude and LISTEN to Me. It's the highest form of worship. The still, small inaudible voice is the most powerful agent on earth. This is the "little child" who leads.

Yes, My magnitude extends to the far corners of the universe, but this all begins with absolute silence and emptiness—pure potential. It ends here also because no matter how deep, wide, great etc., all is meaningless without core contact with Me. True greatness in the Kingdom lies in the ability to become nothing–for My sake.

These are very critical times. Faith comes from hearing the message, but I need TRUE messengers to deliver it; not people who imitate Me, but who allow ME to be I AM through them. The message has many times been delivered in ways that not only DO NOT glorify Me, but actually disgrace and discredit Me. There are many "Christians" who give Me a bad name through self-righteous religiosity and arrogance. Your ability to "love your enemies" and "bear each other's burdens" makes a huge difference in the life of the unbeliever. I have given you much more responsibility than you realize and you WILL BE HELD ACOUNTABLE for it.

You all need a fresh understanding. Yes, put the past behind you, but this means not to get caught in self-pity over your trials. NEVER forget where you came from because the ability to comprehend what I've done in your life is your testimony. Boast about your weaknesses! Yes, My joy is your strength, but MY STRENGTH is manifested in YOUR WEAKNESS.

You need to forget everything that you THINK you already know. Remember, manna was good for one day. That's the way daily bread is also. I am the bread of life, but you cannot live on yesterday's experience with Me. You have to commune with Me each day, but contact, communication, and commitment precede communion. I am ONE with My bride.

Most people don't know Me at all. They just have an idea of me that they pretend to have a relationship with—just like they do with each other. They truly are worshipping an image they have created

instead of the Creator. This is a huge problem, but you can't truly get to the solution without being willing to suffer a little—and to not get your way all the time. You have become entitled, spoiled brats; especially in the United States. Get honest with yourselves about that.

To sum up what I want to say to you all: Please turn off all cell phones, pagers, televisions, and radios! In other words, silence in the court! But this is not a court of law, but a courtship of love. The groom wants intimacy with his bride.

October 10, 2004

It has recently become clear to me that I have been working too much. Today the Lord told me that He already made the sacrifice; that the cross He wants us to bear is a life well lived—that death of self is necessary because "self" creates hardships and burdens. It is His pleasure to *give* us the Kingdom.

Self-will tries to earn or manipulate its way into places and situations that make us "seem" as if we have it all together or are "successful." In reality, simply just knowing Him and accepting *whatever* He wills for you is the Kingdom. Then, in an instant you realize that you have everything you need because you have Him and He is everything. He told me that to honor Him is to honor each other. He said …

Okay, you're unmasked. You know that it's Me living in you—through you—as you. Now what are you going to do? Do you think that I sit around waiting for people to recognize Me or do you think that I go about the business of being Me? The highest realization is that the thing that makes life meaningful is the ability to share it with others. It's not so much about knowing who you are in Me as it is about BEING Me in the lives of others. It's all about balance—between work and play—between worship and quiet time—between giving and receiving—between joy and sorrow.

It's all about Him and it is glorious. What matters is the time alone with Him; the intimacy I share with Him and the people in my life—the relationships. It's the moments of true contact with Jesus and others that I get to take with me.

It doesn't matter what happens from here. I am home because my heart has finally opened. Heaven is not just a nice idea, but a reality. I have everything I've ever wanted because this moment, I am absolutely content to be here now—on the couch with my family—doing what I love most—nothing. There are no big deals because the most awesome thing in the universe is so small that it's invisible. Yes, indeed, Lord—more of You and less of me. It's all about love.

A new commandment I give unto you, that ye love one another; as I have loved you, that ye also love one another.
John 13:34

October 16, 2004

I've kind of been in a funk because things just aren't moving fast enough to suit me. I can say this much, knowing who you are and why you are specifically here is a pain.

Excuse Me, dear, but you are here to enjoy your life! Yes, there are many things that I have ordained you to do, but you have been in a funk because you have been driving yourself towards a goal that you can only reach by being led by Me. You've been making a huge job out of something that's supposed to be a joy. When you're not enjoying it, you've taken over.

That's why you must die to self; not because I want you to sacrifice yourself, but because your "self" gets in the way. Yes, there is work to do, but it is also My will for you to enjoy the treasure that you are to Me. It's all about balance. All play and no work makes a fool, but all work and no play makes a fiend.

Relax and trust Me. I know what I'm doing. I love you!

October 19, 2004

I feel prompted to "capture" this moment, but this is definitely a day when I don't *want* to capture myself. I want to lose myself. I'm so sick of my self.

I've been struggling a lot lately. I'm still attached to the need for recognition: to the need to "make my mark"—to the belief that I am nothing unless I do something or *be* somebody "special," like there's such a thing.

I just don't want to own these shadows; yet another part of myself that I hate. It's all just a Catch-22. I hide—the hiding causes pain—the discovery is too painful—I hide—ad infinitum. Thank God for being Jesus.

He told me to capture all of this so here goes … Either I'm some sort of freaked out crazy weirdo or else—welcome inside the mind of all of us. Welcome to the places we pretend don't exist. Welcome to the depths of sorrow and doubt and discouragement and weariness. Paul had a thorn in his flesh. I have a porcupine in mine. It's like that for us addicts. I suspect that it's like that for us humans, but we're all too busy putting on pretenses to admit it.

I am utterly depressed. There's a part of me that's locked deep inside—screaming bloody murder to get out. No five mile run, anti-depressant, drink, or drug can stifle the plea within me. I know her Hero is on His way, but I see today that this is *all* a part of the experience; becoming seasoned—to be the salt of the earth.

I picked up a dear old friend today, Kahlil Gibran's *The Prophet.* It says so beautifully what I have come to understand to be the reality of existence—of walking with the Lord; whose hands can also be a terribly frightening place to be …

> "When Love beckons you, follow Him, though His ways are hard and steep. And when His wings enfold you yield to Him, though the sword hidden among His pinions may wound you. And when He speaks to you believe in Him, though His voice may shatter your dreams as the North wind lays waste the garden.
>
> For even as Love crowns you so shall He crucify you. Even as He is for your growth so is He for your pruning. Even as He ascends to your heights and caresses your tenderest branches that quiver in the sun, so shall He descend to your roots and shake them in their clinging to the earth.
>
> Like sheaves of corn He gathers you unto Himself. He threshes you to make you naked. He sifts you to free you from your husks. He grinds you to whiteness. He kneads you until you are pliant; and then He assigns you to His sacred fire, that you may become sacred bread for God's sacred feast.
>
> All of these things shall Love do unto you that you may know the secrets of your heart, and in that knowledge become a fragment of Life's heart.
>
> But if in your fear you would seek only Love's peace and Love's pleasure, then it is better for you that you cover your nakedness and pass out of Love's threshing floor into the seasonless world where you shall laugh, but not all of your laughter, and weep, but not all of your tears." [363]

Praise to You, Lord Jesus. Thank You for the privilege of suffering. How sweet the pain—and how great the anticipation of its corresponding joy. For yes, Lord, my pain *is* the breaking of the shell that encloses my understanding—and I understand this: what good is salt if it has lost its savor? Thank You for the seasoning. Thank You for the texture. Thank You for giving me the ability to sit in serenity through the seasons of my grief; to wait in peace through the violent blows of the threshing floor. I stand before You; naked and not ashamed—vulnerable and bleeding, but *not* afraid. How sweet the taste of sadness, Lord, when contrasted to the ecstasy of just one touch of Your seamless garment.

I forever stand in awe of You, Jesus, my King of Kings, my Everything.

epilogue

January 14, 2005

Lift my hands and spin around
See the light that I have found
O the marvelous light, marvelous light
Is Christ in you
No more shame![364]
Charlie Hall

January 14, 2005

I have been editing the journal to its form that will be submitted to publishers. This is quite an experience for me because it continues to blow my mind concerning the faithfulness and thoroughness of Jesus—and the utter depravity of myself without Him.

I came to the part where I had the abortion in 1990. It was so painful to read because I had no regard for the child I murdered. All I could focus on was how hard *my* life was. At least I knew that I was making it hard on myself, but the depth of my selfishness was appalling.

The good news about it is the Good News Himself. He is faithful; even when I fail. He told me that my precious babies are with Him and assured me that they are waiting for me. And then, in His usual way, He pointed out my progress to me. He showed me that the reason I can now clearly see the selfishness is that the beam has been removed much more.

He showed me that all we really ever see is ourselves. If we see others with judgment, we see what we are. If we see with compassion, we see what we have been—or could be. With compassion, we are able to see—both within ourselves and in others—what we are capable of becoming through His love and grace and mercy. To me, that is just beautiful.

Another very clear lesson that He has taught me through the journal is that the "only way out is *through.*" In '89, it is so clear that I took the potential of what was to come and just pretended as if it already was without the "working out" of it all. I fell hard and then realized that what was truly in front of me was sobriety and integrity. The journey of a thousand miles truly does begin with the first step, but *every step* must be taken—in order. It is simple life on life's terms that prepares us for any dream-come-true.

You can't become a teacher without first being an obedient student. I am truly blessed because I have literally been taught everything I know by the Master Teacher Himself, but what He has taught me is that the *foundation* is the most important part of the structure and that the integrity of the whole is *impossible* without the Chief Cornerstone—Him. We cannot build a tower to Heaven, but the Master Builder can construct layer upon layer of deep and examined experience that finalizes in a very "High" structure, but it is an organic whole—not a compartmentalized edifice.

I've spent my whole life dreaming of the time that is happening *now.* He has made my ministry my vocation and the journal has come to its completion point for the book. Yet now I understand that all of this would be meaningless without the deep content and awesome context of my life. This whole world is focused on the outer form of what things look like without understanding that it is the *filling* that is the substance; and substance requires both righteous seed and *fertile ground.*

Let me say right now to those that are reading this (He's prompted me my whole life to take notes for *you*): if you have a dream, dare to believe in it, but understand this …

The simple things in life done well are truly the most difficult tasks: to be patient with a child, to be loving and supportive to a spouse, to be fair, to be honest. The integrity of your own soul is the *most* important thing and the relationships in your life are your laboratory to test and strengthen your living skills. I believe that this has best been said as "*For what is a man profited, if he shall gain the whole world, and lose his own soul?*" (*Matthew 16:26*) It takes much more humility to be a window washer than to be the executive sitting in the leather chair inside the window.

... But back to your dream: do what you love! Do it for free! Do it with passion! He'll make your joy your vocation if you don't give up.

Precious Lord, what more can I say to You but *thank You*! Thank You, Jesus, for saving my life, for making me into a new person (constantly), for giving me wisdom and discernment, for giving me the privilege to serve You. I pray, Lord, that all who read the words of these many pages will be unmasked themselves—that You may be revealed as the One True Identity of all. I am forever Yours.

Paige

1 George Seldes, *The Great Thoughts* (New York, New York: Random House, 1985), 391.

2 David Hazard/John of the Cross, *You Set My Spirit Free* (Minneapolis, Minnesota: Bethany House Publishers, 1994), 131.

3 www.quotations page.com

4 Anthony DeMello, *Awareness* (New York, New York: Bantam Doubleday Dell Publishing Group, Inc., 1992), 30.

5 Richard Bach, *Illusions* (New York, New York: Bantam Doubleday Dell Publishing Group, Inc., 1977), 177.

6 Seldes, *The Great Thoughts*, 414.

7 Henri J. M. Nouwen, *The Wounded Healer* (New York, New York: Bantam Doubleday Dell Publishing Group, Inc., 1979), 34.

8 Nouwen, *The Wounded Healer,* 32.

9 Anthony DeMello, *Awareness* (New York, New York: Bantam Doubleday Dell Publishing Group, Inc., 1992), 29.

10 Nouwen, *The Wounded Healer*, 29.

11 Kahlil Gibran, *The Prophet* (New York, New York: Alfred A. Knopf, 1923), 53.

12 Bach, *Illusions*, 119.

13 Bach, *Illusions*, 71.

14 Hugh Prather, *Love and Courage* (Berkeley, California: Conari Press, 2001), 49.

15 Hugh Prather, *Notes to Myself* (New York, New York: Bantam Books, 1990)

16 Prather, *Notes to Myself*

17 Prather, *Love and Courage*, 28.

18 Mother Teresa, *The Joy in Living* (New York: Penguin Books USA Inc., 1997), 82.

19 DeMello, *Awareness*, 28.

20 *Twelve Steps and Twelve Traditions* (New York, New York: Alcoholics Anonymous World Service, 1952, 1953, 1981), 94.

21 DeMello, *Awareness*, 26.

22 Gibran, *The Prophet*, 8.

23 *Alcoholics Anonymous* (New York, New York: Alcoholics Anonymous World Services, Inc., 1976), 82.

24 Prather, *Love and Courage*, 9.

25 Seldes, *The Great Thoughts*, 450.

26 Prather, *Love and Courage*, 7.

27 Gibran, *The Prophet*, 32.

28 DeMello, *Awareness*, 8.

29 DeMello, *Awareness*, 5.

30 www.quotationspage.com

31 Prather, *Notes to Myself*

32 DeMello, *Awareness*, 55.

33 Gibran, *The Prophet,* 48.

34 A.W.Tozer, *The Pursuit of God* (Camp Hill, Pennsylvania, Christian Publications, Inc., 1982, 1993)

35 Seldes, *The Great Thoughts,* 164.

36 *Twelve Steps and Twelve Traditions*, 44

37 *Twelve Steps and Twelve Traditions* (New York, New York: Alcoholics Anonymous World Service, 1952, 1953, 1981), 72.

38 DeMello, *Awareness*, 71.

39 *The Andrew Murray Daily Reader*, 18.

40 *Alcoholics Anonymous*, 62.

41 James P. Gillis, M.D., *Temple Maintenance* (Tarpon Springs, Florida: Love Press, 1989)

42 Oswald Chambers, *My Utmost For His Highest* (Grand Rapids, Michigan: Discovery House Publishers, 1935), May 2.

43 Templeton, *Worldwide Laws of Life*, 55.

44 Mother Teresa, *The Joy in Living*, 288.

45 www.quotationspage.com

46 Templeton, *Worldwide Laws of Life*, 55.

47 Chambers, *My Utmost For His Highest*, March 16.

48 Gibran, *The Prophet*, 6.

49 *Alcoholics Anonymous*, 53.

50 Hazard/John of the Cross, *You Set My Spirit Free*, 70.

51 Marianne Williamson, *A Return to Love* (New York, New York: HarperCollins Publishers, Inc., 1992), 60.

52 *Alcoholics Anonymous*, 83.

53 Nouwen, *The Wounded Healer*, 38.

54 www.quotationspage.com

55 Prather, *Notes to Myself*

56 DeMello, *Awareness*, 110.

57 Nouwen, *The Wounded Healer*, 41.

58 www.quotationspage.com

59 Chambers, *My Utmost For His Highest*, August 29.

60 *Twelve Steps and Twelve Traditions*, 93.

61 Prather, *Love and Courage*, 137.

62 Andrew Murray, *Humility* (Gainesville, Florida: Bridge-Logos, 2000), 77.

63 *Alcoholics Anonymous*, 58.

64 *Alcoholics Anonymous*, 43.

65 *Alcoholics Anonymous*, 34.

66 Henri J. M. Nouwen, *The Wounded Healer*, 93.

67 *Alcoholics Anonymous*, 61.

68 Gibran, *The Prophet*, 40.

69 *Twelve Steps and Twelve Traditions*, 48.

70 Brennan Manning, *Ruthless Trust* (New York, New York: HarperCollins Publishers, 2000), 21.

71 DeMello, *Awareness*, 88.

72 Gibran, *The Prophet*, 19.

73 Templeton, *Worldwide Laws of Life*

74 *Alcoholics Anonymous*, 64.

75 DeMello, *Awareness*, 28.

76 *Twelve Steps and Twelve Traditions*, 43.

77 DeMello, *Awareness*, 148.

78 Emmet Fox, *Around the Year with Emmet Fox* (New York, New York: Harper & Brothers, 1958), 153.

79 Prather, *Notes to Myself*

80 Seldes, *The Great Thoughts*, 407.

81 *The Andrew Murray Daily Reader*, 212.

82 Templeton, *Worldwide Laws of Life*

83 Anthony DeMello, *The Way To Love* (New York: Doubleday, 1992), 8.

84 *Alcoholics Anonymous*, 25.

85 DeMello, *The Way To Love*, 10.

86 Raymond Bernard Blakney, *Meister Eckhart, A Modern Translation* (New York, New York: Harper & Row, Publishers, Inc., 1941), 172.

87 *Alcoholics Anonymous*, 37.

88 DeMello, *The Way To Love*, 20.

89 Gibran, *The Prophet*, 53.

90 *Twelve Steps and Twelve Traditions*, 73.

91 Prather, *Notes to Myself*

92 Chambers, *My Utmost For His Highest*, February 16.

93 Melody Beattie, *Codependent No More* (New York, New York: HarperCollins Publishers, 1987), 40 – 41.

94 Bach, *Illusions*, 120.

95 Bach, *Illusions*, 120.

96 DeMello, *Awareness*, 45.

97 DeMello, *Awareness*, 145.

98 Chambers, *My Utmost For His Highest*, March 7.

99 *Alcoholics Anonymous*, 28.

100 DeMello, *Awareness*, 86.

101 www.quotationspage.com

102 Mother Teresa, *The Joy in Living*, 103.

103 *Alcoholics Anonymous*, 60, 62.

104 DeMello, *Awareness*, 5.

105 www.quottionspage.com

106 Gibran, *The Prophet*, 43.

107 Oriah Mountain Dreamer, *The Invitation* (New York, New York: Harper Collins Publishers, 1999)

108 John Marks Templeton, *Worldwide Laws of Life* (Radnor, Pennsylvania: Templeton Foundation Press, 1997)

109 www.quotationspage.com110

110 Oriah Mountain Dreamer, *The Invitation*

111 Beattie, *Codependent No More*, 113.

112 Prather, *Love and Courage*, 27.

113 *Alcoholics Anonymous*, 59 – 60.

114 *Twelve Steps and Twelve Traditions*, 15.

115 *Alcoholics Anonymous*, 59 – 60.

116 Chambers, *My Utmost For His Highest*, July 27.

117 Prather, *Notes to Myself*

118 www.quotationspage.com

119 *Alcoholics Anonymous*, 46.

120 *Alcoholics Anonymous*, 54.

121 Prather, *Notes to Myself*

122 Nouwen, *The Wounded Healer*, 41.

123 *Alcoholics Anonymous*, 58.

124 *Alcoholics Anonymous*, 570.

125 Prather, *Love and Courage*, 110.

126 *Alcoholics Anonymous*, 25.

127 *Alcoholics Anonymous*, 52.

128 *Alcoholics Anonymous*, 45.

129 Seldes, *The Great Thoughts*, 88.

130 *Alcoholics Anonymous*, 58 – 59.

131 *Alcoholics Anonymous*, 33.

132 *Twelve Steps and Twelve Traditions*, 76.

133 *Twelve Steps and Twelve Traditions*, 97.

134 *The Andrew Murray Daily Reader*, 240.

135 www.brainyquotes.com

136 *Alcoholics Anonymous*, 63.

137 *Alcoholics Anonymous*, 64.

138 Chambers, *My Utmost For His Highest*, October 4.

139 *The Andrew Murray Daily Reader*, 29

140 www.quotationspage.com
141 *Twelve Steps and Twelve Traditions*, 76.
142 Murray, *Humility*, 21.
143 *Alcoholics Anonymous*, 30.
144 *Alcoholics Anonymous*, 84.
145 Murray, *Humility*, 16.
146 *Alcoholics Anonymous*, 85.
147 www.quotationspage.com
148 www.quotationspage.com
149 www.quotationspage.com
150 *Twelve Steps and Twelve Traditions*, 71.
151 *Alcoholics Anonymous*, 61.
152 *Alcoholics Anonymous*, 72.
153 *Alcoholics Anonymous*, 62.
154 Chambers, *My Utmost For His Highest*, November 17.
155 *Twelve Steps and Twelve Traditions*, 60.
156 *Alcoholics Anonymous*, 164.
157 Chambers, *My Utmost For His Highest*, October 10.
158 *Alcoholics Anonymous*, 450.
159 *Alcoholics Anonymous*, 45.
160 *Alcoholics Anonymous*, 452.
161 Prather, *Love and Courage*, 146.
162 Templeton, *Worldwide Laws of Life*
163 Tozer, *The Pursuit of God*
164 *Alcoholics Anonymous*, 14 – 15.
165 *Alcoholics Anonymous*, 75.
166 *Twelve Steps and Twelve Traditions*, 32.
167 *Alcoholics Anonymous*, 30.
168 *Twelve Steps and Twelve Traditions*, 72.
169 *Twelve Steps and Twelve Traditions*, 21.
170 www.quotationspage.com
171 *Twelve Steps and Twelve Traditions*, 74.
172 *Twelve Steps and Twelve Traditions*, 34.
173 www.quotationspage.com
174 *Twelve Steps and Twelve Traditions*, 90.
175 Fox, *Around the Year with Emmet Fox*, 200.
176 *Twelve Steps and Twelve Traditions*, 125.
177 www.brainyquotes.com
178 *Twelve Steps and Twelve Traditions*, 88.

179 *Twelve Steps and Twelve Traditions*, 80.

180 DeMello, *Awareness*, 151.

181 *Twelve Steps and Twelve Traditions*, 92.

182 *Alcoholics Anonymous*, 66.

183 *Twelve Steps and Twelve Traditions*, 72.

184 *Alcoholics Anonymous*, 44.

185 *Alcoholics Anonymous*, 30.

186 *Alcoholics Anonymous*, 59.

187 *Alcoholics Anonymous*, 58.

188 www.brainyquotes.com

189 Andrew Murray, *Secrets of Authority* (New Kensington, Pennsylvania: Whitaker House, 2002), 457.

190 Templeton, *Worldwide Laws of Life*, 403.

191 DeMello, *Awareness*, 96.

192 Gibran, *The Prophet*, 53.

193 www.quotationspage.com

194 www.quotationspage.com

195 *Alcoholics Anonymous*, 83.

196 DeMello, *Awareness*, 6.

197 *The Andrew Murray Daily Reader*, 64.

198 Gibran, *The Prophet*, 29.

199 Manning, *Ruthless Trust*, 31.

200 Templeton, *Worldwide Laws of Life* 196.

201 Prather, *Notes to Myself*

202 DeMello, *Awareness*, 105.

203 Seldes, *The Great Thoughts*, 452.

204 Murray, *Secrets of Authority*, 287.

205 Prather, *Love and Courage*, 145.

206 *Alcoholics Anonymous*, 67.

207 Templeton, *Worldwide Laws of Life* 1997)

208 *Twelve Steps and Twelve Traditions*, 98.

209 Gibran, *The Prophet*, 25.

210 www.quotationspage.com

211 Prather, *Notes to Myself*

212 www.quotationspage.com

213 DeMello, *Awareness*, 82.

214 www.quotationspage.com

215 Prather, *Notes to Myself*

216 *Epictetus, source unknown.*

217 *Twelve Steps and Twelve Traditions*, 92.

218 Prather, *Notes to Myself*

219 www.quotationspage.com

220 Templeton, *Worldwide Laws of Life*, 433.

221 www.quotationspage.com

222 Prather, *Love and Courage*, 154.

223 www.quotationspage.com

224 Templeton, *Worldwide Laws of Life*, 328.

225 *Alcoholics Anonymous*, 164.

226 Prather, *Notes to Myself*

227 DeMello, *Awareness*, 8.

228 Prather, *Love and Courage*, 10.

229 Prather, *Notes to Myself*

230 *Twelve Steps and Twelve Traditions*, 71.

231 *Twelve Steps and Twelve Traditions*, 74.

232 *The Andrew Murray Daily Reader*, 24.

233 Prather, *Notes to Myself*

234 Prather, *Love and Courage*, 4.

235 www.quotationspage.com

236 Bach, *Illusions*, 60.

237 Oriah Mountain Dreamer, *The Invitation*

238 Oriah Mountain Dreamer, *The Invitation*

239 www.famous-quotations.com

240 Templeton, *Worldwide Laws of Life*

241 Gibran, *The Prophet*, 15.

242 www.famous-quotations.com

243 www,famous-quotations.com

244 Manning, *Ruthless Trust*, 9.

245 www.quotationspage.com

246 www.quotationspage.com

247 www.quotationspage.com

248 www.brainyquotes.com

249 www.famous-quotations.com

250 Gibran, *The Prophet*, 16.

251 Prather, *Love and Courage*, 27.

252 Bach, *Illusions*, 84.

253 www.famous-quotations.com

254 www.quotationspage.com

255 www.famous-quotations.com

256 Manning, *Ruthless Trust*, 9.

257 Templeton, *Worldwide Laws of Life*

258 Templeton, *Worldwide Laws of Life*

259 Chambers, *My Utmost For His Highest*, March 12.

260 Oriah Mountain Dreamer, *The Invitation*

261 www.quotationspage.com

262 Oriah Mountain Dreamer, *The Invitation*

263 DeMello, *Awareness*, 183.

264 Gibran, *The Prophet*, 49.

265 www.quotationspage.com

266 Prather, *Love and Courage*, 78.

267 www.quotationspage.com

268 www.famous-quotations.com

269 www.famous-quotations.com

270 Oriah Mountain Dreamer, *The Invitation*

271 www.famous-quotations.com

272 www.quotationspage.com

273 Prather, *Notes to Myself*

274 www.brainyquotes.com

275 Oriah Mountain Dreamer, *The Invitation*

276 Prather, *Love and Courage*, 50.

277 Gibran, *The Prophet*, 17.

278 Prather, *Notes to Myself*

279 www.famous-quotations.com

280 Mother Teresa, *The Joy in Living*, 343.

281 Fox, *Around the Year with Emmet Fox*, 184.

282 Prather, *Notes to Myself*

283 Deepak Chopra, source unknown.

284 www.famous-quotations.com

285 www.quotationspage.com

286 *Alcoholics Anonymous*, 449.

287 DeMello, *Awareness*, 17.

288 *Twelve Steps and Twelve Traditions*, 68.

289 Templeton, *Worldwide Laws of Life*

290 Nouwen, *The Wounded Healer*, 38.

291 Templeton, *Worldwide Laws of Life*

292 www.quotationspage.com

293 Mother Teresa, *The Joy in Living*, 372.

294 www.brainyquotes.com

295 For more information, visit *www.thejaywalker.com.*

296 Seldes, *The Great Thoughts*, 117.

297 Chambers, *My Utmost For His Highest*, July 21.

298 Prather, *Notes to Myself*

299 *Twelve Steps and Twelve Traditions*, 124.

300 Bach, Illusions, 136.

301 DeMello, *Awareness*, 99.

302 Seldes, *The Great Thoughts*

303 www.unity.org

304 Manning, *Ruthless Trust*, 88.

305 Blakney, *Meister Eckhart, A Modern Translation*, 105.

306 DeMello, *Awareness*, 35.

307 Chambers, *My Utmost For His Highest*, March 21.

308 *Alcoholics Anonymous*, 89.

309 www.brainyquotes.com

310 Blakney, *Meister Eckhart, A Modern Translation*, 127.

311 Prather, *Love and Courage*, 56.

312 Mother Teresa, *The Joy in Living*, 402.

313 Manning, *Ruthless Trust*, 64.

314 Murray, *Humility*), 16.

315 David Hazard/Augustine, *Early Will I Seek You* (Minneapolis, Minnesota: Bethany House Publishers, 1991), 47.

316 Murray, *Secrets of Authority*, 470.

317 *Alcoholics Anonymous*, 68.

318 Gibran, *The Prophet*, 15.

319 www.quotationspage.com

320 Eknath Easwaran, *God Makes The Rivers To Flow* (Berkeley, California: Blue Mountain Center of Meditation, 1982, 1991), 38.

321 Blakney, *Meister Eckhart, A Modern Translation*, 129.

322 www.quotationspage.com

323 Nouwen, *The Wounded Healer*, 40.

324 www.quotationspage.com

325 www.quotationspage.com

326 Mother Teresa, *The Joy in Living*, 47.

327 DeMello, *Awareness*, 41.

328 Gibran, *The Prophet*, 5.

329 Templeton, *Worldwide Laws of Life*

330 DeMello, *Awareness*, 5.

331 Prather, *Notes to Myself*

332 Manning, *Ruthless Trust*, 96.

333 Andrew Harvey, *The Essential Mystics* (Edison, New Jersey: Castle Books, 1998), xiv.

334 Gibran, *The Prophet*, 59.

335 www.quotationspage.com

336 Easwaran, *God Makes The Rivers To Flow*, 63.

337 www.quotationspage.com

338 Manning, *Ruthless Trust*, 39.

339 Nouwen, *The Wounded Healer*, 74.

340 Murray, *Humility*, 11.

341 Prather, *Love and Courage*, 81.

342 www.quotationspage.com

343 Murray, *Secrets of Authority*, 241, 598, 643.

344 Tozer, *The Pursuit of God*

345 Chambers, *My Utmost For His Highest*, September 18.

346 www.quotationspage.com

347 Chambers, *My Utmost For His Highest*, October 5.

348 Chambers, *My Utmost For His Highest*, April 26.

349 www.quotationspage.com

350 Prather, *Love and Courage*, 40.

351 Rich Mullins and Beaker, *Creed.*

352 *The Book of Common Prayer* (New York, New York, Church Publishing Incorporated, 1979), 327.

353 Seldes, *The Great Thoughts*, 23.

354 www.brainyquotes.com

355 Barbara Marx Hubbard, *Conscious Evolution* (Novato, California: New World Library, 1998), 10.

356 Thom Hartmann, *The Last Hours of the Ancient Sunlight* (New York, New York: Three Rivers Press, 1998), 1 – 3.

357 *Alcoholics Anonymous*, 60.

358 Murray, *Secrets of Authority*, 172, 264, 574, 640.

359 Blakney, *Meister Eckhart, A Modern Translation*, 132.

360 Jason Wade, *Revolution Cry* (Cherry Rover Music), 2003.

361 Jon Marsh and Helena Marsh, *Deliver Me* (EMI Virgin Music), 1996.

362 Isaiah 11:2

363 Gibran, *The Prophet*, 11 – 12.

364 Charlie Hall, *Marvelous Light* (worshiptogethersongs.com), 2005.

Tate Publishing & *Enterprises*

Tate Publishing is committed to excellence in the publishing industry. Our staff of highly trained professionals, including editors, graphic designers, and marketing personnel, work together to produce the very finest books available. The company reflects the philosophy established by the founders, based on Psalms 68:11,

"THE LORD GAVE THE WORD AND GREAT WAS THE COMPANY OF THOSE WHO PUBLISHED IT."

If you would like further information, please call
1.888.361.9473
or visit our website
www.tatepublishing.com

Tate Publishing & *Enterprises*, LLC
127 E. Trade Center Terrace
Mustang, Oklahoma 73064 USA

CPSIA information can be obtained
at www.ICGtesting.com
Printed in the USA
FFOW05n1821231016

9 781598 867367